HOW TO LEARN ENGLISH QUICKLY 3:

GRAMMAR

Integrating Vocabulary and Discussion

Michael Mitchell

Also by Michael Mitchell

How to Learn English Quickly
Diadem Books 2009

*How to Learn English Quickly 2:
Topics and Vocabulary*
Diadem Books 2012

HOW TO LEARN ENGLISH QUICKLY 3:

GRAMMAR

Integrating Vocabulary and Discussion

MEMOIRS

Cirencester

Published by Memoirs

MEMOIRS
PUBLISHING

25 Market Place, Cirencester, Gloucestershire, GL7 2NX
info@memoirsbooks.co.uk www.memoirspublishing.com

How to Learn English Quickly 3: GRAMMAR:
Integrating Vocabulary and Discussion

ISBN: 978-1-909544-22-2

Interesting people get interested:

We love to learn and there is a practical point to studying English. We learn quickly by having a willing attitude and repeating the right sort of perfect practice: listening, writing, speaking.

1. PLAN
2. WRITE
3. READ it through and check.

We combine Grammar and Vocabulary as if they are guiding stars leading us to read, to speak and to write simple sentences.

We build the confidence and strength to do research, add detail and improve. As we extend our vocabulary and improve our grammar we copy or write our own sentences and paragraphs. We K.I.S.S. and use all parts of speech. Travel happens as we make ourselves clearly understood.

Integrate all Parts of Speech.
"It's all in the way that we say it."

Every language has evolved from being primitive to become essential for passing on basic messages. Now, several thousand years later we have a wide range of technical information as well as sophisticated fictional and factual descriptions we **love to read and listen to**.

By thinking **globally** we have found we are virtually the same the whole world over. As we can fly to almost anywhere **'isolation'** is both a passed and past tense idea. Like broadcasters, we impart the basic messages we need to help us feel secure and **strong**. We create and pass on stories of optimism or transmit vital news.

Some people make their point through the stories they hand down, while scientific texts such as anatomy books widen our knowledge of what our body comprises and how it works. One day we'll learn how it is that we naturally **laugh** and why it is that when we use the word **'bright'** we are suddenly obliged and inspired to be more **cheerful**.

Language is alive for us as surely as the wind rustles the leaves of bamboos, the sun **sparkles** on waterfalls and the hardiest trees survive and thrive on mountainsides. We fight for life and express ourselves both gently and otherwise for the causes of both stability and change.

Over the past century mankind has emerged from one way of thinking to another. There **used to be** an ignorant suspicion of 'those people over there.' We now discover they have our sense of humour; we all **love** music; they cook interesting food; they too have lovely children who need schools and nurturing. Their skilled people help us as well as us wishing to help them. **Integration is still happening.**

Our effective use of words and language let us overcome what **used to be** corrupt and oppressive systems, including our own. Fresh ideas and **good communication** initiate **change and mutual co-operation**. We now use our words to make everyone aware of our simple wish for things to be better. Do it better; it can't be any clearer than that!

Think long-term:

You are certain to use English sooner or later. You'll need it.

Willing and interesting people are interested in making progress. Improve yourself gradually or quickly and stay ahead of the others:

Let's do this together!

A handstand is a compound noun.
Easy for some!

INDEX

Exercise ANSWER PAGES:.........................

The exercises are extended reading and not too testing.
The easy questions make us focus on the points being made.
The process is simple: extension, extension, extension, detail.

Read one chapter daily; notice the sentences in the exercises.

Focus on the integration of the grammar, the vocabulary and the theme. We are soon comfortable with the general meaning. Repeat, repeat and **copy** and repeat and do **RESEARCH.**

1. PLAN our essay;
2. WRITE from the plan;
3. READ it again.

PREFACE

The **inner richness** of learning a language and experiencing another culture either through its words or by travelling is long lasting. We have a priceless asset for a lifetime. This inner **richness matures**; it is of practical use and eternal as well as something we are proud of.

We confidently make use of English today. In this book, a better-than-average student observes many grammar points. These arise as we: **1st: Observe, 2nd: Do writing and research, 3rd: Read and repeat**. We reflect that we learn mainly through simple correct repetition.

There is a lot of <u>repetition</u> and there is the **integration** of grammar and vocabulary. We imitate. We observe and write sentences rather than spend days doing grammar exercises of gap-filling.

We focus on the points and as **we repeat and repeat we also build**. The **exercises are extremely easy and straightforward**. Their purpose is for one reason: to **OBSERVE** the point being made! No hold-ups. No limitations in our life. The <u>**ANSWERS are at the back.**</u>

We combine grammar, vocabulary and ideas; they are

<u>integrated</u> into each sentence. Our **research** overcomes the ignorance we once had.

First, we appreciate people around us; **second**, we combine words of interest; **third**, we read and write a language which leads to self-improvement. Others do not put these simple ways of thinking into practice. We become **EXCEPTIONAL** and have a major advantage.

We are almost unique because only one person in 10,000 appreciates that the people near to them are special. To our advantage, we keep our **special contacts and take no one for granted**. We communicate.

1. Appreciate making connections; 2. Study and grow; 3. Enjoy the progress. **Others don't. They have a limited life.** What is the result? We will travel, build strong friendships and be a richer person for it.

INTRODUCTION
Clarity and Precision: Communicate Clearly

No matter which country or culture we visit we discover that people are very similar to each other. Those across the seas or just over the border are not from the planet Mars, neither do they possess a different life form. We all have red blood, a good brain and our four-chambered heart **loves** having the ability to **communicate** accurately.

We seek shelter, food and drink because survival is the key. We respect and want to experience other cultures. We are designed to want to perpetuate our species and to have a good place to rear our young for at least 12 years. We prefer to live in a household where there is respect for young and old and the emphasis is on good manners. We **love** and **encourage our sense of curiosity**.

Most relationships begin with smiles, kindness and generosity; we build self-confidence by treating each other respectfully. Once we establish mutual respect then far friendlier events either arise naturally or are engineered. In order to make things happen we **co-operate** and **communicate** very well because we cannot do everything alone.

The fashionable belief is that we, species Homo sapiens,

evolved and emerged from the plains of Africa. Thus, we share a common origin which is yet further reason to agree that we are inter-related. No matter how we dress up our modern society and try to show that being sophisticated is a necessity, we are ubiquitously **more or less the same**, both physically and emotionally. We communicate very well.

Our focus is on how **to communicate adeptly** and we are similarly gifted to do so. We want to put our thoughts into speech and writing. Our **skills of communication give us strength and an advantage**.

For much of the time we get our meaning across by using our **body language**. For example, we put on our coat, get the shopping bag, check our money, put on our shoes and state the obvious: "Okay, let's go shopping!" We communicate mostly by the use of our facial expressions and by speaking. However, the additional or supplementary skills of reading and writing are invaluable too.

Too often when absorbing a language or being told a cooking recipe or learning what to do on the computer, the messenger speaks far too quickly and we make a "Could you repeat that please?" request. There are also times when we dare not ask them to say it again as they will be more than annoyed. 'I've already told you that once before!'

Therefore, when we speak or write we do so politely, **clearly and concisely** by using words the listener or reader understands. It is best to use reasonably correct grammatical constructions. We help the receiver of our message, our child for example, to understand us by being **accurate and showing our care**. 'Having fun' is still allowed. We have a flexible range of words and ways of saying what we mean.

Therefore, in order to show our care we **combine our words and body language**. This might include putting our arm around our listener's shoulders and checking: "Do you understand?" They notice our kind care and **patience**; our words suddenly seem to be clearer. We have a presence and transmit calmness: "I am strong when I am on your shoulders." Our comforting manner promotes maturity.

Dreamers and idealists long for the perfect professor. This person may be beyond our affordability or absent. **We make a compromise and settle** *for who is available*. Together we adopt a good attitude, decide on constructive guidelines and succeed just as well or even do better.

Between the giver and the receiver is a strong mutual wish for our message to strike a chord. **We know what we mean, but do they know what we mean?** Being accurate helps us to save time in the long-run. We construct and design our message carefully, **clearly and precisely**. It pays to be grammatically correct as we state the obvious and what is not so obvious with clarity. We set out on our journey as pioneers as we light up someone else's life as well as our own!

1.

Definite and Indefinite Articles: 'The' 'A' and 'An'

We are starting a journey of study and a tour of observation. Most books undertaking **the** teaching of grammar concentrate on **the** present, past and future tenses. Along the way, we aim to do that too. Just like being thrown in at **the** deep end of **the** swimming pool and being forced to 'survive', in our first chapter we notice **the** constant use of **'the', 'an',** and **'a'. THE, AN** and **A** are called **articles**: **'THE'** is the **definite** article; **'A'** and **'AN'** the **indefinite** article(s).

The names of things we label as NOUNS. Therefore, while absorbing vocabulary we immediately make use of these articles, **'the', 'a',** and **'an'** to go with and precede **nouns** for much of **the** time.

A slight complication occurs when we have to know which nouns in various contexts are either **COUNTABLE** or **UNCOUNTABLE**.

The **flour** we use for making bread is **UNCOUNTABLE** while the **flowers** in the garden are **countable**. We count a dozen roses but we cannot count the amount of flour we need to bake a cake. We do not count rice: we say, "I'll have **some** rice." We use **THE** before common nouns when we are sure of which thing we are referring to. 'The girls are in the car.' We use **A** or **AN** when we are not sure to whom or what we are referring. 'Have you made a choice of career?'

'There was **a** chair by the window and **a** chair by **the** door. He decided to sit on **the** chair by the window. Later, he wished he had chosen the one by the door.' We use 'an' before a vowel: '**an e**ar'.

We do **not** say 'a flour', but we might say, 'a bag of flour'; we do not say 'a rice' but we might say 'a bowl of rice'. We do not buy 'a toothpaste,' we buy 'a tube of toothpaste'. We do not say 'an Earth', but we might say 'the planet Earth'. The usual form of this proverb is, "Too much of **a** good thing is bad for us." But, Mae West, **the** film star said, "Too much of **a** good thing is wonderful!"

Teach yourself: Insert 'a' or 'an' or 'the': _ __ __

"The Tale of Peter Rabbit" is _ collection of stories for children written by Beatrice Potter (1866-1943). She was

2

__ English author who wrote more than 20 children's stories about 110 years ago. Her illustrations of ___ characters added to ___ charm of her books. As __ eager young student she was interested in nature and ___ countryside. As _ child from _ privileged family she had many pets and at __ early age drew many sketches of them and developed _ love of ___ natural world. She especially loved going to ___ Lake District and later in life bought_ farm there. She was also_ student of fairy tale stories and presumably began to imagine stories involving her pets. She wanted to marry her London publisher in 1905, but ___ tragedy of her fiancé's death meant she spent longer in ___ Lake District and engaged in her writing. ___ friendship with her solicitor who helped her buy land developed into _ romance. They were married in 1913 and stayed together until her death in 1943. The place she liked best was _ village called Sawrey where she bought _ traditional Lakeside farm. She built __ extension to the house for ___ farm manager and his family to use. They created _ beautiful English cottage garden. Many of her subsequent stories were set in ___ scenery of this area. Beatrix always had _ deep interest in being _ conservationist and she eventually donated many of her fifteen farmland properties to ___ National Trust. Her original Hill Top farm is still visited by thousands of visitors each year. Stories written by Beatrix Potter are well-known to all British children. She has shared her love of ___ impression ___ countryside and animal life made on her with so many readers. Her words and paintings have endured for over _ century.

2.

Using 'The' for Proper Nouns, Specific People and Places

When something is unique or we are being **specific** as if there is only one of them we use 'the': **The** United Nations; the USA; the French; the sea; the earth; the Moon; the village where my aunt lives; the best day since June; the capital of China is Beijing; the best dressed girl. Have you seen the movie "*The Good, the Bad and the Ugly*"?

When someone says they are going to the bank or the cinema or the football match we are usually sure which one they are referring to. "I'll meet you in the classroom." "It's not a good idea to look at the sun." "Most people use the knife in the right hand and the fork in the left." "The idea of having ice-cream for breakfast is a bit unusual."

We compare and ask: which is **the** longest river; the most beautiful lady; the fastest sprinter; the slowest of the runners? Which city has the most pollution? Which is the highest mountain? If Jack and Jill stand together we can see who is the tallest. Are they the same? What is the difference? The sooner we go home **the** better!

I have to go to **the** dentist and **the** doctor. Hurry up or you'll miss the train and **the** last bus. What is the speed limit on this road? The baby is expected in June or July. I must visit **the** clinic soon.

'**The** sedative drug thalidomide has been banned.'

'The use of chemical diuron has been suspended by farmers near **the** Great Barrier Reef.'

'India is **the** largest consumer of the insecticide DDT. We are unsure of **the** effects of DDT on human health. The decline in **the** bald eagle population is attributed to **the** overuse of DDT.'

'Stop at the kerb. Don't run across the road! Is **the** message clear?' We use '**the**' either when we are being **specific** or there is only one. "**Oh, darling, you're the only one!**" Have you said this many times?

Teach yourself: Explain the following:

1. **The** final straw that broke the camel's back.

2. **The** king is dead. Long live the king.

3. When he heard **the** bad news it was like **a** kick in the guts.

4. **The** early bird catches the worm.

5. You decide. **The** ball is in your court.

6. Many people want **the** best of both worlds.

7. You can't burn **the** candle at both ends.

8. You've known each other for 4 years? When will you tie **the** knot?

9. The bigger they are **the** harder they fall.

10. Why are we waiting? We'll be here till **the** cows come home.

Here is the radio news: Add the missing letters:

The no_se made by **the** explos_on was _ncred_ble.

The n_mber of people seeking asyl_m is less this year.

The short_ge of te_chers is re_ching _ crisis point.

A p_nsion_r's home was burgl_d today. His savings w_re stol_n.

The _wner of the pr_perty had saved the m_ney f_r twenty years.

The intern_tional _irport h_s been unus_ble since the earthqu_ke. However, the milit_ry airport ne_rby is und_maged.

Charity w_rkers are wanted to help the p_ _r and needy. H_wever, it takes a l_t of guts to d_ the j_b.

The mess_ge is th_t _lcohol _nd tob_cco c_use c_ncer.

To get the mess_ge across _dvertisements must _im at the t_rget _udience. The aim is not to al_rm people but to tell them of the risks. The _dvice is p_rticularly import_nt for those with _ f_mily history of c_ncer. To be **specific**, we looked at the evidence of cancer of the bre_st, the liver, the bowel and the thro_t.

Finally, T_e Beatles said t_at t_e best t_ings in life are free, but just give me money! (Strangely enough, 'money' is uncountable.)

3.

Be Observant when Listening to Radio Programmes

When wishing to observe English we **listen to informative radio programmes** which have news broadcasts or factual discussions. If we try to take notes we will soon lose count of the number of times that first 'a' or 'an' is used and then quickly followed by '**the**'. The message is:

Be OBSERVANT, FOCUS and NOTICE.

During a News Broadcast copy down as many relevant **sentences** which contain the word '**the**'. This might be three per bulletin which adds up to about six or nine or twelve per day. These may be of a diverse nature, but within a few weeks our English will be better due to the observation we are making and the sentences and the styles we are copying. **Like chaos theory, by concentrating on the smaller part we absorb very many other aspects of English**. This we term as 'a hidden way' of learning as we **CHANGE** by **improving our powers of observation and noticing everything in each sentence**.

What are **the facts of life**? The facts of life are **the** realities of life beyond **the** theoretical. Things in **general**: no 'the': we know where babies come from, of pregnancy and sex education; but, **the** wedding.

What is **the standard of living** like in your country? What is **the** origin of the wealth in your country and are **the** people generally well off or living **a** life close to desperation? Is it getting better or worse?

Then there are **the rates of taxation** in your country. What is **the** rate of income tax or the resources tax? At what age do you get **the** pension? Who pays for **the** police service? We become observant!

What facilities does your town have? What is **the** transport system like? Are the hospitals any good? What about the schools and universities. Do you ever go to the library or the park? Give examples of what you do in your leisure time. Do you go to **the** cinema?

Teach yourself: Matters in the News: Using 'the' and 'a'

1. What is in the news t_day? What is **the** g_ld price today?

2. Is **the** _iamond in_ustry in _ecline and losing its sparkle?

3. Perhaps big c_rporations can earn m_re from the ir_n _re mines.

4. A sp_cial submarine has b_ _n to the floor of the d_ _pest part of the Pacific Ocean, the Marianas Trench, 11 km b_low the surface.

5. The King of T_nga is dead. L_ng live the king.

6. The Aff_rdable Health Care Act was a bill crafted by **the** United States H_use of Representatives in 2_ _9.

7. The F_k_shima n_clear disaster was **the** worst in 25 years.

8. One year later, the nuclear _ndustry says _t's almost back to normal. The d_saster prov_ded many lessons.

9. W.A. is the St_te th_t le_ds the n_tion but it is being denied the investment it needs to support _ once-in-a-century boom. The economy is ch_nging; the government's policy must change.

10. In court, people swear to tell ___ truth, **the** whole truth and nothing but ___ truth.

11. Where is it best to keep your money? Under ___ bed?

12. What is ___ traditional belief about investing in the stock market?

13. The Esperance drug rehabilitation centre is one of ___ biggest and **the** most effective of its kind. It carried out ___ analysis yesterday.

14. Mr Smith was taken to ___ police station and charged.

15. He may spend many months at ___ local psychiatric hospital. ___ programme there is very strict. He must show _ commitment to recovery. Many find ___ regime is too strict.

16. Many of ___ young people entering university are ill-prepared for the tasks ahead. At ___ same time, the government foolishly encourages underperformers to enter university who, in **the** end, will not graduate. ___ students need _ broader pathway.

17. We need ___ brightest students to enter ___ teaching profession.

4.

Using 'the' for Proper Nouns:

The names of places, geographical locations and people usually begin with a capital letter and often have the word 'the' associated with them. For a start, oceans include **the** Atlantic, **the** Pacific. Islands include **the** Cayman or **the** Cocos or **the** Philippines or **the** British Isles. Soon after visiting **the** Galapagos Islands, Darwin wrote *"The Origin of Species"*.

Many famous books use a definite or indefinite article: *"A Tale of Two Cities"*, *"The Secret Garden"*, *"**The** Road Less Travelled"*, *"The Quiet American"*, *"The Old Man and The Sea"*, *"A Christmas Carol"*, *"The Tempest,"* *"The Outsiders"* *"**The** Three Sisters"* *"The Orient Express"* *"Tess of the D'Urbervilles"* *"The Third Man"* *"The Catcher in the Rye."*

Tourists visit **the** Great Wall, the Pyramids, **the** Tower of London, the Eiffel Tower, the Oracle at Delphi, the Taj Mahal, the Great Barrier Reef, the Grand Canyon, the Colosseum, the Empire State Building, the Black Sea, the Himalayas, **the** Alps, the Bay of Bengal, via the Panama Canal.

We may want to visit **the** White House or the Sydney Harbour Bridge but other places do **not** carry 'the': Singapore, Buckingham Palace, Big Ben, Canterbury Cathedral, St Mark's Square, Wall Street, Beijing Lu, Africa, France, Bolivia, Suez, India, China, Iceland, Bermuda, Jersey, Sardinia.

We want to see **the** Principal, the Dean, the Heads of Department, Mrs. Thomson, Mr. Thomson, the Thomsons. President Nixon, the Prime Minister, the Queen of Sheba, Sir Winston Churchill, the Lord Mayor.

The majority of the Earth's population lives in **the** northern hemisphere. Cape Town is in the south of South Africa and Cairo is in the north of Egypt. From Delhi we have to travel north-east to Calcutta and go south- west to Mumbai. The Chinese book is *"Journey to the West"* and many people are advised to 'go west young man' or travel around **the** world.

The Orange River is in South Africa and Orange County is in California. We cross **the** equator and the Sahara Desert, but we eat chocolate dessert.

Teach yourself:

Sardinia is just to the s_uth of C_rsica.

Haiti is located in ____ Caribbean Sea and occupies ____

14

western portion of ___ Island of Hispaniola. It is bound by ___ Dominican Republic to the east and ___ Atlantic Ocean to ___ north.

When staying in London, we will probably not be able to afford a week at Claridge's (Hotel), ___ Ritz or ___ Savoy or ___ Dorchester.

Going to ___ cinema is probably cheaper than going to ___ theatre.

If it's cold in London, go to ___ Cote d'Azur in ___ south of France.

From there go to Venice to see the canals, St. Mark's, and ___ Bridge of Sighs. In Florence (Firenze) is ___ statue of David and in Rome, ___ capital of Italy, is St Peter's Cathedral and ___ Vatican.

In New York tourists visit ___ Statue of Liberty, theatres on Broadway and Times Square. The baseball team is ___ New York Yankees. Have a rest in Central Park or leisurely walk round ___ Metropolitan Museum of Art. Two islands to explore are Staten and Manhattan.

The underground railway is called ___ Subway in New York, le Metro in Paris and ___ Underground or ___ Tube in London.

In Australia is ___ University of Western Australia. Other prestigious universities include Oxford, Cambridge and Yale.

Some rivers are difficult to spell: ___ Mississippi, ___ Thames, ___ Orinoco, ___ Seine, ___ Yangtze. Easier: The Po and Yellow Rivers.

Seas difficult to spell are ___ Mediterranean, ___ Caribbean, ___ Sargasso. ___ Antarctic Ocean is also named ___ Southern Ocean.

Other seas include: ___ Gulf of Carpentaria, ___ Gulf of Mexico, ___ Bay of Biscay. In French, ___ English Channel is called La Manche.

Names associated with colours include: Greenland, ___ Red Sea, ___ Blue Danube, ___ Yellow Sea, ___ Black Sea, ___ Coral Sea. Orange.

Where are ___ Middle East, ___ Far East, ___ Orient, ___ wild west, ___ Fremantle Doctor, ___ West Indies, ___ northern lights?

5.

Change: We have to use: Past, Present, Future

One of the advantages of having a well-developed brain is that we can cope with, adjust and adapt to **CHANGE**. This leads us into another hidden way of learning our language, in our case English. We are forced into using **past, present, future** and **modal verb forms**: We may as well

Observe and Notice CHANGES

By observing changes in our everyday life we have a daily way of concentrating on what is happening and changing. We **must describe how changes affect our behaviour** and of those around us.

We observe the weather. We notice an innovation, a new bus or train or a new electronic gadget. To state the obvious: compared with one hundred years ago, technological advances in, for example, aviation and communication make today's world totally different. We take a long-term perspective as we describe the changes, what **has changed**.

17

Some things never **change**. Everyone still wants to feel important and cared for as such. Human beings are spiritual and share a philosophy of wanting to be as decent to others as they are to us. When life is peaceful we have few dilemmas; when life is **unfair** there is likely to be jealousy, crime or fighting on the streets. People must have self-esteem or high status or they will want to struggle for dominance.

These characteristics do not **change**. However, the 24 hours a day news service **thrives on change**. We are forced to use past, present and future tenses. We state what used to be, what the situation is now and plan for the future. We absorb English in a hidden way and learn simple sentences as well as looking for '**the**', '**a**' and '**an**'. Reports and sentences contain **a subject, a verb** (someone does something) **an object**, and descriptive words: **an** adjective and **an** adverb. We observe these parts of speech in: '**The** beautiful Brazilian couple used to dance the samba smoothly. Now they perform **the** Salsa. They might get married.'

Teach yourself:

We use the **past** tense(s) a lot. These are most useful when we say what happened or **used to** happen and, for advanced exams such as IELTS, we have to be able to discuss **what has changed** from the past until now and speculate about the future. What did we do yesterday? We usually add 'ed' or 'd' to dance=danced, rehearse=rehearsed, play=played, suck =sucked, divide=divided, look=looked, trust=trusted, believe=believed.

It soon becomes **not** too difficult to remember the past form of irregular verbs such as catch=caught, drink=drank, think=thought, write=wrote, buy=bought, see=saw, have=had, say=said, is=was, are=were, fly=flew.

The past participle: e.g. begin, began, begun; As soon as I had begun talking someone else in the room began whistling. Do, did, done; What have you done. Yesterday I did the washing; I have just done the ironing. When did you last visit? I came yesterday and I've come again today.

Infinitive	Past	Participle	Infinitive	Past	Participle
Arrive	arrived	arrived	Lay	laid	laid
Expect	expected	exp_cted	Lead	led	l_d
Admit	admitt_d	admitted	Leave		
Begin	began	begun	Lend	l_nt	
Bite	bit	bitt_n	Lose		
Blow	bl_w	blown	Make		
Break	brok_	brok_n	Mean		
Bring	brought	brought	Meet		
Build	built	built	Pay		
Buy	bought	bought	Put		
Can	could	been able	Read		
Catch	caught	caught	Ride		
Choose	chos_	chos_n	Ring		
Come	came	come	Rise	ros_	ris_n
Cost			Run		
Creep		cr_pt	Sag	sagg_d	
Deal			Say		
Dig			See		
Draw			Seek		
Drink			Sell		
Drive			Send		
Eat			Sew	Sew_d	S_wn
Fall			Shake		
Feed			Shine		
Feel			Shoot		
Fight			Show		
Find			Shrink		
Fling			Sing		
Fly			Sink		
Forbid			Sit		
Forget			Sleep		
Forgive			Slide		
Freeze			Sow		
Get			Speak	spoke	sp_ _ _ _

Infinitive	Past	Participle	Infinitive	Past	Participle
Give			Spend		
Go			Spring		
Grind			Stand		
Grow			Steal		
Hear			Stick		
Hide			Strike		
Hit			Swear		
Hold			Swim		
Hurt			Take		
Keep			Teach		
Know			Tore		

Some words are the same in all three cases: hurt, hurt, hurt; shut, put, cut, bet, burst, hit, let, spread, set and cast. Words worth recalling are: **write, wrote, written**; tell, told, told; win, won, won; wear, wore, worn; lie, lay, lain; learn, learnt/ed, learnt/ed; will and would.

Teach yourself: Past tenses:

1. She's so old! She _ _ _ born last century!

2. The train co _ _ _n't wait and w_ _ _ without him.

3. What hap_ _ _ _ _ to the Titanic?

4. The Titanic s_ _ k on April 15th in 1912.

5. The Wright brothers fl_ _ their first plane in 1903.

6. Their first business _ _ _ a bicycle shop.

7. They d_ _n't claim the invention of the flying machine, but

8. adapted and dev_l _ _ _ a reliable method of pilot control.

9. Not all plays ascribed to Shakespeare w_ _ _ wr_ _ _ _ _ by him.

10. We know a few facts about Shakespeare's life (1564-1616) but he _ _ _ respect_ _ in his own lifetime. He marri_ _ Anne Hathaway in 1582. His son Hamnet died at the age of 11 in 1596. Shakespeare _ _ _ _ _ the play Hamlet between about 1601 and 1603. Shakespeare di_ _ in 1616 and w_ _ bur_ _ _ in his birthplace in the village of Stratford, England.

11. Have you ever b_ _n to Shakespeare's birthplace?

12. No, I've never visit_ _ England. I've o_ _y been to Scotland!

13. Whisky tastes good, but is too strong. I _ _ _ giv_ _ some to drink when I _ _ _ there. I drank the first sip and fe_t fine but when I dr_nk the next sip I kn_w I w_s ge_ _ing drunk! I h_ _ to lie down and I haven't touched it since.

14. I w_nt to English classes in Edinburgh. I stud_ _d tourism too. I m_t lots of students from all over the world, especially Europe. They h_d b_ _n learn_ _g English for years. We tour_ _ many parts of the Scottish highlands and th_ _ght the scenery w_ _ beautiful.

15. We c_ _ld hardly understand the Scottish accent at times, though when we underst_ _d it we start_ _ to speak like it!

16. Therefore, I have now b_ _n learning English for four years, since 2009. During these years I have lear_ _ to speak naturally.

17. I us_d to be shy, but I h_ve become fluent and now speak up.

6.

The Present Tense

We use the **PRESENT Simple** tense in a few ways:

a. When we ask for or state a **fact** or say what is **generally true**.

b. To say what we normally do or don't do, all the time; our habit and how often we do it: "I clean my teeth every day."

c. We also state our **theory**, or **promise** or **suggest** or **apologise**. E.g. when listening: 1. <u>R</u>eceive; 2. <u>A</u>ppreciate; 3. <u>S</u>ummarise; 4. <u>A</u>sk

d. We use the present continuous to talk about now or the future, such as, "We are playing tennis next Sunday."

e. We state what things are happening: "Pollution is getting worse." "They're building a new hospital." "The climate is changing."

Present tense: Fill the gaps:

When we f_ _l too hot we h_v_ the choice of d_ _ _ g several things. We c_ _ remove our clothes and r_st in a cool place, splash water on our skin and h_ _ _ a cold drink. When we _ _ _ too cold we m_v_ to a warmer place, put on more clothes and st_y busy and active. These conscious actions h_lp us to k_ _p our body at a fairly constant temperature of 37 degrees C.. In the heat the hypothalamus part of our brain sign_l_ to the blood vessels near our skin surface to become wider and g_ve off heat. We l_ _k red and our sweat glands rel_ _se sweat. This ooz_s onto the skin's surface, dr_ _s or ev _porat_ _ and draw_ further heat from the body. Each sweat gland _ _ a knot of tubes and cells in the skin's dermis layer. We h_ve about 3 million sweat pores; they a_ _ most numerous in our armpits, between our legs and on our forehead. In cold weather our blood vessels near the skin r_duce in size and we r_tain heat. We prod_ce goose-bumps and st_rt to shiver. When the hairs on our skin st_nd erect we a_e tr_pping warm air close to the body which _cts as a heat-retaining area.

Teach yourself:

1. I'm try_ng my best to save money but my b_lls are so h_gh I keep spend_ng all I've got and I'm runn_ng out of cash.

2. Well, doctor, when I'm throwing the ball my _lbow ach_s and wh_n I'm batting I can hardly lift th_ bat.

3. We use 'd_' and 'd_es' and 'd_n't' quite _ften. For example, when making c_nversation while dancing we ask, "Do y_u come here often?" The answer is "Yes I do" or "N_, I don't"

4. "I'm d_ ing my maths homework. D_ you know what this letter means? What d_es this symbol mean? It's all Greek to me!"

5. It shows you ought to l_arn your Gr_ _k alphab_t.

6. "Wh_t are you doing?" "I'm doing the w_shing up. It's got to be done h_sn't it?" "It doesn't need to be done yet, does it?"

7. "How do you do? What d_ you do? What are you d_ing?"

8. "It doesn't matter much does it?" "Oh, I th_nk it does!"

9. "Who are you? What's your n_me? Where _re you from?"

10. "My n_me is Bond, J_mes Bond. I'm a spy from Engl_nd."

11. "That's good. We've nothing to hide. I'm telling you the tr_th."

12. We are always looking for h_roes. "I am Spid_r-Man. With gr_at pow_r also comes great r_sponsibility."

13. Look _p in the sky. It's a bird, it's a plane, it's S_perman. We may adapt Superman's claims: He is more powerf_l than a locomotive, leaps tall b_ildings in a single bound, changes the co_rse of rivers, races a speeding b_llet, bends steel with his bare hands, and fights a never ending battle for tr_th and j_stice.

14. Muhammad Ali, the boxer, used to s_y: "I am the gre_test!"

15. In disasters: The water is r_sing. It's snowing. The lava is flow_ng. The f_re is burning out of control. The sh_p is s_nking.

16. The flow_rs are blooming, th_ birds are singing. The sun's out!

17. "Are you g_tting married?" "Not unl_ss I have to!"

7.

The Future Tense: 'will' and 'going to': Speculation

"I want to be remembered for my willingness to help others. Therefore, I must educate and improve myself because in the future I **will** travel and provide education for others. I'm **going to** be a pioneer. I know I'm **going to** succeed in this! I know I **will**!" In order to talk about the future we usually use the words "will" and "going to". When making arrangements we use the **present continuous**: "I can't see you. I**'m playing** football on Saturday and watching a DVD on Sunday."

When we have a definite intention of doing something or we know something is virtually certain to happen we use "**going to**". "I'm **going to** learn to be a helicopter pilot. I must. I promise I will!"

When we suddenly decide to do something we use "**will**". "Someone's at the door." "Okay, **I'll answer** it." Or, "Who has been the best behaved? Let me see. I think **I'll choose** you today."

We use **will** when making a **promise**: a wise and kind mother may say to her child, "You may not get what you want from me, but I'm wiser than you; I'**ll** give you something better." When wanting to live together we promise, "I'll support you, I'll be loyal, I'll care for you, I'll love you." We might reply, "You'll be better off without me."

We wonder what will happen or **is going to happen**. If we break a mirror **will** we have seven years' bad luck? Sport matches hold the crowd's interest and are unpredictable. In a movie a card game or waiting for a verdict in a court of law holds the audience in suspense. Who's **going to** win? What **will** happen? What **will** the jury decide?

For "going to", we give the example of, "Look at those clouds, it's **going to** rain." Another: "Look at her; she's **going to** have a baby soon!" "I've made my **plans**; I'm **going** to write the book next year." **"I will"** for **immediate action**. For **planned events: "going to"**. **"I'm going to plan my essay first, write it and then check it."**

Teach yourself:

1. Bring your plates here. I'm g___g to do the washing up now.

2. When I go shopping you w___ have to give me some money.

3. We are definitely _____ to need some more rice and potatoes.

4. I remember. I think I'__ get some tomatoes and onions as well.

5. Our visitors ____ be here at any minute now.

6. I'__ answer the door while you make the coffee.

7. You're carrying too many. You're _____ to drop some of them.

8. Well, I'__ come, but if it rains, I'__ return home immediately.

9. I've been told it's almost certain I'm _____ to pass my exams.

10. If it doesn't rain soon we're _____ to have a drought.

11. How long it'__ go on for we don't know.

12. No one is exactly sure what is _____ to happen.

13. Anyone who has had a deep cut ____ be left with a scar.

14. The use of plastic surgery ____ improve its appearance.

15. As the years pass by, our skin ____ lose its elasticity.

16. I don't know what we're _____ to do. I haven't got any money.

17. One of us ____ have to get a job. I suppose it'll be me.

18. No, I ____. I've already been told I'm _____ to start next week.

19. The car w__'t start. I'__ have to take yours.

20. For every pretty girl there ___ be a long queue of boys.

21. The match was close. No one knew who was _____ to win.

22. "We sh_ll never surrender!"

An oddity is that instead of "will" we sometimes use "shall" but ONLY for first person singular and plural, 'I shall', 'we shall.' Often it is used dramatically: "Oh my love, shall we ever meet again?" "We never shall!" "I shall not be here tomorrow; I shall go to the doctor's." "Hurry up and get better, we shall miss you." "Forget the past; today is the start of what I shall, will and am going to be."

We make **suggestions** and **speculate** about the future. How shall we feed ourselves when the population is 10 billion?

8.

Modal Verbs and Grammar Associated with Change

An important concept to appreciate is that everything **changes**. Therefore, we spend a lot of time describing how things used to be, stating how things are now and suggesting or speculating on how things should be in the future. We say how things **used to be**. We give dates; we try to understand and appreciate the circumstances, context, culture and beliefs of those times. Everything changes.

Scientifically speaking, there is no better topic than climate change. We explain what is happening now, such as extremes of weather and natural disasters and we attempt to give the causes. It is highly possible that human beings with their industries and farming methods are contributing to those gases in the atmosphere which envelop the Earth and cause heat to be retained instead of being released. We state what **used to** happen, what we are doing to make matters worse and what we **ought** to do in the future in order to improve this situation or, at least, **not** make matters too much worse. Will we give up cars?

When a patient goes to see the doctor then questions will be asked about what is happening, what used to happen and what solution or pathway ahead is recommended. 'You should rest.' We have to use **modal verbs** such as: **should, may, can/could, shall/will/would, ought to, might, must** and we **"had better" use "have to"** in a similar way. We give advice, make a request, give permission, talk about ability and discuss possibilities. 'We must adjust and adapt.' When making recommendations we use '**need to**'. Some people even consider '**dare**' as a modal verb. Dare we use it too?

The future will be different from the past. There will be astrological activity and the scenery on Earth will change. Our attitudes will change. It is a fact that everything is temporary; there is growth, but we must accept the inevitability of decay. In order to create **order from chaos** we **must** make **PLANS** and be **good communicators**.

Teach yourself:

1. In English exams we will have to discuss "issues" and speculate.

2. Wh_n we w_re at school we used to write stories and

33

adventures which often ended, "And th_n I woke up. It was only a dr_am."

3. Now we h_ve to discuss m_tters such as : television; _dvertising; equ_l rights; clim_te ch_nge; educ_tion; libr_ries; popul_tion growth; city planning; the environment; he_lth c_re and exercise; poverty; tr_nsport; _nim_l rights; w_ter; money and fin_nce.

4. We also h_ve to discuss change. We used to belong to an extended family; now we have a nuclear family and we m_y want to bring families back to being in closer touch again. Wh_t must we do to bring about this change? Offer **suggestions** and recommendations.

5. It has been said that all b_sinesses m_st fail. Therefore, they must adapt and adj_st. It is a challenge to us to realise that we sho_ld change with the times. The best example is the amazing man_al typewriter which now has become virt_ally obsolete and replaced by the comp_ter. We have to embrace change. Typing _sed to be something done by the girls in the typing pool. Now, both men and women may be expected to engage their own keyboard skills.

6. When m_ddle-aged couples talk about their marriage they usually pick out three d_stinct stages. There used to be the incredibly 'oh so much in romant_c

love' stage. Between the ages of 30 and fifty they devote themselves to cop_ng with bringing up children. They then look forward to relying on each other for support during their elderly years of ret_rement and old age. They realise they should have saved more money and invested more w_sely. Their grown up children can hardly afford the_r own house and so it is hardly worth relying on their ass_stance. They m_ght be able to help.

7. Following yesterday's heavy rainfall there may be f_rther showers today. As a res_lt of the floods there might have been more loss of life than we know of so far. Everyone sho_ld stay out of flood water, beca_se it is likely to be highly contaminated and there might even be snakes swimming along in the flow of water. The water levels will s_bside soon. The dro_ght we used to know may now be replaced by the health hazard of unclean water s_pplies.

8. In many sp_rts players could do worse than look at the rules of their game. Even the referees have t_ revise the rule amendments each seas_n. M_st likely, changes will have been made.

9. When stud_ing for an exam it is possible to remember some ke_ phrases and even sentences. We can make our own list. The_ should be words which could be applied to man_ topics in general.

10. When we define 'empathy' we _sk, "Wh_t would it be like if I were in their shoes? C_n I see it from their point of view?"

11. We m_st stand together; we must work as a team. We must learn to live together. We must develop and maintain the capacity to forgive. Wisdom born of experience sho_ld tell us that war is obsolete. Hate cannot drive out hate; only love can do that!

12. Even tho_gh we may not be religio_s, all religions have things to teach us abo_t what how we should treat our neighbo_r.

13. In a game of chess wh_te must go f_rst.

14. Not only must we p_y our t_xes, we have to; otherwise we will be breaking the l_w. There is no might, perhaps or maybe.

15. Would y_u prefer me to c_ _k dinner or are you g_ing to do it?

16. "Sh_ll I sleep here?" "No, you c_n't sleep here. You'd better go now. It's time my p_rents c_me b_ck. They might see you."

17. In future we need t_ reduce mankind's carb_n f_ _tprint.

18. C_uld I use your ph_ne please? Could you give me her number?

19. "W_uld you like m_re tea?" "C_uld you make it h_t please?"

20. He suggested that I should dr_ve slowly on my dr_ving test.

21. "Could you p_ss the s_lt please?" "Of course, here you _re."

22. D_ct_rs say _ld pe_ple sh_uld have an annual wellness check.

23. 'Must' is stronger th_n 'should'. 'Ought to' is sometimes used inste_d of 'should'; should is usu_lly more n_tural to use.

24. _hat I told you was confidential. You shouldn't have told anyone. You ought to kno_ that. Can't you keep a secret?

25. 15—40. He shouldn't have hit the ball into th_ n_t. He mustn't do that on this point. He n_ _ds to win the next four points.

26. Jane sho_ld be here by now. She m_st have missed the b_s.

27. I s_ppose we needn't h_rry. We've still got lots of time.

28. Sports f_ns like to know the score or the result. Good

writers should give b_sic f_cts and figures and not _ssume the re_der knows them. The wise writer d_re not leave the reader guessing.

29. Thank you for doing the washing up. You n_ _dn't have don_ it.

30. Oh, it's nothing; it's what I sho_ld do. Thank yo_ for the meal.

31. You o_ghtn't feel g_ilty about it. There's no need to. You can leave that, I'll do it later. You m_st get ready to go. When you get home you m_st telephone to tell me. You must stay again next weekend. My parents will be o_t. At least, they sho_ld be.

32. I m_ght, I m_ght not. If you th_nk I should then I will.

33. W_it and see. Would it be better if I came to st_y with you?

34. I think we c_uld have _ne weekend in the city and the next here _n the farm. It depends which _ne you prefer. Do y_u prefer to go sh_pping or w_uld you rather have s_me fresh air?

35. We could have the best of both w_rlds c_uldn't we?

36. When sh_ll we get m_rried? Can you w_it until next ye_r?

37. Act_ally, I can't wait. I j_st think we o_ght to be careful.

38. As it's a l_ap y_ar you should ask m_ if I will marry you.

39. Well, I m_y do just that, mightn't I? C_n we _fford to?

40. We m_st get serio_s and start saving; we'll have to grad_ate.

41. I'll th_nk it over. Would you like to go travelling f_rst?

42. Well, we could _o to_ether. Or would you rather _o alone?

43. Do I need to be asked? Wh_ don't you sta_? Must you go?

44. We must make plans. Plan a project or your next five years.

9.

Do, Does and Did

After the auxiliary verb forms **to do** and **did** we have the infinitive. This is most clearly seen when we ask questions. "**Did** you enjoy the movie last night? **Do** you want to see it again?" "Yes, I liked it a lot and so **did** my friend. And yes, I **do** wish to go to see it again, but only if you come with me. **Does** that answer your question?" "What **do** you think of me? What **did** you think of me when we first met?"

DO, DID and **DOES** are useful words to be aware of and to use very often if only to find out: "And then, **what did you do next**?"

These words tell us about what we **did** yesterday, what we do for a living or what he or she does for a job or hobby. They help us to construct **questions** and to make conversation. We are always asked about what we do for our hobby, or what our parents do, or what our sister does or what our grandparents did or used to do.

They are simple short words and it is good to make endless use of them rather than just see them as exercises **to do** in the grammar book. Once we regard them as **useful friends** then we overcome an obstacle as if it wasn't there. In essays we are advised not to use contractions: in **good university academic writing** we do <u>not</u> use 'don't', 'doesn't' or 'didn't'. As a reverse rule: '**don't use don't**'.

We remember to use **doing** and **done**. "What are you **doing**? This is the city centre. You can't be sick here. Oh, what have you **done**?" In school or when working on a project we are asked, "What are you doing. **How much have you done**." I'm **doing** these calculations. I've **done** twenty-three of them so far; I've got another seven to **do**."

Some people create a **crisis**: "Oh my God, what have you done?" And the future is "We just don't know what you're going to/will do next!" A famous children's book is "*What Katie did next.*" A significant question to ask is: "What do you aim to be doing 5 years from now?"

Teach yourself:

1. What we d_d years ago today's teenagers are also d_ing today.

2. Have they agreed to _ _ the work? We want it d_n_ by July.

3. "Is this tablecloth clean enough?" "Oh, it will d_, I suppose."

4. When we d_ the housework we always _ _ the floor last.

5. "Tell me more. Then what d_d you d_? What happened next?"

6. The hospital said grandpa is d_ _ _g as well as can be expected.

7. He should have d_ _e what I told him to _ _: stop smoking!

8. If he d_ _s he will live longer. If he do_ _n't he won't last long.

9. He'd better get used to d_ _ _g what he is told.

10. A lot of charities _ _ very good work for very worthy causes.

11. What d_d I tell you? I told you you could _ _ it didn't I?

12. I'm just a talker. You're the d_er. You're the pioneer.

13. 'Anything you can _ _ I can _ _ better. I can _ _ anything better than you.' D_ _s this always apply? If we d_ _'t try we won't know.

14. What are they d_ _ _g in Nanning? It d_ _n't use to be so big.

15. Most people **used** to wear a hat a hundred years ago, but I d_dn't **use** to do that. In the 70s a lot of people used to have long hair, but I d_dn't use to. Most people used to smoke, but I didn't use to. Most people us_d to go to church, and so did w_.

16. Just because he's playing football, d_ _s he have to spit like that? Surely, we d_n't have to watch that on television d_ we?

17. He didn't spit d_d he? He was just watering the grass.

18. D_ you have to keep looking at me? I'd be glad if you d_dn't.

19. This d_esn't even need thinking about. It's a "no-brainer!"

20. "Go ahead and d_ it! Just do it!" "Don't rush me. Let me think."

21. A famous poem: "*D_ not go gentle into that good night.*"

22. "*Do not stand at my grave and weep, I am not there. I do not sleep.*"... "*Do not stand at my grave and cry, I am not there I d_d not die.*" (Mary Elizabeth Frye.)

10.

Difficult Prepositions such as 'during', 'since', 'for', 'from'

When asked to define words such as 'during' and 'from' it is difficult to explain these without giving examples. In the dictionary the word **'during'** is associated with 'throughout'. We also use the word 'between' implying a starting and finishing time. And we use 'from' to tell us between the beginning times and until an end. "In British history, the First World War lasted **from** 1914 until 1918."

"**During** the match some heavy clouds came over the ground. It rained hard **from** half-time until five minutes from the end."

'From' is a preposition we use to indicate times or places. "We walked **from** Parliament Square to the Palace. Then, **from** 11.30 until 1pm we had our picnic in the park and fed the pigeons." We usually substitute the word 'between' for **from one place to another** and 'between' when **indicating times** and 'during' for **an event**.

"**During** the lecture, our professor wandered **from** one topic to another. I could hardly follow what she was actually talking about."

'**Since**' indicates the start of a time. "Oh, it's good to see you again. I haven't seen you **since** you were a little baby, twelve years ago."

"I have had a pain in my leg for fourteen months since at least last year. Six years ago I had a sore ankle and I have hardly had a day without some slight pain ever **since**."

Prepositions are difficult to define, but their roles are more readily shown when put **into** use. We hear them used in a court of law when a witness is asked for evidence: "How long did the burglar stay in your house **for**? Can you say when, **from** what time to what time? **During** those hours, were you frightened? Have you ever seen him again **since** then? And this happened six months **ago** did it?"

Teach yourself:

1. I have been trying to get in touch with you _ _ _ most of the day.

2. D_ _ _ _g your year's stay in France did you enjoy the food?

3. Famous poems by Robert Browning are: "*How they brought the good news f_ _ _ Aix to Ghent.*" "*Home thoughts, _ _ _ _ abroad.*"

45

4. Movies: "_ _o_ here to Eternity." "Escape _ _ _m Alcatraz."

5. Many farm labourers work _ _ _ _ dawn till dusk.

6. We ask: "What has changed d_ _ _ _g your lifetime?" "How have you changed _ _ _in_ the past seven years?"

7. We use a time or a date when we use 'since'. "Has anything happened _inc_ we spoke yesterday?" "What changes have happened in your life s_ _ _ _ 2007?"

8. We use 'for' to state a period of time: "I've been studying English f_ _ ten years. I've been living here in Canada _ _ _ a decade."

9. I had my milk teeth _ntil I was about seven years old. S_nce then I have had my permanent teeth. D_ring my teenage years I had to have my teeth straightened. Sin_e then I have felt more confident. If I want to keep my teeth f_r the rest of my life I must be careful. I haven't spoken to my classmates si_ce we were at college ten years ago. It will be good to meet up again if only f_r a weekend. During our absence fr_m each other many of us have become parents. I suppose we have become more mature sinc_ then but we will remain young for a long time in each other's eyes.

10. Full length swimsuits were used in swimming competitions f_r about ten years. A lot of swimming records were broken d_r_ng that time. S_nce these swimsuits have been banned the number of world records being broken has reduced dramatically.

11. You have been married f_r 30 years. Did you **use** to have a lot of boyfriends bef_re you were married? D_ring that time, did you consider for a moment marrying someone else? And s_nce then?

11.

More Prepositions

As students, in order to learn and get used **to** which **prepositions** are used **in** various contexts, we need **lots of EXPERIENCE**. We **MUST** <u>focus</u> and concentrate and observe. Concentration **on** our part helps us clearly notice that prepositions occur or come **along** in almost every sentence. Congratulations **<u>on</u>** making that observation!

We never get **tired of** learning English. It comes naturally **to** people of even the least intellectual capacity to absorb its basic principles. It is pointless getting frustrated and then angry **about** it or angry **with** our teacher. Rather **than** expecting to improve within just a few days, it is a matter **of** practising and becoming more fluently comfortable every month. Soon, everyone will know what we are talking **about**.

Lots of examples emerge when we talk **about** travel. "We have **to** leave **on** time at 8 o'clock sharp. I will go **on** holiday **with** or **without** you. We can go **to** the station **on** foot, go **by** train **to** the airport and travel **by** air. **On** the plane we can read a book **by** a writer who tells us **about** how to learn English quickly. We can have a hot drink **with** or **without** sugar; at the half-way point we will have a meal and eat **with** a knife and fork or **with** chopsticks. It's no use being **afraid of** foreign food. We all just have to like it and get **on with** it."

Overseas, things are a bit different **from** what we are used **to** but most city centres are just **about** the same now everywhere. We just make a commitment to get **on** well **in** our new environment. We read **about** the places before we go, listen **to** the news or watch **for** information **on** television. We have to find something we're good **at** or interested **in** and not be afraid **of** anything. Like it or not, we have to **get on with** it and don't feel sorry **about** it. We shall only feel **sorry for** ourselves if we don't enjoy the holiday **on** the coast. By the way, we prefer to pay **in** cash **rather than by** credit card.

Teach yourself:

Some people succeed **by** forming a partnership; others tell of its disadvantages. Whether as friends or **in** business, the relationship **w_th** each other can be tested and strengthened or disastrously torn **ap_rt**. There is definitely a demand **f_r** patience and tolerance.

The advantage of travelling or living alone is that we can

do what we want. Otherwise, when in a partnership the likelihood is that we will have to make compromises almost entirely **thr_ugh_ut** every day. The causes _f many arguments arise **fr_m** when we have different solutions to problems or when deciding **on** which direction to take. We don't agree **w_th** each other on everything!

The idea of marriage continues partly because human beings as a species reproduce **b_** engaging two people, male and female, usually _n sexual intercourse. There has to be a warm relationship and prolonged and continuous co-operation **between** the two parents for many years together. Children prefer **t_** have two caring parents to look **aft_r** them. With both parents encouraging them and providing secure discipline the child will feel a sense safety. Children try to see _f they can create a division or break _p between Mum and Dad, but they are glad when they are not the cause _f any disunity.

B_ the time children leave home they want to go travelling. In a new country they have a wide variety of places to see. If they disagree _n where to go they will, in the end, have to travel separately. A substitute word for frustration and boredom is anger. It is easy to be bored with a place and then get angry **w_ _h** each other. We can be impressed **b_** or amazed _t what we see for the first time, but then get fed _p _ith it after a while. It's best if we are generous **to**

each other and appreciative **of** the partner's wish to be independent.

Teach Yourself:

Fill the gap: **at, between, in, off, out, for, about, on, of, with, up, to, until, against, by.** (Notice: unisex names)

1. I'm older and grown up now. I'm fed _ _ with this hairstyle.

2. I hope everyone is shocked _ _ my new hairstyle. Is it terrible?

3. I'm not afraid _ _ what people might say.

4. Most people's comments only reflect a portrait _ _ themselves.

5. They tell us so much _ _ _ _ _ themselves when they criticise.

6. I used to get annoyed b_ criticism, but now I realise....

7. Most people only talk _ _ _ _ _ their own self-importance.

8. It goes without saying, they don't really listen _ _ anyone else.

9. Eventually, we only feel sorry _o_ our poor critic.

10. Later they have to be good _ _ repairing the relationship.

11. We meet a lot of prepositions when talking _ _ _ _ _ love.

12. We fall _ _ love. When we fall _ _ _ we lose a friend.

13. We break _ _ w_ _ _ our partner and walk _ _ _.

14. Sam is keen _ _ Stacey, but Stacey has a crush _ _ Alex.

15. Alex is going _ _ _ _ _ _ _ Casey, while Casey has fallen f_ _ Coby. I don't know what they see _ _ each other.

16. Dale is getting married _ _ Drew unless they split _ _.

17. It just shows what a thin line there is _ _ _ _ _ _ _ love and hate. Gwyn had an affair _ _ _ _ Jade last year until Kerry found

    o _ _ a_ _ _ _ it. Actually, they had been cheating _ _ each other.

18. Leslie was engaged _ _ Madison but they broke it _ _ _.

19. They're still fond _ _ each other and the best _ _ friends.

20. Mickey got engaged _ _ Riley but their parents were a_ainst them getting married and told them to wait _ _ _ _ _ they are 18.

21. But they might get interested _ _ someone else before then.

22. Unless they still only have eyes _o_ each other.

23. They flirt _ _ _ _ friends but their love is a friendship set _ _ fire.

24. After all, a friendship can be shattered _y an affair.

25. In my speech I would like to take this opportunity to thank everyone _ _ _ attending tonight. You must have taken a lot of trouble to come so far _ _ _ _ _ your way.

26. I've decided _ _ stand as your Member _ _ Parliament _ _ _ three reasons. First, I'm not impressed _ _ _ _ the present state _ _ affairs regarding the economy. I am most concerned _ _ _ _ _ the falling value _ _ our currency and the rising cost _ _ living.

27. Second, we must try to **mitigate** climate change _ _ decreasing our carbon footprint. Therefore, I propose that, _ _ _ _ immediate effect all use of fossil fuels should be banned. All means _ _ transport using petrol should stop before we run _ _ _ _ _ fuel.

28. Third, we will have to find other means _ _ transport.
As you know, good means _ _ communication are _ _
the utmost necessity. Therefore, you will be pleased _
_ know that taxes o_ bicycles are going to be
dramatically reduced when I'm _ _ power.

29. I know some of you will be annoyed _ _ _ _ _ all this
while others will say it is good _ _ me to improve _ _
what others have done. I'm not apologising _ _ _ my
plans and proposals for giving us all something to
think _ _ _ _ _. I hope you approve _ _ them.

30. I'm depending _ _ your support _ _ _ me in the
election. You might be surprised _ _ what I have
recommended. You need my wisdom to protect you _
_ _ _ the effects _ _ climate change. We cannot be
blamed _ _ _ that; we can blame it _ _ someone else.

31. We rely _ _ our cars far too much. No wonder people
suffer _ _ _ _ obesity and the effects _ _ not
exercising. We don't want a rise _ _ high blood
pressure numbers or dying _ _ a heart attack. Don't
fall i_ _ _ the trap of complaining _ _ _ _ _ air
pollution.

32. If we care _ _ _ _ _ anything we must care _ _ _ others
around us by searching for answers _ _ these
problems and crises. It would be generous and polite
_ _ you to weigh _ _ my proposals.

33. Do you prefer _ _ take my word or my opponent's promises?

12.

Comparing and Opposites: We must CHANGE and ADAPT

There are many opposite fortunes in life. This fact is recognised in a wedding ceremony where we hear the promises of the bride and groom to care for each other: **"for richer, for poorer; for better, for worse; in sickness and in health** and to love you as a part of myself." We can go to the extremes or reach for compromises.

It is worthwhile improving our ability to compare. In exams we might either be asked to compare or *WE take the initiative* and spend a paragraph making comparisons. This principle is especially applicable when discussing statistics, graphs, charts and tables of facts and figures. We use phrases such as **smaller** or **greater than, a dramatic rise** or **fall, a steady decline in sales**. We do not wait to be asked!

A useful list of words to classify things under is: '**opposites**'. In daily life we quickly calculate a fair price:

fair; fairer; **much** fairer; the fairest. We talk about **money a lot** especially whether things are dear or cheap or a good buy. We have **relationships**: friends and enemies, love and hate, happy and unhappy. When we talk about our **status** we use higher or lower, top or bottom, senior or junior, promotion or demotion. Have we made ourselves clear or are we misunderstood?

In order to make things different we have to **change** and take a risk about making matters better or worse. We seek harmony and peace rather than disunity and strife. Do we prefer life to be very orderly or is it better to be spontaneous and impulsive? Are we mature or immature? We benefit from being optimistic, but we use caution.

Superlatives are the words which describe the **best or worst**, **most expensive or cheapest**, sunniest or cloudiest, best friend or worst enemy. It is best to have the **brightest** and **most** optimistic view that English will be of the greatest benefit to us and **most life-enriching**.

Teach yourself:

1. What colour shall we paint the room? Red is warm_ _ than blue.

2. Is it b_tt_r to be extrovert or introvert? Find a balance of both.

3. The wind howls b_t the mountain remains quiet.

4. Solitude is strength; to depend on the presence of the crowd is weakness. Anyone can give up; it's the easi_ _t thing in the world to do. B_ _ to hold it together when everyone would understand if you fell apart, that is true strength.

5. The strong_ _t man in the world is he who stands alone.

6. Reflect that in a crowd or as a part of our culture it is difficult not to concur with the opinion of the crowd o_ the group.

7. Pay great_r attention to how News bulletins, newspaper opinion pages and reports are constructed. They usually keep it simple.

8. Which is m_re important: having a higher I.Q. or having the application and ability to get the job done day by day?

9. Beware of those who speak constantly l_udly, either they don't want to make room for you to grow or they lack inn_r confidence. Speak s_ftly and gently see if they can run the show without you.

10. For many comparisons when stating our integrity we add the word 'more' or 'less'. He is **more**: h_nest, r_liable, tr_thful, l_yal, p_tient, s_rious, t_lerant, r_sponsible, p_rsistent, p_rsevering, d_ligent, r_spectful, r_spectable, upr_ght, c_nsistent, cr_ative.

11. Research shows that tw_ce as many people believe university r_search states the obvious and is more unreliable than r_liable.

12. Men and women are m_re or l_ss the same; if so, is it only the glass ceiling that is preventing their progress?

13. The chart clearly shows that a h_gher than before percentage of advertisers promise us far more free time if we purchase their product. However, do we prefer to rest or to stay busy?

14. Compared with 40 years ago, many more people are living f_r beyond the age of 60 while the number of children in families is far fewer. Thus, the great_st problem for future generations is taking care of the elderly, many of whom are unable to get jobs.

15. Life and employment us_d to be far simpler. It is getting h_rder and hard_r to find employment for those who are unfamiliar with mod_rn technology. A sign_ficant number of old_r people will require homes and nursing care as the population ages. This will create m_re employm_nt in this care industry and more homes will have to be built and staffed. Therefore, the government must not expect impossibly high standards that are impossible to reach, oth_rwise carers will find that home improvements and adequate staffing will be much t_o expensive to augment and implement.

16. Wh_reas in Europe the month of June has the long_st hours of daylight, the southern hemisphere, by contrast, has its shortest days and longest nights. "Winter's days are not long enough!"

17. Gen_rally, we agree on m_st matters and our opinions only vary sl_ghtly and are marg_nally or only fract_onally d_fferent.

18. It is difficult to say why shark attacks in this ocean have varied so c_nsiderably in the past twenty years. We have been hoping the numbers would have dropped dram_tically by now. We have had b_tter supervision of the beaches and **far more** surveillance by spotter-planes. This year has seen the w_rst number of deaths.

19. I don't know wh_ch is m_re relaxing and distracting: going swimming or singing karaoke. I feel s_bstantially more at ease after work by doing either. I wish my colleagues at work would complain l_ss; some of them are the l_ast appreciative people.

20. Generally speaking, things are bett_r now than ev_r.

21. The man who shot more th_n 60 people in Norway said at his trial that to be declared insane would be a f_te worse than de_th.

22. Some investments are said to be 'as safe _s houses'. However, house prices as well as the stock market prices can dr_p dr_matically. Compared with the

original situation some buyers may find that their mortgage will be far high_r than their house is worth. There c_n be cr_shing f_lls on the stock m_rket too.

23. We are all keen to make progress and to impr_ve. Going into r_verse and getting w_rse in our behaviour is called 'r_gression'.

24. A Tale of Two Cities: It was the b_st of times, it was the w_rst of times; it was the age of wisd_m; it was the age of f_ _lishness.

25. When **c_ntrasting and c_mparing** we use words which lead us towards variati_ns, opp_sites or similarities. Opposites include: c_nversely, on the c_ntrary, in c_ntrast to this, in comparis_n, h_wever, yet, n_netheless, nevertheless, th_ugh, even though, instead, even if, in spite _f, despite, alternatively, whereas, while, whilst, on the one hand, on the other hand, as a result, theref_re.

26. When things are **more or less** the s_me we use: simil_rly, likewise, _lmost the s_me, ex_ctly the same.

27. When talking about sales statistics we say: reached a p_ak, climax_d; declined; soared; rose/dropped dramatically; went into a trough; decr_ased; grew; improved; recovered; reached a plateau; bottomed out; but hardly _nough to be of significance.

28. Find opposites of: atheist, agreed, opinions were poles apart, discrepancy, fertile, responsible, consistent, world of difference.

29. The opposite of: fair, justice, co-operative, success, attractive.

30. Employment used to be cert_in and predict_ble: women were not expected to work; this was the m_n's role; there were not so m_ny old people to look after and there have been **far more** radical ch_nges in the workplace. These ch_nges mean that jobs are **no longer** as secure and **as** s_fe **as** they used to be. We must **adjust**.

31. Use the dictionary to find opposites of: regular, responsible, lucky, strong, nephew, m_ral, true, appear, healthy, justice.

32. He roared **like** a lion, just **like** you. **More or less** like you. Similar to you. Vaguely l_ _e you. Okay, not the **least** like you.

33. **In comparison, by comparison, compared with** Sam you look more and m_ _e **just like** her. Or do I mean less and less? The older I get the younger I feel. Strange isn't it? Stranger than fiction.

34. As we age we are **far less** naïve. We are **f_r more** mature and **less** inhibited and have **much more** fun.

April Easter holiday school trip 40 years ago.

Barge in springtime: Snow is an uncountable noun. We love the beauty of its whiteness and we willingly want to talk about comparisons and contrasts. Causes and effects. Climate change. Description. Of course, the scenery undergoes rapid CHANGE; we again write about the past, the present and the future.

13.

In Exams: Causes, Consequences and Results

People like to find **reasons** (for) **why** things happen. These reasons may be sound enough, but some of them (always given in hindsight) qualify to be of the utmost nonsense. However, we prepare ourselves for the fact: logical reasoning is a requirement of university-speak. We encounter bias and the use of very suspect and selective evidence.

We need look no further than discussions regarding education, which always **generate** hot air. Schooling is recommended for all, whether or not it is suitable for all. For a chosen few, an academic education enables them to fulfil their potential in literacy, while others are forced to undergo what is to them: sheer torture. Only one side of the story is told. It is difficult for non-academic students to adjust.

In an IELTS or a TOEFL exam we will not be asked to give reasons for a medical diagnosis or a physics question in which we suggest ways of improving engine efficiency. The questions are very **general** in nature and we need only give the conventional answers.

To be frank, the causes and reasons for events are usually incredibly interwoven, complex and complicated. Everyone makes a plea for the aim of 'keep it simple'. Thus, to reiterate, the principle is: go along with conventional middle-class values expected on naïve talk-back radio or fashionable theories. Do not upset or shock them. They live a long way from the realities of life and wear rose-coloured glasses.

When it comes to the writing of essay answers, it is in the student's interest to give reasons they believe to be in line with these 'valued principles.' Climate change may be due to mankind's overuse of fossil fuels or it may be the judgement of the gods or it is due to the fact my grandmother hung her underwear on the clothesline upside down. Just give conventional and fashionable answers!

Give essay graders the desired reasons in a conventional answer. It is wisest to supply the usual reasons with facts carefully selected to suit.

Teach yourself:

Some grammarians like to see the correct and precise use of 'due to' and 'owing to'. We use **'owing to'** as a synonym of **'because of'**. 'Owing to' serves as an adverbial while '**due to**' modifies a noun and is a synonym of '**as a result of**'. Nowadays, these are more or less interchangeable and a fairly safe general rule is to **put 'owing to' at the start of a sentence.** Most teachers are unaware of the difference, thus we leave this fine line decision for the advanced course!

1.   **_wing to** the wet r_ad c_nditions the tw_ cars skidded.

2.   The subsequent crash was **du_ to** the downpour of rain.

Students will do well to remember that their favourite word should be '<u>**because**</u>'. Just by saying this word the conversation or explanation is certain to continue and the answer extended. Instead of struggling to talk for half a minute when we use the words 'because', 'however' or 'although' we are forced to add far more and go on for two minutes.

We might make a terrible start when explaining cause and effect but we have to practise and practise and we will find some wonderful friends in the following words and phrases: **the reason for; thus; therefore; as a result of; as a consequence; hence; consequently.**

In formal essay writing, especially when opening a key

sentence of importance, it sounds weak to use the word 'so'. Use '**therefore**'.

3. The children played football every day; **c_ns_quently** their shirts and shorts had to be washed daily **bec_use** they were muddy.

4. The **r_as_n f_r** travelling to China in 1998 was to help hundreds of students with their study of English **bec_use** they knew their country was opening up to the rest of the world.

5. It is vital to make a good impression early on, **oth_rwise** we may be judged poorly in a prematurely unfair and unjustified way.

6. Being well-prepared for the exam is extremely important. **Th_r_f_re** the student must arrive early, check the instructions and read every question thoroughly.

7. Being economically prudent is essential. Over-expenditure and poor financial judgement by many banks l_d to the crisis of 2008.

8. The res_lt was that house prices plummeted and employment increased for many years after.

9. Historians still find new caus_s of old wars. Their research provok_s and l_ads to a lot of unanswered questions.

10. The First World War was sparked off by the assassination of the Arch Duke Franz Ferdinand. No doubt, there were many other underlying causes and reasons for the provocation, but this pr_t_xt was enough to g_n_rate conflict. The roots of the problem dated back several decades. The Duke's death s_t in train a series of events which br_ught about outrage and culminated in four long years of the senseless slaughter of young soldiers. The unfairness of the spoils of war, including borders and territory, pr_mpted Germany, China and Japan to resume the struggle for the return of their motherland in the 1930s. The c_uses of present day antagonisms st_m back at least 100 years, if not longer.

11. The purpose of my l_tt_r is to expr_ss my et_rnal gratitude_.

12. I am on a tour of Cambodia. My a_m is to see as much as I can.

13. The res_lt will be that I will fall in love with the country or someone and consequently stay (t)here forever.

14. We can ask what the aim or purp_se is. We are having a meeting with a view or visi_n of planning the new railway line.

15. The **result** can also be the upshot or outcome or implications. The ups_ot of the meeting was that the construction of the railway would go ahead but the cost will be more than expected.

16. Acc_rdingly, always expect c_sts to be far more than stated.

17. We state and compare situations. More than, less than. Most. We use 'although', 'whereas', 'while/st' to start our sentences. We use 'as...as', He went as red as a beetroot, Why? Because....

14.

There are, There is, There might be

"**There might** or will be a high price to pay if we find that mankind is contributing to climate change. **There** will be more droughts, tornadoes, floods, snowstorms and cyclones."

When assessing the IELTS essay writing, one sign of a good writer is the use of '**there**'. When the student uses '**there** is/are/was/were' it is not remarkable, but as with so many aspects of life, **other students do not use it**, partly because they are unsure of how to do so.

We point out a fact: '…. There are a few Chameleons that are viviparous and they are all zygodactylous with fingers and thumbs'.

The difficult sentences give a forewarning of what we are about to say: **There** may be trouble ahead. **There** you go again, always complaining. '**There** are three main reasons for this opinion. First, …'

We introduce a person: **There's** someone here to see you.

Something happens or occurred: **There** were three loud explosions.

We say 'in that place': 'Duck-billed platypuses are found there.' 'Oh, there you are, you're here.' 'Where is it? It's over there.'

When we notice or make an observation: 'There have been significant advances in medical science this century.' 'I'm okay. There's nothing wrong with me! It's you!' 'There is a chance of rain this afternoon.' 'There's a close resemblance between that and the map of Tasmania.'

<u>Idioms</u>: There's more than one way to skin a cat.

There's many a slip between cup and lip, something might go wrong.

There's no such thing as a free lunch.

There's no fool like an old fool.

There, but for the grace of God go I.

Teach yourself:

1. Okay, you've made a mistake. Th_re's a lifetime left to correct it.

2. The f_re services arr_ved there w_thin two m_nutes.

3. It's too late now. The_e's no point in crying over spilt milk.

4. What d_ you want? There isn't any c_ffee, is there? Do y_u like tea? I hope there's s_me h_t water in the kettle, isn't there?

5. Oh yes. Shanghai is a lively city. Have you ever b_ _n there?

6. Once upon a time, there were three blind m_ce.

7. There's str_ngth in numbers.

8. Just c_ll my n_me and I'll be there. I'll be there to comfort you.

9. Was there a l_brary here? There used to be; now it's a w_ne bar.

10. *There once was an _ld man of Esser*

    Whose kn_wledge grew lesser and lesser.

    It at last grew s_ small

    He knew n_thing at all

    And now he's a c_llege professor.

11. Everything's g_ing sm_ _thly. But there's sure to be a pr_blem.

12. There's alw_ys a w_y to overcome any obst_cle. Where

there's a will there's a w_y. It's not too l_te, there is alw_ys hope.

13. There is s_fficient evidence to show a strong correlation between the ability to play the piano and learning a lang_age.

14. There's every ch_nce our rese_rch will be completed soon.

15. There is a tendency for some th_ngs to become fash_onable quickly and to become unfashionable just as qu_ckly.

16. There's every likelihood that your b_siness will be s_ccessful.

17. Ow_ng to the overuse of ant_biotics there seems to be inferent_al evidence that many v_ruses are now more res_stant.

18. There is a virt_al certainty that the world's pop_lation within ten years will exceed 8 billion people.

19. When comforting: 'Th_re, there. No n_ _d to get too upset.'

20. There are m_ny choices and v_rious ways of coping with this problem. First, there is the question of finding enough food _nd shelter. Second, there is a gre_ter

need for educ_ting people about contr_ception. Third, there is the question of he_lth care.

21. There is a distinct chance that many animal species will become extinct. There is already t_ _ much p_llution of their habitats.

22. There are many reasons why you will like my hometown. There are se_eral beautiful parks and from Kings Park there are wonderful views of the ri_er as well as the distant hills. Among the disad_antages, there are too many sets of traffic lights.

23. There sh_uld be en_ugh m_ney in the bank to pay this bill.

24. There _ught to be a l_t of pe_ple there. It's today's big match.

25. There w_s h_rdly anyone there a fortnight ago.

26. There were tw_ classes of sch_ _lkids, an old man and his d_g.

27. There's no s_ch thing as a certainty; no one knows the f_ture.

28. There us_d to be a lot of respect for t_achers, but there is very little these days. There is good r_ason to pr_fer the old days. As there is no _mpirical data we have to r_ly on anecdotal _vidence.

29. There must be sufficient scientific pro_f. _therwise it's hearsay.

30. "Did _nyone phone?" "There was a call from your dentist at 2.30. I'm afr_id to say there wasn't any mess_ge."

31. The w_rst people believe 'there is no sm_ke without fire'. I am telling you the truth and there is no reason to d_ubt my w_rd.

32. M_ke the me_ning clear so there is no ch_nce of ambiguity.

33. There is usually a str_ng b_nd between a m_ther and her child.

34. There is one big questi_n: deciding on the r_le the father plays.

35. There are 365 days in a ye_r but in a Le_p ye_r there are 366.

36. There's gold in those hills and there's plenty more where that came from. There's no need to be gr_ _dy. There's pl_nty for everyone. There will still be some there tomorrow.

37. He was a f_ _l to believe her. There's one b_rn every minute!

15.

Reasons, Comparisons, Give, Giving, Create and Generate

We <u>integrate</u> 'comparisons', 'cause and effect' and statistics into much of our writing. The trouble with selecting 'cause and effect' or 'comparison and contrast' is that we isolate that specific theme. The point is though, these ways of writing are what we do in every essay whether or not we are asked directly to compare or **give** reasons. We integrate comparisons as well as give cause and effect all the time.

'Even in the developed world, 20% of children go to bed hungry.' In every essay we use statistics. We compare and write about: the past and present; the rise and fall of profits; improvements from what **used to be** to what is now. By knowing the past we understand what has given rise to the present and future trends.

Events **give** cause to or **give** rise to other events which again **generate** further ripples. We begin speeches with "It **gives** me so much pleasure to be here tonight because….." We use **'give' a lot instead of 'cause'**. "Smoking cigarettes almost certainly **gives rise to** many people **developing** lung cancer whether directly or by passively inhaling the smoke of others."

The words used in **cause and effect** and **comparison** essays include variations of the following (note the accompanying prepositions): **Although, whereas, while, give rise to; produce; spark off; give; generate; bring about; change into; develop, owing to; due to; as a consequence of; result in; trigger (off); stimulate; influence (a person to); provoke; promote; induce; contribute to(wards); accounts for; facilitated (by); derived from; motivated by; thus; positive/negative outcomes/expectations; analogy between; more, most, less, in contrast to; compared with; effects of; difference between/from/in; affected the outcome; analysis of.**

We also include 'advantages and disadvantages' as well giving a plain description of a process. For a process we will use the passive voice much of the time. When giving advantages we use **superlatives** or comparatives: 'greater than', 'is similar to' 'not as many as' 'least'.

A key word in life is our act of **'giving'**. As a philosophy, the concept of 'giving' is a fundamental principle. We are extra kind to people and give them assistance or pleasure and **ask for no reward. A good result is enough.** We are **charitable** and **donate** our time or money.

To be blunt, it is easy to make a case that in every city there are the 'haves' and the 'have nots'. There is the risk of demonstrations, riots or mass street violence. Unfairness **gives rise to** violence.

When there is a **need we must act**. A high proportion of a community needs special help or endures unpleasant surroundings. The length of the list of schools that cater for people with special needs is a major surprise. In addition, we have to look after the elderly and those who are left behind in the daily rush for jobs suitable only for those who have either earned or cheated their way to degrees of all levels. This situation **gives grounds for believing** that no one cares enough and **gives** us many **reasons** to plan programmes to help those who need assistance. Many of these programmes **generate** good **results**.

Difficult people or problems **give** us a pain in the neck or **cause** us a lot of trouble. These problems force us into **generating** ideas and being **creative**. We **create solutions** rather than wanting to **create** further problems. We test our ideas and put them into practice. Then we **produce** a report which states any success or otherwise.

The prefix 'gene' implies giving birth to. As well as generating electricity we might **generate** controversy or extra income or interest and enthusiasm through effective marketing and advertising. There is always a need for **creative** ideas, though these **new approaches** must be practical. They have to be properly implemented. The members of staff involved are usually fully motivated to care about the standard of their work or to **adopt** a **caring attitude**. Equipment has to be provided and **its ongoing maintenance has to be allowed for**. Ideas are easy to dream up. Implementation is the difficult 'real' work.

Contributions and commitment should be recognised and appreciated with each person **warmly acknowledged and praised**. A caring and appreciative attitude gives rise to caringly made products and better service. If the workplace is a factory **then** the resultant measure would be the more **productive output** of quality-made **products**. We use words such as **'give'**, **'generate'**, **'produce'**, **'develop'** and **'create'** to describe a process.

We use **'therefore'** in preference to the weak 'so'. Take digestion as our example. Students of English should acknowledge that medical matters, bowel cancer or diet are of utmost importance and **therefore** the correct use of English is obligatory. We use a strong connecting word **'Therefore'**, when leading to significant results.

As a general rule, we use **'owing to'** (as a result of) at the start of a sentence and 'due to' especially **'is due to'** (on account of) fairly centrally within a sentence. "Owing to heavy overnight rain the match has been cancelled." 'Due to' must be attached to a noun. "The reason why we slowed down was due to the fog which suddenly descended." For either or both we can get away with: **'because of.'**

When stuck for ideas when speaking or writing then we reach for **'because'** and **'however'**. By using 'because' we are forced and **stimulated** into extending our sentences. When we finish one idea we add more and put forward another point of view by using the word 'however'. **Consequently**, we give rise to more ideas. Life is a battle, but these useful words **generate** new strength in us to carry on.

Just like asking the **result of one hand clapping so we realise that at least two things come or go together to produce cause and effect.** All our exercises on comparatives and superlatives become useful.

<u>Teach yourself:</u>

1. One eff_ct of tornadoes is houses being knocked to the ground. The res_lt is a trauma for the homeowners too.

2. A pay rise for one group of workers usually sp_rks off pay claims by other groups. Widespread pay rises will g_nerate inflation.

3. The eff_ct of the stim_lation of the economy through tax cutting delays or s_ves a country's economy from g_ing in_o recession.

4. The referee's decision to award a penalty most certainly aff_cted the result of the game as well as br_nging ab_ut the g_ving of the red card to the offender.

5. "I us_d t_ suffer from anorexia nervosa. Starvation can c_use structural changes in the heart and brain; this le_ds to long-term cons_quences. Now I feel much bright_r and I am at a h_althier 54kg, m_ch h_ppier, m_re resili_nt and studying again." She was so moved and m_tivated by the dedication of the hospital staff she decid_d to enrol in a nursing degree. **The result is** that her peers in her class serve as and g_ve her an understanding support system.

6. "As a physiologist, some clients fear over-exercising bec_use of the risk of injury or have suffered a setback d_e to injury. I help them to dev_lop skills and body awareness to help avoid injury. B_ild your strength, flexibility and endurance slowly. Be m_tivated to impr_ve steadily rather than c_use yourself injury. Steady exercise res_lts in long-term improvement and f_cilitates a willing desire to continue. **Th_refore**, do not go full out too soon."

7. Exercise **c_uses** glucose to be tr_nsported from the blood stream into the body cells. Exercise brings about the lowering of blood sug_r and **gives rise to** lessening the chance of getting diabetes.

8. Children have plenty of reason to exercise. **Owing to** their bad eating habits or sedentary lifestyle kids do worse in school and in general mental functioning. Exercise prod_ces better r_sults.

9. What can they ask? _ompare and contrast. _ause and effect. Debate an issue. Every essay: **PLAN: WRITE: _HE_K!** Read it again.

16.

Countable and Uncountable Nouns

More often than not, we use the **indefinite article 'a'** or **'an'** with **countable** nouns. And we do not add 's' to the plural form. We can have ten bags of flour (bags being countable), but we only use flour (not 'a flour') to make 17 cakes. We say we have 'a lot of' or 'haven't got any' or 'have no' (money). Flour and money are 'uncountable.'

Strange as it may seem, we become aware of 'countable' and 'uncountable' when discussing money. We can demand, "Give me the money!" but we do **not** say, "Give me a money." We can count the money notes and coins in our pocket, but 'money' is uncountable. Things that **flow**, such as water, are **uncountable**; whereas **glasses** of water are **countable**. Other **uncountable** nouns include:

Milk, champagne, happiness, love, art, advice, rice, sugar, butter, information, news, music, improvement, electricity, gas, fun, power, luggage, baggage, furniture, wine, travel, poetry, pollution, health, homework, scenery, work, machinery, harm, leisure, chaos, luck, research, evidence, accommodation, photography, progress, mud, sunshine, housework, weather, cutlery, shopping, applause, rice, coffee, tea, clothing, chess, assistance, violence, cheese, cash, light, camping, safety, courage, rain, snow, equipment, sand, ice, flesh, intelligence, food, china, worth, transport, magic, stuff.

We have containers: a **liquid** such as beer is usually uncountable but we use a container: a barrel of beer. We also say: I'll have a beer. Generally, we might usually have courage and show no **fear**, yet, in a particular case, have a fear of snakes. **Thought**: "That's a good idea; I'll give it some thought" or, "I've just had a bright thought." We have to be aware of different meanings: while we may want to "rent a room" we may look and say: "There isn't much room in here."

Also we use singular uncountable nouns: e.g. The Department of Education; we say that "a good education is such a good asset."

<u>**Teach Yourself**</u>: Make a long list of uncountable nouns and integrate and absorb them as a part of your English, grammar and vocabulary:

1. My ed_cation was more in the sch_ _l of life and hard knocks rather than at un_versity. The adv_ce is: to value both.

2. What things flow? Fl_ur, s_lt, w_ter, b_er, t_othpaste, w_ne, hair.

3. "Happy birthday. We didn't know whether to give you ch_colate or a box of chocolates or some c_ffee or a coffee pot. Go on, have some chocolate; resistance is useless.

4. I like to give my girlfriends j_wellery as a birthday present.

5. Some people like to have fun by giving und_rwear as a present.

6. When we give cl_thing we have to guess the s_ze.

7. Buying furn_ture is a bit too costly. We need a lot of m_ney.

8. Let's do some shopping. We need che_se, sug_r, m_lk and r_ce.

9. At school I studied Chemistry, Physics and Biology. I like living things but I also like des_gning m_chinery.

10. Over a year we will see pr_gress and impr_vement.

11. S_ccess is more likely if we stay in good h_alth.

12. Our good c_nduct and beh_viour allow the teacher to teach.

13. There is anecdotal evid_nce that conc_ntration on music or a hobby helps us to concentrate on learning a language.

14. It does no h_rm to believe in luck, but it takes hard w_rk and we have to make our own luck. This is not n_nsense.

15. After we have graduated we can enjoy tr_vel and sights_eing.

16. With co-op_ration we can book ahead for the acc_mmodation.

17. I have exp_rience of this. We need t_leration and p_tience.

18. No one is prepared for the unfores_en. We don't need perm_ssion to believe in good or bad fortune.

19. We need inf_rmation or everything could end up in ch_os.

20. We won't lose our l_ggage or get any d_mage to our b_ggage.

17.

The Passive uses the Verb 'to be' and the Past Participle

We use the **passive** voice when talking about the causes of an event or illness. Thus, when describing bodily parts, anatomy and causes of illnesses we find it difficult to avoid using the passive. We use the **'active' tense** or voice to say "The parasite called Plasmodium causes malaria", or use the 'passive' and switch our emphasis by saying, "Malaria **is caused** by a parasite called Plasmodium which **is transmitted** via the bites of infected mosquitoes." The passive **is formed** by using the verb 'be' (in this case 'is') and the past participle of the next verb (in these cases, 'caused', 'transmitted', 'formed').

However, the **past participle is** more clearly **seen** when we use an irregular verb such as 'see' which becomes 'seen'. Most books use 'build' and 'built' as examples of a way to revise this difficult verb. "The Great Wall of China **was** first **built** in the 7th century B.C. when China **was** still **divided** into many smaller states. In 221B.C., the Emperor of the Qin dynasty united China, linked the three parts and rebuilt the Wall. The Great Wall we see today **was built** in the Ming Dynasty between 1368 and 1644. In some areas two Walls **can be seen**. The Great Wall **was built** using local materials and bricks."

In anatomy an example is 'are attached to'. "The two heads of the biceps muscle in our upper arm **are attached to** the scapula or shoulder blade." "The triceps has three heads and these **are connected** to the humerus and scapula bones in the shoulder."

In the eye "the light waves entering the eye **are bent** by the cornea." "Nerve pathways make the connection from the eye to the visual cortex at back of the brain where the visual centre **is located**. In the condition of optic neuritis there is pain in the eye when it **is moved**."

In pregnancy, "The 46 chromosomes **can be organised** into 23 pairs." "The placenta grows along the lining of the uterus and **is attached to** the baby by the umbilical cord. The placenta **is made up of** a combination of cells from both the mother and the growing baby." "Pregnancy **is broken down** into weeks and **is divided** into three parts called trimesters." "Fathers feel more of an attachment when the baby's movements **can be seen** on the mother's stomach." "The attachment between the parents and the baby **is created** together."

In architecture: "Architectural works or buildings **are** often **perceived** as cultural symbols; historical civilisations **are identified** by their surviving architectural achievements." "Frank Lloyd Wright developed Organic architecture in which the form **was defined** by its environment and purpose." "Ludwig van de Miles said that 'architecture begins when two bricks **are put** together'." By contrast, other architects **are satisfied** if the building has three qualities: *Firmitas, Utilitas, Venustas*: Durability, Utility and Beauty."

In adolescent psychology: 'Researchers believe the brain **is** not fully **developed** until at least the age of 24. Adolescents are ill-equipped to be able to exert self-control and are vulnerable to bad decision-making regarding sex, drugs and alcohol. The adolescent brain **is handicapped** in the rational assessment of risk. The age of 18 **is** not now **regarded** as the start of adulthood. Fifty years ago people got married at 18; now this milestone **is delayed**. Parents who **are involved** in their teenagers' lives are less likely to have problem adolescents. The damage **can be limited** by effective policies. A greater commitment **is needed** in the care of teens.'

Regarding many issues, we can always say: **The situation is serious; something <u>must be done</u> about it before it is too late!**

'**Better communication**' **is regarded** as the first improvement to make by a committee making an Official Enquiry into a tragedy.

Most problems have complex causes. These are complicated by multiple factors. As our wordpower is limited, try for simple answers.

Teach yourself:

As writers we **are** always **advised** to **avoid** using the passive as it apparently weakens the impact of our writing. However, when we are describing anatomy or a process and we are unsure of who did what then we resort to the passive. Texts which **are written** in the passive voice **are said** to be vague about their claims while the **active voice** is that in which we **make statements with confidence**.

1. It **is all_ged** that three teenagers broke into the house.

2. It is believed that Mr Keywood w_s murd_red.

3. They suggested that he w_s killed by someone seeking revenge.

4. She said she w_s disapp_inted with that conclusion.

5. It is reported that North Korea has b_ _n misunderstood.

6. It is argu_d that more countries should adopt a one-child policy.

7. The house had been br_ken into but nothing w_s taken.

8. The girl _as either m_rdered or had been kidn_pped.

9. **Sometimes we can be quite definite**: e.g. I was b_rn in 1948.

10. The door was locked. The pub was cl_sed on police orders.

11. The research was c_rried out over a period of a year.

12. The results w_re sh_wn to be inconclusive.

13. The defendant was f_und guilty and was fin_d.

14. The news of Ghandi's death was rec_ived with much sadness.

15. Ghandi was k_lled by an assassin's bullet. He w_s shot at 5.15 on January 30, 1948, and the assassin wa_ immediately seiz_d.

16. The thoracic cavity, our chest, **is encl_sed and prot_cted** by the ribs, the vertebral column and the spine; these **are separated** from the abdominal cavity by the muscular partition or diaphragm. Blood **is**

coll_cted in the heart where it **is pump_d** around the body via the arteries. The heart **is surr_unded** by the pericardium and the membrane around the lungs **is kn_wn** as the pleura. The outermost layer of the pleura **is refer_ed** to as the parietal pleura; the innermost layer is kn_wn as the visceral pleura.

18.

Integrating various verb tenses: Have Solar Panels Fitted

Every day we **use** various verb tenses: the past, present or future. 'We **are having** solar panels fitted on our roof today. Our neighbours **had** theirs **done** a year ago and they **encouraged** us to go ahead. We're having it done so as to cut down on our electricity bills. Thus, next Friday, I **will** phone you to say **we've had** them **fitted**.'

Someone is **going to do** it for us or someone **did** it for us last week or 37 days ago. We **might be having** it **done** today or next week.

Perhaps we are using our phone while we are **having our hair cut**. "Are you having your hair cut soon too? I think you should have it cut. It looked good last time, when you had it done by Tom. I'm just having my hair cut by Sally. I hope she's making a good job of it. I wonder if I have had too much taken off? I'm **having it dyed** next."

Advertisers are always saying they <u>can</u> do something for us (for a price): we can have our house insured. We can get our teeth seen to and fixed. Perhaps we can have our house decorated by a professional painter. We can get transported to the station and booked into a hotel.

We **want** our car repaired. We used to have it repaired by a good mechanic, but he moved away. Our new mechanic is good; he had the job fixed and done by lunchtime yesterday. I'm using it tomorrow.

Tom and Jane are cooking dinner for us at their house because we are having our old cooker replaced. I'll invite them again next Sunday when we can make a Sunday roast for them. Problem solved.

I had my CV written for me last year, but because I have had a better computer programme installed I'm having more details added.

Get it done! I'm having an operation done next week. I'm having my nose straightened. I've had it done before, but I'm having it done again. I saw the doctor again yesterday. I've been seen three times now. I don't want to have it operated on ever again!

Teach yourself:

1. When I get off the train I will h_ _ _ my shoes cleaned by Sue.

2. I've had my shoes cl_aned by Susan every w_ _k for a

y_ar.

3. T_m_rr_w I'm having them d_ne f_r the last time.

4. Ann and I are getting m_rried. No, we h_ven't got to. We w_nt to.

5. I've h_d to order the flowers for the church _nd the reception.

6. We've had _ll the invitations done.

7. I've had to tell every_ne h_w to get there.

8. I told them th_y have to r_ply: "Repondez S'il Vous Plait."

9. My p_rents h_ve h_d to organise the tr_nsport.

10. One p_rson has to have a wh_ _lchair.

11. I'm h_ving my h_ircut this _fternoon.

12. The catering has had to be d_ne by pr_fessionals.

13. W_ haven't had the time to organise v_g_tarian m_als.

14. We've had t_ get very expensive ph_t_graphers.

15. We'll have to h_pe the weather f_recast is f_r a fine day.

16. We w_re supposed to check the w_dding rings, but we haven't had time to have th_m adjusted. I hope they fit. They'll have to!

17. Today, I'm h_ving the c_r serviced re_dy for my big journey.

18. I've alre_dy h_d four new tyres fitted.

19. I've _sked to have the water checked and the oil ch_nged.

20. We haven't had that done for s_x months now.

21. You'll have to have your p_ssport inspected _t the docks.

22. I forgot m_ne last t_me. I had to get my parents to br_ng it.

23. I had to have m_ visas last _ear, so I've had mine done.

24. You've had ple_ty of time to get yours do_e, haven't you?

25. Last y_ar the car brok_ down we had to hir_ one.

26. By the t_me we had it done the cost of the tr_p had doubled.

27. We h_d better h_ve he_lth and _ccident insur_nce.

28. If we have to have m_dical tr_atment w_ will be bankrupt.

29. I've **pl_nned** my ess_y; I'm **writing** it. I will **check** it over.

19.

Reported Speech

"Ann, are you coming to our house this evening?" "Tell Mark I'll be there at 8 o'clock; I've done my assignment. I'll bring my laptop. I've had my haircut, so don't make fun of me. Are your parents there?"

What did she say? She **told me** she **would** (be coming) come here half an hour from now and she'd bring her computer with her because her assignment's on it. She added that she had had her haircut and so we had better not make fun of her. She asked me if our parents were here. I told her they weren't. She said she was pleased about that."

In reported speech we say or report what someone said or told us; therefore, we use various past tenses. 'Is' becomes 'was', 'do' becomes 'did' and 'will' and 'can' become 'would' and 'could'. Usually, the present perfect becomes the past perfect, but in the example above instead of using 'had had' we could have used 'has had' as the evidence of the statement remains true. And 'were here' could be 'are here'. Mostly, when reporting, we move back one tense.

We use 'instructed me' 'asked me', 'told me'; and 'This

place, here' becomes 'That place, there'. We might say 'he replied' or 'her reply was'. Pronouns change: 'my handbag' becomes 'her handbag'. 'Come over to our party' becomes 'We've been invited to their party.'

We also use 'that' very frequently to mark from where her reported remarks are being stated. "I've lost my handbag." She said **that** she had lost her handbag. We call these '**that-clauses**'. However, when there are a few too many uses of the word 'that' in a sentence or paragraph we may be forgiven, even by experts, and drop one or two.

I've been told **that** as a way of improving our English these exercises may be approached with a sense of fun. We can usually keep it simple, but we can also get very confused and start laughing as our communication becomes more and more misleading! In this particular instance we realise and are advised that only a few of us are perfect!

Teach yourself: Report these sentences: Be precise or flexible:

1. "I love Mark." She told me (that) she loves Mark.

2. "We'll graduate in July. We'll go on holiday then." She said you'd both graduate in July and you would go on holiday after that.

3. "I want to go to Italy." She said that she wante_ to....

4. "Mark wants to go to Greece." She s....

5. "I'll never forget being 22." He said he w....

6. "It's an age I'll remember forever."He said that he w...

7. "I really enjoyed being at university."

8. "And we graduated too."

9. "I'm having the best time of my life."

10. "I used to be naïve."

11. "I've learnt so much."

12. "Some of it in the classroom."

13. "I've improved my singing."

14. "I've always been good at it."

15. "But my singing teacher, Ann, has made me twice as good."

16. "I improved because I practised and concentrated on getting better. She told me to learn from my mistakes now, not later!"

17. "I've learnt some French songs."

18. "My confidence in speaking French has improved so much."

19. "I also learnt a speech in French."

20. "I had to enunciate properly and speak clearly."

21. "That practice certainly made a huge difference."

22. "Of course, when we had that fortnight in Paris together I was really immersed in French. I matured. I grew up!"

23. "Oh, I shall never forget the year I was 22."

24. "I really believe this experience means I am going to get far more out of life from now on."

25. "I've developed so much confidence through doing all this."

26. None of us is perfect. None of them was perfect either.

20.

Clauses: Defining and Non-defining

'Michael, **the one who used to work here seven years ago**, was the most patient man I've ever met in my whole life.' This is an example of a defining clause. We put a comma before 'the one' and a comma after 'years ago' as if we are using brackets to say exactly <u>**which**</u> Michael we are talking about. We often include 'who' or 'whom' ('with whom I worked 7 years ago') to assist us group our words and indicate precisely. "Jenny, the one who lives in Dover Road, is the best swimmer in our team."

Some relative clauses are not so necessary. "The piano tuner, who lives across the road from me actually, is going to France next year." This is just extra information.

Sometimes we use 'which' or 'that' at the opening of our clause. "The Sirocco, which is a warm and humid wind that originates in Northern Africa, travels eastward over the Mediterranean Sea. It reaches a peak in March or in November which is when it is very hot."

We use 'which' to add more about something, usually the subject of the sentence: "These flowers, which were picked this morning, are for your birthday." "This poem, which at first is a bit difficult to appreciate, will become more meaningful to you later."

We also use **'when'**, **'where'**, **'whereby'** and sometimes **'why'**. **'Whose'** is used when we refer to something belonging to or associated with a person. "Burke was an explorer whose pioneering travels will always be remembered in Australian history. Melbourne, 1860, is where and when he met that other famous explorer, W. J. Wills."

"We were eventually offered a good price for the house, which we accepted." Other non-defining clauses add extra information but are not so vitally specific. "My sister, who now works in the library, used to be one of the best ballerina's in this city."

Teach yourself:

1. A student wh_se aim is to pass exams is well-advised to do extra research into his or her hobbies and interests too.

2. Most of our class, wh_ch is mainly girls, want to travel next year.

3. China and Brazil, wh_ch are lands of contrast and

diversity are enjoying a change in their economic situations.

4. Brazil, wh_re the nuts come from, has an abundance of many natural resources. The Amazon, wh_se estuary opens into the Atlantic, is the world's longest river and flows through Brazil.

5. Jack, wh_se suggestion it was to go camping, wasn't able to go.

6. Camping, whi_h is not my favourite pastime, was therefore left to the rest of us to organise. Actually, the campsite, whi_h is next to the beach, is one of the best. Therefore, we were glad to choose the week th_t turned out to have the longest hours of sunshine.

7. The campsite had a new restaurant wh_ch we frequented often.

8. The food they served there was better than ours. They had a different menu each day wh_ch was carefully chosen to please all.

9. The restaurant, who_e owner was Italian, made the best pizza.

10. The decision about where to go next year, which won't be difficult to decide, will be made soon. They might

decide to go elsewhere, in w_ich case I won't go. We leave that decision to the committee whose ruling we have to stand by and respect.

11. Where_s I used to be enthusiastic, I now need to be persuaded.

12. Although I don't want to go, I expect I'll do wh_tever they say.

13. We need a committee who_e members are more active wh_reupon they'll rejuvenate keenness in the rest of the staff.

14. Enthusiasm is an attitude th_t would bring benefit to everyone.

15. I used to say it is better to be poor and happy. I've learnt that it's best to be rich and happy wh_ch shows how much I've changed.

16. We notice neglect, w_ _ _h is where things start to go wrong.

17. We should be kind to those wh_ are placed under our care.

18. Some bosses make a salary offer wh_ _h is not to be sneezed at. They make an offer that is hard to turn down.

19. They should employ staff whose mutual success depends on the company doing well. Surely, this approach to people is one that is not too hard to conceive. It is an idea _hose time has come.

20. One of my sisters, the one wh_'s just had twins, has decided to get married. Another sister, the eldest one, has just got divorced. My brother, the one _ho broke his leg last year, has just returned to playing football and rugby and is getting married next year.

21. He has found th_t he is not as nimble as he used to be.

22. The doctors have advised him th_t he should not play competitively. He respects their opinion, but he is the one w_o has to make the final decision about whether or not he plays.

23. My sister's husband is the typical person w_ _ sits at the computer too much. It's his lack of exercise th_t has led to him putting on so much weight. He is a person wh_ is more familiar with the Internet than playing sport. To us, it is a choice th_t's not difficult to make: his improved health or isolation in his room.

24. It is not something th_t is good to witness happening.

25. He could get out and do some voluntary work; there are plenty of people wh_ could do with some help.

26. I have a friend wh_ runs a charity called 'meals on wheels'.

27. They deliver meals to those who are unable to go out shopping or cook for themselves. He could give the sort of help wh_ch is always welcome. He's a good person whose computer skills would be most useful. He would be doing something that is useful for the community. He has many skills; several of wh_ch are needed now!

28. My family is one which is full of contrasts and diversity. No doubt, I'm not the only one who can claim this. Each person is one wh_ is admired, wh_ch is more than can be said of most families.

21.

Participle Clauses: -ed and –ing forms

"**Having broken** and shattered the silence by break**ing** the window, the burglar was shocked to have set the alarm bells ring**ing**."

We sometimes use the **'-ing' form** followed by the past participle for going on to give **reasons, results** or for using **time** descriptions:

Hav**ing** not **told** him, we began by surpris**ing** Tom about the wedding.

Having **lost** another match the team moved closer to relegation.

Being shock**ed** by the news she knew there was not a moment to lose.

Many adjectives end in **'-ing'** or **'-ed'**, **i.e. past tense**. 'She was late. While park**ing** she could see that the shop had just closed.'

Striving to be precise in language use is a means by which we train ourselves to **clarify** our thoughts **concisely** and get things in order.

The teacher observed that "**being bored**" was a sign of frustration, of a limited mind and of self-criticism. He told his students **that** they should not use the word. Moreover, "**I am boring**" is incorrect use of English. Hav**ing** taken the effort to get to class then adopt**ing** an improved attitude is advised. Clearly, **being bored** is self-criticism.

Examples of **'-ing' words** to begin a sentence include: "Sailing down the river; glancing around the room; reading newspapers; listening to the radio; watching television; observing closely; noticing how some people speak; smelling the lovely perfume; offering to help."

'-ed'/past participle: Being injured is no way to… Having published your book, what will….? Being made in Germany is… Having grown up in France… Being woken so early… Having stolen her heart, what will….? Having repaired my car…. Being built of sand … Being arrested at 4am is…. Having thanked everyone I will now…

Teach yourself:

1. **B_ing s_tisfied** with what we have helps us to relax.

2. The incident, **h_ving cl_sed** down central London last

Friday, brought out large numbers of riot police onto the streets.

3. H_v_ng needlessly hailed a taxi we apologised to the driver and then proceeded into town by train.

4. Ge_ _ing married is many people's desired hope, for others it is merely a cultural obligation and someone to live with.

5. Having acquir_d the money through his consistent work ethic he was reluctant to share it with a family th_t he hardly knew.

6. L_ _king ashamed, the man in the crowd decided to give the baseball he had caught to the child next to him.

7. B_ _ng interested in butterfly life, Sheila decided that she would go to Thailand, a country renowned for its beautiful specimens.

8. H_ _ _ _g impressed the air force recruitment officer with her CV she was offered the post. Being interested in flying, she accepted. Though being very young, she had great self-confidence.

9. B_ing slim, the doctor told many of his patients they were obese.

10. Being overweight, the doctor rarely told his patients they were obese. His nurse, b_ _ng slim, told overweight patients the truth.

11. Having cri_d himself to sleep, he decided to rip up all of the love letters (that) they had exchanged since 1990.

12. Since he now had room in his private desk, he thought he would only collect investments wh_ch were of long-term value.

13. Th_ugh acting as a bit of a clown sometimes, he was actually very intelligent, shrewd and broadly educated in many aspects of art. He was a man wh_ kept his talent hidden.

14. Being overlooked, he decided, was to the disadvantage of others rather than to him s_nce it was their loss, not his.

15. He concluded that being reg_rded as stupid actually gave him an immense advantage. Turning lemons into lemonade was his aim.

22.

Giving Reasons: because; so as to; in order to

There are certain ways of ensuring we extend what we have to say and one of those ways is to use the word: **because**. Merely by adding the word **'because'** after our opening statement we force ourselves to go on, to continue to say more **because** we must say **why!**

Young people do not fully mature until about the age of 21 or 22 and many regard 25 as the age of full development. **In order to** mature we have to become a 'thinker' and this attribute is seen in us in our twenties. We develop ways of thinking our way through problems; these might include winning a football match or getting through a university course. Being practical becomes an obligation **because** using common sense is still a major virtue. Many teachers or exam setters expect a seventeen year old to be fully mature. This unfair situation is **due to** all concerned having set too high expectations.

Thus, although the word 'strategy' implies **being practical**, a strategy to employ includes the simple suggestion of including the words '**because**' or '**however**'. When asked to talk for two minutes and we dry up within only 30 seconds then we use these words so as to steer us in the direction of making further logical statements.

The word '**as**' is sometimes used instead of '**because**' at the start of sentences; it has the same usage as '**because**' and is marginally better used there. "**As** we are now approaching mid-winter there will be less hours of daylight." We use '**since**' when giving reasons: '**Since/As/Because** he was learning Chinese he thought he may as well go there on holiday.' '**Owing to**' is adverbial. If we can use 'because of' we use 'owing to'; '**due to' (caused by)** is adjectival. We also use '**due to**' after the word 'is/was' rather than 'owing to': 'My lateness was **due to** a traffic delay.' (Although '**owing to**' and '**due to**' are not always interchangeable, an amusing rule is: use 'due to' in mid sentence and 'owing to' as our sentence's opening words!:)

Teach yourself:

1. Bec_use the cost of a holiday in my own country is so high we decided to fly to Bali, have a good time and spend less.

2. We have to make good investments because history shows th_t prices of land and good works of art usually increase.

3. Because Australia is a large and exciting country it is very easy to overspend. Many students go home d_e to running out of cash.

4. A_ the price of new products, such as the latest phone, actually drop after a year, it is best to buy one later.

5. S_ _ing _s you have lived all this time without one, it is highly likely you can exist a while longer without spending so much.

6. D_spite the recent rise in gas prices, gas is still the cheapest fuel.

7. **Ow_ _ _ to** the unprecedented demand for iron ore there is going to be a huge increase in jobs in the mining industry.

8. In summer, ow_ _g to the fact that many people leave their windows open, thieves find burglary an easy occupation.

9. Most burglaries **are d_e to** us not locking up properly.

10. O_ _ _g to the generosity of neighbours, we have been told to form our own 'neighbourhood watch' so as to prevent theft.

11. We feel safer d_e to the fact that we care for each other.

12. The more we travel the more we are open to discovering, learning and tolerating what was previously unknown to us. **On acc_unt of** this fact, our life can be compared to a journey. **In the light** of realising how other people live and by experiencing other cultural habits we can widen our experience. **O_ing to** the certainty of being surprised by things new to us we will lose our naivety and might have to show flexibility in our moral code.

13. There are sev_ral reas_ns why you should come and see my home town mainly bec_use it has many beautiful parks and interesting people. The wonderful climate is d_e to ….

14. The reason we _ust **PLAN** before we **WRITE** is so that we will keep cal_. As we write we have the steps to expand upon. Then we **READ** it over.

23.

Though, Although, However, — Contrasting

Our chapters continue to point out the varied ways of extending our writing or speaking. We may as well **integrate the vocabulary and grammar points**. We use 'there', 'reasons', '(al)though', 'comparing and contrasting' in every essay. **Linking words** help us to be coherent and logical as we **move smoothly** from one thought to the next:

We write **cohesively: 'Even though** John stands alone as the greatest player in the history of the sport, he found that he was losing his appetite for the necessary hours of practise required to stay at the top. The statistics tell the story. **However**, he will be remembered for his amiable personality as much as for his undoubted talent and skill.'

We can employ similar tactics again:

'**Although** there are some people who achieve high status and their lofty elevation sees them worthy of being criticised for their decisions, we have to remember that these people are only human. When students or complainers want things to be different then, **rather than** protest, all they have to do is get into parliament and change things themselves. They will soon see **there** is a need for more mature thoughts and responses.'

Our job is to study lots and lots of examples of writing in magazines or newspapers and **observe CLOSELY how other writers put their essays together.** They use 'although', 'however', 'but' and 'due to'. Some newspapers use **'but'** far too often, their reason being that they want to **hold the reader's attention**. Readers are free to read the article or not, **yet** may completely overlook its importance unless the wording is **short** and the 'news' is very easy to digest.

The IELTS essay writer has to consider this technique, **yet** also impress the examiner with a range of writing skills. A fundamental requirement: use **several paragraphs** and a **range of linking words**.

<u>Teach yourself:</u>

1. It is difficult to make a distinction between 'c_mpare' and 'c_ntrast'. C_mparisons usually look for similarities. C_ntrasts look for and highlight the distinct differences or the 'c_nverse'.

2. As we **compose** our essay we need alternatives to

'howev_r'. For example: 'Nev_rtheless', 'y_t', 'even so' and 'notwithstanding'.

3. We had our irritations with each other; n_v_rtheless, despite what we may have feared, we worked together to succeed in completing the journey regardless of any diff_rences of opinion.

4. C_ntrary to expectations, we were the best in our group.

5. The contrasts betwe_n living in hot and cold countries are apparent in the diff_rences in the intensity of sunlight and the nec_ssity for air-conditioning.

6. It is sa_d, possibly without just_fication that under d_fferent leadersh_p there would be a marked contrast _n results.

7. There is a m_rked contr_st or difference between sitting in the conference room and experiencing the practic_lities of cl_ssroom man_gement. It is as different as ch_lk and cheese.

8. Some twins are so alike we a_e compa_ing peas in a pod.

9. In Physics, 'cont_ast' is the difference in luminosity or when watching television the diffe_ence in the brightness of colours.

10. In science we sometimes find that res_arch figures and subsequent opinions pr_sent conflicting views.

11. We will probably notice a contr_st between rur_l and city life.

12. Alth_ugh people on the farm probably engage in less academic activities, we w_uld be bigoted if we said they are less intelligent.

13. On the one hand, a lot of credence is pl_ced on liter_ry and m_thematical skills. On the other h_nd, practical skills such as sailing or playing tennis or out-thinking an opponent in a sport are dismissed by those who lack physical prowess. How silly!

14. When writing an essay, we must not sh_w contradictions between our intr_duction and conclusi_n.

24.

Ergative Verbs Express ACTION: e.g. 'change'

We need not get too detailed about the different types of verbs. Our principal aim is to have experience of new vocabulary and their grammatical forms. **Ergative** verbs are those associated with **ACTION**! The important topic chosen here is that of: <u>**CHANGE**</u>.

Verbs which express **change** often take an object (transitive) yet can also be used without an object (intransitive). These include: improve, accelerate, cut, chop, crash, break, burn, burst, crack, sell, melt, move, cook, boil, warm up, mark, continue, develop, fill, damage, destroy, empty, grow, increase, open, quicken, rot, shut, spoil, stop, expand, decline, weaken, strengthen, double. The drip dropped (on the floor).

From the family home to the office to the on-site workplace, whenever there is **change** then other unexpected changes, unrest and unsettled disturbances occur. The situation may improve or worsen. We may expect things to be or get worse at first, which they probably will for three weeks. However, more often than not, movement, improved teamwork and a greater sense of responsibility on behalf the participants eventually lead to improvement. Those whose talent was suppressed come through and have a chance to display their intelligence and people skills. **MOVEMENT** generates further movement.

Consider movement, cooking, breaking, change and size. We can crash our car, crash into someone we haven't seen for years or say the computer crashed. Situations **improve** or **worsen**. We **improve** or **worsen** our prospects of a bright future: 'I **increased** my salary, but at the same time the size of my family **has increased**.' 'Some laws **have changed** society, but some say nothing **has changed**.' 'We move on.'

There are chemical changes such as in **science** or in **cooking which are permanent**. In business some people cook the books. Some even admit that their books **have been roasted**! From the fire and ashes the Phoenix arises and **flowers bloom when allowed the room to grow**.

Teach yourself:

1. The athlete almost b_rst his lungs trying to win the race.

2. The financial bubble bur_t just like a collapsing air balloon.

3. Ling Ling has co_ked the rice. The roast duck is already coo_ed.

4. Sit down. Don't move. On hearing the news her face d_rkened.

5. Please, go away, never dark_n my door again.

6. Let these photographs dev_lop.

7. Her shoes were new and she devel_ped a large blister.

8. Water the plants and let them gr_w. G_ow them in a pot.

9. His h_ad turned when the young lady ent_red the room.

10. The d_g turned its head when he heard the sheep.

11. He told the ex_minees, "Ple_se begin."

12. "Where shall I b_gin?" "Just start! Begin at the b_ginning."

13. This is a cl_se match. It rests _n a knife edge.

14. Go ah_ad. Sit and think. R_st your head on this pillow.

15. He empt_ed the rubb_sh _nto the b_n.

16. _t the end of the m_tch the st_dium emptied.

17. The dr_ver stopped the car. The pedestr_an stopped too.

18. In the Titanic _isaster 1523 people _rowned or froze to _eath.

19. When we feel fed up we might dr_wn our s_rrows.

20. At n_ght we close the curta_ns. We say we draw the curtains.

21. It is to_ late to g_ sh_pping. The market has cl_sed.

22. The pi_neer's sailing adventure has c_ntinued.

23. Please read on, c_ntinue the st_ry.

24. The trad_rs split up the money betw_ _n them.

25. Due to dis_greements the p_rtnership h_s split up.

26. While trying to pick up the hot sa_sage he b_rnt his fingers.

27. My ch_nces of p_ssing the ex_m have improved.

28. I h_ve recently improved the st_ndard of my h_ndwriting.

29. We can dissolve parli_ment. Sugar is e_sily dissolved.

30. At my age, sometimes I sit and think. Sometimes I just sit.

Pagoda at end of Pathway

Half way up may be a tall Pagoda where it is good to have a rest and to take photographs. We indulge in adverbs and adjectives to say there are spectacular views. The climbers have a sense of fulfilment, they experience spiritually uplifting moments as well as believe or smile about having the fortune reader tell them about their future: what is going to happen!

25.

Compound Nouns and Adjectives: The Snowball Effect

We put 'snow' and 'ball' together, both literally and figuratively to make a snowball. This is a **compound noun**. Another interesting word to make use of regularly is 'exponential'. In mathematics this term is expressed in an algebraic formula; in our case we say it is like **compound interest** in a bank.... from a slow beginning growth increases in an accumulative way. It can accumulate quite quickly!

By using English, after a year we have a few friends; after ten years we have a network of connections **world-wide**. "Ten years ago I hardly knew anyone **overseas**. Now, on my world tour, I will stay with friends in seven countries. First stop: **Hong Kong**, then Hawaii, followed by Chile, Canada, the U.K., Spain, **South Africa** and Bali." The rolling snowball **accumulates** and gains momentum.

The intention here is to have a look at some **compound nouns** and **adjectives** and, without necessarily learning any words, broaden our mind through some grammar exercises. In our vocabulary book we have the verb 'to snowball' or a compound noun, 'snowball', but in our case the connotations and **snowball effect** of this one word is seen in our world tour. The **upshot** is: we extend our **word-power** and our imagination brings us the benefits of **inner enrichment**.

Because the term 'snowball effect' is a cliché, we avoid using it in the best writing. However, in this instance, this **adjectival** usage is appropriate. We start from an insignificant beginning, but we see a beneficial reward later. In maths it is a geometric progression. In our life it creates one opportunity after another. It **builds upon itself**.

The list-making **homework** can be treated as merely a matter of fun with the hidden way of learning. The bonus: the rewards of our **never-ending list-making**. We are upstanding students. What's your opinion, where do you stand? We do not have to do **handstands**. We understand and withstand. **Hatstand; grandstand; washstand;...**

Teach yourself: Look for these combinations:

1. This grammar book is my **passport** to me learning **state-of-the-art** English. It is a **matter of fact** way of a_ _umulating **general knowledge** and using my

common sense. I get onto my **personal _omputer** to find out all about **day-to-day _urrent affairs** and even do some reading about **natural history, s_ience fiction** or go **job-hunting**. I like learning **modern languages** because I have a **catlike sense of _uriosity** and in close collaboration with my **travel agent** I want to travel not just **nation-wide** but **world-wide**. I have left university and I want to travel and join the **labour force** and resear_h the **labour market**. I must **skill-up**, go on to **higher edu_ation** and do a **post-graduate degree** next year. I'm not very keen on paying **in_ome tax** and I want to go through the **duty free section** of _ustoms **and excise** wherever I go. My **motherland** is _hina and my **mother tongue** is Mandarin. Travelling is like doing an **educational course** in **so_ial studies**. I will take **traveller's _heques** with me and if I stay long-term in one place I'll open a **bank a_ _ount**. My length of stay depends on the **cost of living** there. I will respect **race relations, _ultural traditions, civil rights** and **human rights** in each _ountry. All countries rely on **law and order**; for example, I mustn't take drugs into Indonesia because they have the **death penalty** and believe in **_apital punishment**. My awaiting **bride-to-be** is almost at the age of consent. She doesn't want to be a **one-parent family** and so we have dis_ussed **birth _ontrol, contraception and family**

planning. We don't want to add to the **human race** just yet. I will stay in **youth hostels** everywhere I go and give her the relevant **telephone number**. I want her to keep her **blood pressure** down. I hope she manages not to worry and not have a **heart attack** or any **heart-a_he** while I use the **swimming pool**. She has the **food processor**, **washing machine**, **mi_rowave oven**, **vacuum cleaner** and **central heating**, despite **worrying about the greenhouse effect** and in spite of being **eco-friendly** and leaving no **_arbon footprint!** She is in the **women's movement** and thinks I am a **good-for-nothing** using **pollution-making airports** and **airlines**. She thinks I should go by **hot-air-balloon** or **hang-glider**, or **rowing-boat**. I told her we're not in the **Stone Age** and I would prefer the **space-shuttle** rather than being **ship-wre_ked**. I want **around-the-world flights** or **luxury ya_hts** or a **nuclear-powered submarine** would suffice. I must avoid **nu_lear power-stations**, nuclear **meltdowns** and any leaking **atomi_ energy**. I want the **open air** and try a culture different from my own **upbringing**. People talk about a **generation gap**: well, I think there is a **_ultural gap**. I want all sorts of **pop-music** and different **clothing brands**. I want to try **Fren_h-fries**, **chewing gum**, **mineral water**, **baked beans** for **breakfast**, **fish and chips**, **fast food**, **junk food** and to use **tea-bags**. I don't want to get a **stomach ache** or **headache**. I will try to get a **part-time job** in information te_hnology or as an **air-traffic _ontroller, fruit picker, petrol-pump attendant, hair dresser** or do **_ommunity service**. I want a **_redit card** so I can go to **department stores** to buy her present of **earrings, make-up, underwear** and an **over_oat**. I'll leave **pi_k-po_keting** and **shoplifting** to others. I want to do a bit of **sightseeing**, visit an **art gallery, safari parks** and **nightclubs**. I'll see **waterfalls** and go **ro_k-climbing**. I'll watch sports in the Olympic Games such as **baseball, horse-riding**, the **long jump** and the **hop, step and jump**. When there are no **thunderstorms** I'll stay at **_amp sites** or **guesthouses** as long as I am **_redit-worthy**. I don't know what the **ex_hange-rate** will be for my **_urrency exchange**. I'm not a **mira_le-worker** and I'll do my best to stay out of the **newspaper headlines**. I'm praying for a happy **out_ome**.

26.

Hyphens: Well-being, well-known, self-respect, self-reliance

Most words have connotations and they set us off thinking about the extensions of the ideas they generate. We can play with hyphenated words. By going off at a tangent, such as using hyphens, we create discussion of either serious matters or just comically-amusing nonsense. As with other grammar exercises, the aim is to notice and to **observe,** to create a <u>mind-shift</u> and to **start talking**!

The word 'welcome' seems at first glance to be a compound of the words **well** and **come**. The original old English usage was 'according to my **will**'. The host was happy; it was his or her desire or pleasure for the guest or 'Cuma' to arrive. Today's hyphenated words such as 'well-known' may also evolve in this way. The language evolves from separation to connection and to fusion, though for many words the fusion may not happen entirely. Thus we have hyphenated words.

Clearly, numbers such as thirty-four and fifty-five are

closely linked **Fibonacci numbers**. Meanwhile, some people when asked, what is the meaning of life might reply, "Forty-two." This number is seriously meaningful for some mathematicians. Others joke that just as politicians can give apparently logical reasons for and justify the strangest decisions they make, so the number **forty-two** can be used similarly as if **self-evident**. At least, we write numbers correctly.

A **well-known** rule is well known: **we use hyphenated words when there are two or more adjectives expressing one idea.** When we are doing our accounts, we lose friends immediately if we are incorrect about money matters or if we underpay. We like **cut-price** sales, **low-budget** flights and **tax-free** incentives. Australians pay income tax on a **pay-as-you-earn** basis (P.A.Y.E.). They want to be given a fair go in a **fair-go** community. Teamwork relies on **first-rate co-operation** and we should plan for both **long-term** and **short-term** aspirations.

Teach yourself:

1. The **b_tt_m line** in **double-entry** accounting is the **end of year** profit or loss. We don't want staff who are **sec_nd-rate** and nor do staff want to be **l_w-paid**. We need both **well-balanced** books and employees. Employers need to be both **str_ng-minded** and **kind-**

hearted. Most businesses do not want rapid staff **turn_ver**.

2. When are you: **cl_sed-minded, narrow-minded, broad-minded, _pen-minded, single-minded, fair-minded, health-minded**?

3. Are you: **easy-g_ing, well-behaved, well-mannered, well-off**?

4. Are y_u **stuck-up, big-headed, bad-tempered, tw_-faced**?

5. In _rder to face up to criticism we have to be **thick-skinned**.

6. Critics actually reveal and give us their **self-p_rtrait**.

7. At the age of 15 we devel_p a sense of **self-respect** and stop being **ill-advised** and behaving like an idi_t. At the age of 22 we definitely develop into being a 'thinker'. We imp_se on ourselves **self-responsibility, self-discipline** and gain **self-c_nfidence**. We bec_me **quick-witted** and THINK about how to pass an exam; we think about tactics for getting through a **j_b interview**. We get into the habit of being **well-dressed**. We take care of our _wn **well-being**. We are **self-reliant** and d_n't have time to take sick leave.

8. We are **y_ung at heart** and young physically until we feel **run-down** at 55. We are **sh_rt-sighted, burnt-out** in the **workplace**, need heart **by-pass** surgery and have to have c_ntact lenses.

9. At 85 we are: **absent-minded, grey-haired, _ld**, a **second-class citizen, br_ken-down, beyond caring, bent-backed, hard-up, pig-headed,** an excellent **baby-sitter** and **in sec_nd childhood**.

10. We can ask the person wh_ knows the meaning of life the more difficult **present-day** question: why do w_men wear **high-heels**?

11. How do we make people **panic-stricken**? Say: "D_n't panic!"

12. We are resilient and **sh_ck-resistant**; we spring back.

Flick-flack: This boy is demonstrating the hyphenated word: flick-flack or the compound noun backspring or back handspring. It isn't easy is it?

27.

You Concentrate on Yourself; I'll Concentrate on Myself

Reflexive pronouns indicate that the subject and object of the sentence are the same. "It's okay, **I'll** do it **my**self." "Make sure **you** take care of **your**self." "When we play football we don't think too much about them; **we** concentrate on **our**selves and our opponents concentrate on **them**selves. The **referee** takes care of **him/her**self."

When full of pride we say, "We did it, we're proud of **ourselves**." When we admit our fault we say, "It's my fault, I blame **myself**." When Jessica Watson sailed round the world at the age of 16 she was proud of **herself**. A boyfriend and girlfriend look after **each other**. Fifty years later they might not recognise **one another**.

A fundamental question in life regarding relationships is whether to live alone or to live as a couple, as when getting married. It is difficult to manage everything completely by **ourselves** and when wonderful things happen we love to share such moments with **someone else** who also enjoys the experience. To travel **alone** or to go with a partner is a difficult decision. Having complete **independence** and going along with our own choice is preferable to compromising and missing out on what we, **ourselves** want to do. "Make a choice. Please **yourself!**"

The choice to live on our own is **itself** a perplexing question. We face the same dilemma: when we live **alone** we then long for **someone** to help us or to **share** our joys and responsibilities with. Can we tolerate **each other** for long? At other times we yearn to be by **ourselves**. However, can we always help **ourselves** or cope **alone** such as in emergency situations or when waiting for tradespeople to do our house repairs or when we are looking after a baby? What if we burn, cut, fall or hurt **ourselves**? The infirmed, elderly and little children can hardly dress and feed **themselves** let alone apply their first aid. **People need people**. We have to protect and care for **each other**.

Teach yourself:

1. It comes to us n_turally but it is also wise to push **ourselves** to communic_te better rather than avoid **each other**.

2. As we have a r_ght to be here there is never any need to feel ashamed of **ourselves** for being gently assert_ve.

After all, other people do not hes_tate to assert **themselves**. Assert yourself.

3. We have a s_nse of achi_vement and humbly say, "I did it **myself**."

4. As a young child we have stages of growth towards independence: "She can dress **_erself**." "He can tie his shoelaces by **_imself**."

5. Life is sh_rt; we may be pleased with **ourselves** merely by surviving. We look at ourselves in the mirr_r: "I can still see **myself**. I'm still alive. Today I must push **myself** to do s_mething!" At other times, when pe_ple think we have behaved unethically they ask, "How can you face **y_urself** in the mirror?"

6. Many people h_ve a high skill level. However, if we believe in **ourselves** we can often be as good _s most **others**.

7. When in a new c_untry or in new surroundings we have to adapt and acclimatise **ourselves** to all c_nditions, not least the culture.

8. When in a c_untry new to us we get the most out of both cultures because they complement **each other**, e.g. c_ _king food.

9. When v_siting **someone** we will be offered food and told to "Go ahead. Help yourself. I know it's good, I made _t myself."

10. "L_dies and gentlemen, I'm afraid the meeting will be del_yed due to a technic_l fault. Talk among **yourselves** for 5 minutes."

11. "Okay. Let's begin. First, I will introduce **m_self**. M_ name is …"

12. I w_uld also suggest that we keep what we say in this meeting c_nfidential and to be kept to **_urselves**."

13. We are not here to c_mpete with each other. Rather, we want to collaborate and co-_perate in a positive way with **one an_ther**.

14. When st_dying, we can work **individ_ally** or with **each other**.

15. Our cat looks down on us. It pleases **itself**!

Epsom Derby Horse Race Day crowd: A great crowd for a great day. Communication is vital for when having fun or when being serious.

28.

Nouns and their Possessives

This is yet another aspect of grammar that offers us a lot of **amusement**. Mistakes are easily made and seen daily. We either smile about them or we are disappointed. My own error once was that I put an apostrophe in 'lets' and wrote "Our boss **let's** us go early," instead of '**lets**'. This **embarrassing error** was spotted by a student!

However, here we are talking about noun forms. In this case the apostrophe shows who owns or **possesses** what. We might say, "We are going to Jack's house in Jane's car." The house and the car belong to Jack and Jane respectively. When asked about where the party is and whose car we are going in we use ellipsis and omit words and say, "It's at Jack's and we're going in Jane's." We are pretty clear about to what and to whom we are referring. "We are coming back in Jim's car." When we go shopping we say, "I'm going to the baker's and then the butcher's. I'm going to spend next week's money now." "The government's dilemma is whether to raise taxes or not."

Names ending in 's': e.g. Charles's car, we can use Charles' car with or without the apostrophe 's'. When we talk about Tom Jones and his voice we keep the Jones and either use the apostrophe or apostrophe 's', "People love Tom Jones' voice." or Tom Jones's voice.

For a plural such as children we add an apostrophe 's' as in, "They like playing children's games." Sometimes we may omit the 's' in a title. "I attended Dover Boys Grammar School." We could put Boys'. In 'scissors' there are too many 's' sounds and so we are reluctant to add another and we talk about 'the scissors' blades.'

The **INCORRECT** forms are amusing. These either attract attention and business or they drive customers away: taxi's, ladie's, 5 house's, 3 flat's, difficultie's, green leave's, top mark's, Pari's, Lo's Angele's!

Teach yourself:

1. Is that M_zart's Pian_ Concert_ No. 21 as used in *Elvira Madigan*?

2. Which do you pr_fer: B_ _thoven's Ninth Symphony or his Fifth?

3. Which is c_rrect: Charles Dickens' *"A Tale of Two Cities?"* or Charles Dickens's *"Great Expectations"*? Either. B_th are correct.

4. When we want a good proj_ct for research purposes

then we can choose Mendel's Gen_tics which describes genetic inh_ritance.

5. Apostr_phes show that a letter is missing. We now say "9 o'clock" but it used to be "9 of the clock." P_ssessive pronouns include the word: its. "It's time for the cat to have its evening meal isn't it?"

6. To be basic, the men's toilet r_ _m is called the "Gents" the w_men's is the "Ladies". It is amusing to see, "Comfort Rooms".

7. Which do you pr_fer? The B_atles' music or The Rolling Stones'?

8. Or the Beatles's music _r The Rolling St_nes's music?

9. We ref_r to last night's television programmes or say that yesterday's newspap_r is today's wrapping for fish and chips; last y_ar's fashions are so out of date and we may not like last c_ntury's way of thinking or Victorian 19th century attitudes.

10. The ex_ression on your face and what you look like by the age of forty is no one else's res_onsibility but your own.

11 People alw_ys fall in love with the most perfect aspects of each other's person_lities.

12. The desire to get married is a basic primal desire in _omen; this desire is superseded by the _oman's instinct to be single again.

13. Some char_cters in books are really real —- J_ne Austen's are.

14. F_nd a pr_nt of and research Durer's *The Praying Hands*".

15. Research m_ny artists' and authors' lives. Read about Van Gogh's life and tr_vels, or read Bunyan's, "A Pilgrim's Progress".

16. Empathy invol_es seeing things from another's point of _iew.

17. Does a g_rl's mind turn to marr_age before turn_ng to love?

29.

Word Order

This is another grammar exercise which provides a little bit of fun. When being descriptive we use adjectives in the following **order** (when available): **Size; age; colour; from where; made of; noun.**

The large, new, green, Indian, cotton shirt is a perfect fit.

If we give our **opinion** we put that at the beginning, such as: "The beautiful, large, new .... shirt...."

In the world of antiques and business dealing every descriptive word may help to increase the price in the auction room when 'a beautiful, unique, ancient, Ming Dynasty, blue and white, Chinese, earthenware rice bowl in very good condition' comes up for bids.

We state what our senses tell us about flowers, music, the weather or food: tastes good; terrible weather; sounds wonderful; they smell beautiful; feels on top of the world; **looks magnificent**. I gave up golf because I wasn't **much good** at it, but now I play the piano **very well**.

There is a difference between **adjectives** and **adverbs**. We may be a quick thinker or fast learner and so be able to learn English quickly. We may not be beautiful or handsome, but the asset of being a **confident cheerful person** who faces **life cheerfully and confidently** is of higher value. Tourists say they like to haggle to get a **cheaper price**, but we would be better off to buy something **reasonably cheap** which will last for a long time. **Metaphorically**, it is absolutely ridiculous to buy a **dead duck** if we want to trade in **golden eggs**.

When selling a house we can say that our pre-loved home is in need of care and attention and has **enormous potential** rather than naively say that this **old place** is in need a lot of repair. It is **terribly** unfair to make **false claims**. We **hardly** need to be told to be **totally** honest. This practice is both **morally wrong** and unethical, but we **simply** turn a blind eye and hope our offence is not taken **too seriously**.

Teach yourself:

1. **Notice the word order and abbreviations in this real estate advertisement**: Impo_ing well located near new townhouse with own _treet frontage. It offers 4 dble bdrms, 2 with ensuite toilet, one of which is downstairs to cater for all age_. Beautiful bamboo timber floor_

give warmth & easy care. Quality stainless steel kitchen fit-out for the di_cerning cook, ducted inverter air con., alarm and video intercom. The two sep. living area_ allow for family harmony & there is a sep. _tudy for the busy person. No maintenance yard, ideal for ca_ual entertaining. View today!

1. **Impre__ive advert! Notice: word order and compound nouns**: Atop the highest hilltop in Kallaroo's north shore, no expen_e has been _pared in the creation of this secluded premium home built in 2012 and _urrounded by native bushland. From the central feature wall made entirely from Donnybrook _andstone, to the poli_hed porcelain tiles imported from Holland and the commercial grade German bench-top in the uber-chic kitchen, class abounds. The spla_hback in the kitchen is made from metallic formica while the alcove in the family room is fa_hioned from Balinese hammered lime_tone. In the outdoor entertaining room the impressive copper water feature wa_ handcrafted by a local artisan and in the bathrooms marble plays the _tarring role. Despite the grand nature of its de_ign and the materials employed throughout, the property _till feels like a relaxed home. "It's not just the ocean view_, but it's the beautiful trees and surrounds. The pines are

gorgeou_ and it's just so secluded and peaceful. The home mixe_ modern and classic styles – we wanted a low-maintenance home, but we also wanted to give it _ome warmth, comfort and style." Upstairs, the gorgeous main _uite with a walkway with treetop and ocean views steals the _how.

30.

Prepositions associated with Fear and of Being Afraid

Of huge psychological influence in our life is our sense of fear and of being afraid. In a contest we might play a psychological game of warning our opponent to "Be afraid, very afraid!" They might be!

Can we overcome our fear? Advertisers know the potential of most people to be **influenced by** greed, fear and greed or by fear, greed and fear. We may be filled **with** fear or afraid of nothing: "I fear nothing, I am afraid **of** nothing!" However, we might actually be **full of fear**.

Our greatest fear is the **fear of failure**. We can be terrified, scared stiff, fearful or fearfully afraid. We might take fright if the teacher asks us the next question. We have phobias and are afraid of heights, **scared of** the dark, **frightened of** open spaces and **panic** in the presence of insects. We are **concerned** and **worried about** the future and of **running out of** money. We **dread** failing exams or being sent to prison. We are **alarmed by** strange noises in the night. We are **apprehensive about** being chosen for the school team and we may be **quaking in** our shoes. We daren't ask for a dance and we **tremble at** the thought of speaking to the object of our desire. There are **dangers in** growing old and fears of any sudden **calamity** or **disaster**. We may be in **awe of** the power of our God and so we treat him or her **with reverence** and **deep respect**. On the ocean there is rough weather and we pray for those **in peril on** the seas. On land we are **nervous and uneasy** even **about** the mention of snakes and spiders! When buying food we are **anxious about** whether the sandwiches are freshly made.

We are not **chicken-hearted about** going overseas. We are bold, brave, courageous and confident; we show **no signs of** trepidation. We are lionhearted rather than let the lion smell our **fear**. We stand up **for** ourselves and overcome our apprehension. It makes sense to be **strong enough** to hold fast to our beliefs and to 'go forward' **with** a mixture of courageous fearlessness and a sense of wise caution.

Teach yourself:

Notice the **gr_mmar, vocabulary, comparisons** and **prepositions**. When c_ught stealing, our knees will knock and our hair stand on end, our blood will run cold, our skin will creep. We m_y experience goose bumps or pins and needles. We might even be un_ble to move, turned to stone or petrified. We will either blush red or our skin will turn p_le and as white as a ghost. We might not control our bowels. Therefore, notice these physic_l reactions.

The great diffic_lty when tackling this topic is that, j_st as with the word 'bored', once we hear the word we might gravitate towards it and become it. Therefore, the objective is to overcome fears by knowing of the words associated with being **brave**. We think first, consider it and then go ahead and do it! We <u>hold fast</u> to our <u>confident self-belief</u> as we enjoy the advent_ro_s ride.

The worst that can happen is that we _ail. Many do. We are a_raid of failing or failure. With persistent perseverance we succeed. The worst that can happen is that we fail: 'Oh, so what? Who cares? Something better is meant to and is going to happen.'

Life is not for the faint-hearted. We are fitter if we work and struggle. There is a battle to survi_e in our gas-filled atmosphere as we endure the extremes of climate. Our existence is fragile, yet we have the inner resources and in-built desire to sur_ive.

Medical e_perts and 'climate change' exponents try to have their moment of importance by **scaring** us to death or **out of our wits**.

Fear of failure can inspire us to st_dy for exams and this

has long-term benefits. We feel **nervo_s**, yet preferably not worried sick.

During or after a _ad experience we may be distur_ed, agitated, in a state of shock and endure insuffera_le reactions. It is distressing, awful, upsetting and the load too much to _ear,

If we behave b_dly I'm afraid there will be a terrible price to p_y.

A s_dden death or accident may have the harshest and direst res_lt and we may have a tremendo_sly tra_matic reaction.

31.

The Grammar of Making Progress and Doing Well

Lady resting before continuing to carry water bottles up the mountain

Water carrier: This slim and very fit lady carries vital water supplies to the mountain top twice every day in winter and summer. The boxes of bottles are a significant weight and she has stopped at a viewing point for a brief rest. She regards her enormously hard work as a duty. The heat is extreme in the summer and it snows in winter. She exemplifies ergative verbs: work, action, movement!

Having spent a chapter overcoming fear we now select and highlight as many sensible words as we can in order to steer us towards **doing well** and **being successful**. If we have lived this long, then we are already successful! We know we can pass the exam and as intelligent **thinkers** we **plan out** how to pass. We **learn** a lot **from** our mistakes and **although** we want to pass first time, we become all the wiser. We then make **a habit of doing research and repeating the words associated with how to make progress and succeed.**

The words we repeatedly use give us ideas. Olympic athletes know very well that they should not take drugs. They know what is banned, including diuretics. A diuretic stimulates the kidneys to secrete urine and it helps to reduce the stock of excess water in places **such as** our legs and ankles. Once an athlete knows of the word and the chemical then first the **imagination** is stimulated and then the kidneys. Next is the **plea of innocence to** the charge of taking drugs. While they are **distracted** we **go towards** and

associate with the words we repeat: **adopt and persist with smart habits**.

Success is often seen as being unexpected or a surprise. In fact, success happens because we **persist** while others give up. Another **pathway to success** is to copy what good people do and then become innovative, different and individual. When we go overseas we want to know the native language; our colleague does not and so we **gain an advantage**. While we are active our travelling companion is less so. **We make plans and carry them out; our friend does not**.

Our friend goes home early, knows what to do next time and might prepare better. We are already ahead and may stay in this position. We **thrive** and become **prosperous** by being confident and efficient. The reasons **for doing so** may be because we want to be pragmatic and to **succeed** because we dearly enjoy the **sense of achievement**. Our **sense of achievement** has a good friend called 'Happiness.'

Teach yourself:

1. We **succeed in** a pioneer**ing** adventure by plann**ing** for the known and the unexpe_ted; then we persist **on** and **with** our journey.

2. Success is sometimes thought to be due to lu_k. However, it only o_ _urs to active participants and usually to those who have practised for years. After many years of work the result seems to be easy to achieve, yet we should never undervalue our effort.

3. Just like writing a book or diary, if we make progress day by day then, within one year we have a substantial **a_ _omplishment**.

4. Our prolonged effort over a long period of time **at last** bears fruit.

5. Whether or not we pass our exam at the end of a _ourse of study we still have that edu_ation and insight for as long as we live.

6. It is for each of us to de_ide how we measure success. We have to **decide for** and **against** several criteria, e.g. accumulating inner wealth and _ontentment or _ounting money and investments.

7. Some like to attain fame, others are glad to be alive for another day. Wealth is sometimes **measured in** monetary terms, but for most of us it is **through** our feelings of **growing** inner enri_hment.

8. We can **su_ _eed by** being a tower of strength to others, though if we don't **think of** our own welfare too we are **missing** the point.

9. We warn against giving advi_e because each person knows best how to run their own life. We _ongratulate them **on doing** well.

10. We step aside and don't **stop** others **from showing** their **talent**.

11. We **look forward to** them **prospering** in their own way.

12. They graduate from university and _ome out fighting. **They insist on proving** their worth and gradually **gaining** their fortune.

13. There is **hardly** a person who is not interested in making progress, doing well for their _hildren and being well-off.

14. We **approve of** most people **aspiring** to their peak or zenith.

15. We _an **hardly prevent** anyone **from fulfilling** their potential.

16. We overcome a fear of public speaking by planning our words. We are cheerful; make three points and highlight key words.

32.

Questions lead to Conversation and Writing Factually

When we wonder about whether or not to go and see the latest movie in town we ask many important **questions** without any hesitation. As with most topics in life, when we are paying out money we soon become an expert. "Where is the movie showing? Who's in it? What is the setting and when did it take place? Is it romantic? Is it a chick-flick? Why was the child scared? How does it end? How long is it? What did you think of it? Do you think I should go? Will my friend like it? Will we cry? Will we need a box of tissues?"

Once we know **the facts** we think it over and consider. When we know the facts we can write factually without omitting or overlooking what our reader is dying to know. We answer questions, state the obvious and do not neglect what is important. A good example of this is when we turn on the radio during a sports match and no one tells us the score. Several times we shout at the radio, **"What's the score?"** We are annoyed **when what we want to know is overlooked.**

Thus, we use **obvious** ways of **asking questions** as if they are a compulsory list of **research** objectives, even though the answer may appear to be "oh so obvious". **They are obvious to some but not to others** and we need only to hear a computer expert say, "It's easy!" and we are certain to add, "If you know how!" Experts with years of experience find it unbelievable that we are so ignorant. We all have to be told several times or **do research** or we have to **ask questions** no matter how much the answers are 'obvious' to others.

When unsure of how to extend our relationships or of how to make a conversation endure then asking questions is a part of the solution. **Open-ended questions** may be difficult to answer, but they allow a variety of thoughts to be put forward: "What do think about this situation? How do you feel about that? **What should we do**?"

Teach yourself:

1. Whi_h are you going to do? The washing or the drying?

2. Whi_h bus goes to Mount Lawley? Is it the 41 or the 62?

3. When they got to the _rossroads, which way did they go?

4. Who's been eating my porridge?

5. Who's been sleeping in my bed?

6. Who's been sitting in my _hair and broken it?

7. Who's that over there? Is that my friend from _ollege?

8. Who's afraid of Virginia Wolfe?

9. Who's the boss in your family, your mum or your dad?

10. Ex_use me, where's the post offi_e please?

11. Where do you _ome from? When were you born?

12. You look pale. Have you seen a ghost?

13. Do you believe in ghosts?

14. What's the most frightening experien_e you've ever had?

15. How long did it take you to get over it?

16. How do you feel when you are in a graveyard at night?

17. Do you have any superstitions? Tell me of some.

18. Will I get 7 years' bad lu_k be_ause I broke the mirror?

19. I'm sorry, I _an't help it. _an a leopard
change its spots?

20. How have I upset you? How _an I make it up to you?

21. Why do you get upset over little things?
Give me a reason.

22. What do you think they should do about this pla_e?

23. Should they kno_k it down and start again?

24. When will you apply for new jobs? Whi_h ones?

25. What do you think we should do about grandma?

26. Would you like it if they did that to you?

27. When is she moving in with the new boyfriend?
She's entitled to? What do you think she should do?

28. If I _ould fly to the moon one day
I'd be amazed, wouldn't you?

33.

Tag Questions Help to Make Conversation, don't they?

Using tag questions at the end of our comments is an excellent way of getting a response from our partner. **First**, the listener has to show they are listening by responding appropriately and then, **second**, they usually give a response at some length. We may get a short reply to "It's a beautiful day, **isn't it**?" Or our partner may like being given the invitation to make the relationship closer by giving a lengthy reply. "Yes. What shall we do? You'd love to go to the beach **wouldn't you**? I would too. It'll be a better day than the last time, **won't it**?" A positive is followed by a negative tag or vice versa.

Tag questions are attached to the ends of sentences to check up on what the other person thinks or we do it simply to confirm a fact. "Whose hat is this, yours or mine? I think it's yours, **isn't it**? Mine's got the red logo **hasn't it**? It doesn't matter much anyway, **does it**?"

Apart from asking a controversial question, we hardly ever use these tags when writing, **do we?** And we usually use a form of the verbs 'be', 'have', and 'do' such as 'is' 'are', 'were', 'was', 'has', 'have', 'had', 'do, 'did' or 'does', **don't we**? For native speakers these question forms arise naturally; however, for the language student they take a surprisingly long time to get used to, **don't they**?

To begin with, we practise being fluent in this skill while, at the same time, we make lots of amusing errors, which is fun. We eventually get down to serious conversation or offer to help with the question tags. We prompt the listener to agree, disagree or confirm what we say and to add their opinion. We look for variations to this style of conversation. Our suggestion, **offer** or invitation might be quite strong: "You should come and stay with me, **shouldn't you**?" And our reply might be: "Should I? Well, yes, I'd love to, **wouldn't I**?"

Teach yourself:

1. How much could we spend on the Nat_onal Health Service? Well, that's l_ke asking 'how long is a p_ece of string', _sn't it?

2. She looked b_autiful at the w_dding didn't sh_?

3. And the bride w_sn't b_d either, w_s she?

4. I have no need to _sk, h_ve I?

5. You've alw_ys liked Jane, h_ven't you?

6. And I think she's alw_ys made eyes at you, h_sn't she?

7. I th_ught she'd forg_tten about y_u, hadn't she?

8. But it s_ _ms not, do_sn't it? Sh_ told m_ all about it.

9. She d_dn't tell you about the letters, d_d she?

10. You kn_w she t_ld me everything, d_n't you?

11. Not _ll lovers can keep a secret c_n they?

12. There's no n_ _d to tell anyone else is th_re?

13. Well, that puts me in a m_ral dilemma d_esn't it?

14. But it's none of your bus_ness, _s it?

15. I'll have to make it my busi_ess though, wo_'t I?

16. I'll never be c_nfident ab_ut you keeping a c_nfidence, will I?

17. You know _ou can always rel_ on me, don't _ou?

18. Sometimes, to sh_w we are a g_ _d listener we ech_ back to the speaker to show _ur interest and we use a p_sitive question tag: "S_ you were in a car crash, were y_u?"

19. They kn_w who was going to g_t the job befor_hand, did th_y?

20. I expect th_t w_s upsetting for you, w_sn't it?

21. I _xp_ct you don't want to go through that again, do you?

22. S_metimes we are _bliged to d_ s_mething: "I think we sh_uld give far m_re money as f_reign aid, sh_uldn't we? We sh_uldn't be s_ wasteful, should we? You _ught to kn_w, _ughtn't y_u?"

23. I'_ _ te_ _ you a story, sha_ _ I?

24. Th_s is a good way of mak_ng conversant_on, _sn't it?

34.

From One Preposition to Another

Somewhat surprisingly, apart **from** observing nouns and verbs we also learn a lot by noticing prepositions. Thus, we broaden our ways of learning English by playing with such words as '**from**' or 'for' or 'with' and several others too. This is similar to noticing 'active' and 'passive'. When concentrating on one specific feature we also learn the rest of the sentence as if by coincidence or by the way.

When asked to give a definition of the word '**from**' our teacher will be lost for words apart from showing how it is used to express a range in a set of numbers, distances, time elapses and schedules. There are actually very few instances of its use as a phrasal verb; that is, **combining a verb and a preposition** so that they are dependent on each other for their meaning as a new verb.

A famous movie is "*From Here to Eternity*" indicating from one place to another which included a sensuous kissing scene on the beach. When we are young we learn with great pride our ABC **from** A to Z and as we count from 1 to 100. We know how far it is **from** home to school and how long it takes to walk from here to the bus-stop. We get warm wishes **from** everyone on our birthday and **shy away from** auntie's kisses when receiving presents from her at the party. We have to be **protected from** relatives who observe how much we have **grown up from** being just a little baby. After, we **suffer from** overeating.

One way of making conversation is to ask our new acquaintance, "Where do you come from?" Before long we tell them we love them **from the bottom of our heart** or we might **die from a broken heart**. A worthy attribute in life is to **recover from** a setback just like a **phoenix arises from** the fire and ashes. It is good to observe students who **evolve from** being apparently ordinary and then go on to achieve their fullest potential. We **emerge from** being weak into being confident and fearless. We **benefit from** pursuing our interests.

Teach yourself:

1. Good judges have decided that we compare by using **'different**

    f_ _m' rather than 'different to.' Never: 'different than'.

2. It is clear we are not descended **f_ _ _** modern monkeys, but we may share common ancestors. We are

also curious to know and consider if we emerged _ _ _ _ a long-ago existence in the sea.

3. From this idea we then see that passing on life and wisdom _ _ _ _ one generation to another is an obligation hard to escape f_ _ _.

4. Ideas evolve very far fro_ asking the key question of "What if....?"

5. We find many useful words connected with 'giving birth to' such as: make, generate, conceive, evolve, bring into existence, grow, originate, create, cause, breed, produce, develop and form. We use 'from' with many of these. What are we derived _ _ _ _?

6. A useful expression is to say we have 'eclectic tastes' in music and literature that we draw inspiration _ _ _ _ many genres.

7. We acquire and collect knowledge _ _ _ _ a wide range of sources.

8. We conduct research and learn from many books, original scientific observation or _ _ _ _ anecdotal sources.

9. We can be selective and hide, conceal or keep the whole truth fr_m others about what happened. Errors are eliminated from sight.

10. We are prohibited from plagiarising and discouraged ____ copying. We can use quotations from books, yet remember to state our sources. Informal expressions should be omitted or excluded from our university assignments.

11. Between the ages of ten and twenty-five we change ____ being a child to being a careful, thinking and responsible adult.

12. A parent or teacher is our guide and discourages us from developing bad habits and stops us ____ doing silly things.

13. We drive carefully so we are not banned ____ driving or eliminated from use of the road. We benefit from this.

35.

Love Affairs, Vocabulary and Phrasal Verbs

There are a good many phrasal verbs associated with **falling in love**. Perhaps the best sex education advice parents can give is to say that being **attracted by** or to someone is most certainly permissible and virtually inevitable at some time in our lives. The recommendations are to 'be sensible' and to 'behave with a **sense of responsibility.**'

In private the friendship **blossoms into** hours of tender skin to skin touching. At about the age of twenty the desire to be intimate is virtually unstoppable and physical intimacy becomes what we should be doing rather than not doing. We are **crazy about** them; we have a passionate '**pash**' on them. With their increasing and impending sense of independence and feeling of maturity a young couple is going to **go further than** they have experimented before. They should.

The word 'friendship' is usually a basic essential circumstance for intimacy to **proceed with** mutual willingness. We **fall for** someone and **fall in love, fall head over heels in love** or, as in the song we are '**falling into you**.' As in all aspects of life there are positive experiences and negative ones too: we might **fall out of love**!

A century ago many people were married by the age of eighteen. Sharing enjoyment, giving and receiving pleasurable experiences and fulfilling the act of procreation arise naturally and **add to** our spiritual health. The word '**responsibility**' impresses itself upon us. Fun is a central theme as it flows and is **channelled through** our general liveliness, dancing, tenderness and softly spoken conversation.

We **communicate** and generate "unbelievable" heights of sensitivity hitherto unknown **prior to** intimate loving. Including us, every species **wants to** perpetuate their kind and Mother Nature **creates** the settings and circumstances **for** this to be made possible **in** the most natural of ways. Inevitably, money matters are of serious concern. "Who's **paying for** it? Where's the money **coming from**?"

Teach yourself:

1. Having been **stood _p** by several ex-girlfriends and **broken _p w_th** them I decided to **go _ut with** Lucy. We didn't have to chat each other up. We had **built _p**

a friendship when we got t_gether in school and then **paired _ff** and got **dressed _p** for the annual dance. The feeling of being **switched _n** by her really began then and we have been going _ut ever since. We not only **get o_** well, we remain mutually **attracted t_** or even **obsessed by** each other. We left school and went of_ t_ different universities but we **meet u_** every weekend or **drop i_** to see each other at home. Surprisingly, we haven't **grown ap_rt**. We respect, **look u_ t_** and **look aft_r** each other and it wouldn't surprise me if we moved i_ together soon. We could ask someone else to go o_t w_th us but we don't want to break u_ or walk o_t of this relationship. We meet u_ at weekends and **pour o_t** our troubles or anxieties and that **cheers** us **_p**. We often go to the cinema and cuddle _p or we eat o_t at our favourite café. We warm t_ each other in many ways. Our feelings haven't **worn _ff** and it seems likely we will **settle d_wn** and possibly get married or **hitched _p** as they say. I suppose we could **get _ver it** and **drift ap_rt** or see if we are **missing o_t o_** other opportunities. There is no hint of two-timing and so we don't have to keep _p appearances or go showing _ff to other potential lovers. We feel comfortable together and get along well. There are no secrets to keep fr_m each other or feelings that we are **letting** anyone **d_wn** with high or false hopes. We **drop i_** on friends and don't pass up the chance to be invited o_t to parties. Generally though, we like to keep ourselves to ourselves. There is a sense of trust betw_en us and the thought of **splitting u_** would not stop us from remaining life-long friends. We would get ov_r it, but keep i_ touch forever as though we were made f_r each other.

36.

Diverse Phrasal Verbs and Key Concepts of Change

Typewriters are out! When our business grows to become successful there is always a sensible wish to be innovative and to diversify. All business ventures have to adapt, innovate, diversify and **change** in some specific and particular way. Businesses rapidly fail or **fade away** unless they **diversify** or **change from** what they used to be.

If their computer skills are too limited, a one-time scholar who was literate and academically brilliant some years ago may now possibly be deemed illiterate and **out of touch**. To use the current buzz-word, we have to **up-skill**. We have to **cope with** change; **adapt to** it and not **put it off** for too long. We must not **lag behind** our rivals. We have to change and decide to **get on with it** with a sense of urgency.

As staff we prefer things to remain **steady** and **stable** as we **blend into** the environs of the workplace and avoid close **scrutiny of** our performance. We sustain our average effort. Change brings renewed enthusiasm if only for the sake of survival. Today's big effort **differs from** yesterday's ordinariness. Change makes an **impact upon** us: we **take on** a willing attitude and **embrace** innovation **with** open arms. We **adjust to** and **bring about** advancement rather than experience inertia and stagnation. We like good ideas. We neither have **conflict with** resisting progress nor **throw** the baby **out** with the bath water.

To diversify: we **alter, evolve from, move on** and **metamorphose into** something new. We adapt and adjust, instigate innovation and **bring about** fresh plans. We differ **from**, contrast **from**, convert **to** or diverge from or swap **from** the old pathway to new methods. We **branch off;** branch **out;** and **shift from** one thing or place to another. We **vary** or **deviate from** the norm. We **catch on to** new ideas. If we fall **back** we **fight back** and **forge ahead**. We don't **mess about**. We welcome, **go through with** and **concentrate on** change.

Teach yourself: An optimistic speech from the new boss:

"When we **run up** against the tide of progress we have to overcome our weakness and embrace change. Previously we burnt a lot of coal in order to produce electricity; now we are adapting t_ using solar power and solar panels. We are in business; we must diversify; we will convert fr_m delivering coal to making solar panels.

Although we are fearful of change, our business is vulnerable to losing our clientele base. We must **move aw_y fr_m** and **give _p** our old methods because we can't **get aw_y w_th** inefficiency now. We must modernise and **throw _ut** redundant practices and modify past strategies. There are new ways of thinking and we must **keep _p**. We used to **eke o_t** a living; but now we **look forw_rd** to **tearing** our competitor **ap_rt** by **setting f_rth w_th** new methods and enterprise.

When there's a technological breakthrough we have to seize the moment and make the most of it. We **break thr_ugh** the old barriers and **launch i_to** using modern scientific methods. Let's **look ah_ad** and **splash o_t** on state of the art computer controlled systems. Unless we are **bang _p to date,** our business will **ebb aw_y** just like the outgoing tide. We have to **stay on top**. There is no **going b_ck!**

First, we have to **think** things **thro_gh, break w_th** tradition, **come _p w_th** and **embark on** creative ways of being inventive. We will recycle waste and **make use _f** it; what used to be inefficient we will **improve up_n** and make profitable. We will be pioneers, **drum _p** new business and become market leaders again. We'll have to **train up** the staff and use a new broom **to clear o_t** old ways of practice.

It's no good to just **scrape by**. We will **invest in** new technology. This transition and sudden **change fr_m** the old ways to innovation is for those of us who want to **press ahe_d**. We must diversify and be **ready f_r** it! It will be interesting and in our own interests!"

37.

Times and Places

We want to know **when** and exactly **where** we are meeting. "It might be at 7.30 tonight or tomorrow morning at 11. We'll see each other under the clock tower at 7.30 p.m. or 11 a.m. Then I'll be away from April 23rd for six weeks until I come back early in June." **Being clear about times and dates** is of enormous help in both our everyday conversation and when writing a book. When a history book has a date of an event on each page then the reader is clear about the order.

Our use of **'time adjuncts' assists us**. If the TV repair is going to be done at 7 o'clock then it is useful to know if this is in the morning or the evening on Monday or Tuesday. **Dawn** is when the sun rises and **dusk** is when the sun sets. 7 o'clock may mean suppertime or breakfast. Confusion arises regarding 'dinner'. The working classes have their dinner at noon while those who wish to show they are not working class have **dinner** in the evening. The midday meal is **lunch**. There is considerable tautology in the observation that, "After reveille at 6.30 a.m. first thing in the morning we'll have breakfast."

In the eastern world the question might be, "Will our house be built and ready before Spring Festival?" In the Christian parts of the western world meanwhile, the request is to want it to be completed and ready by Christmas. It is also best to state *which* Christmas we mean: this year or next? The eastern Spring Festival's date (January/February) and the Christian Easter festival (March/April) are very much associated with and depend on the lunar calendar. Christmas Day, December 25th, is just after either the shortest or longest day of the year, depending on the hemisphere, north or south. The season has definitely changed from autumn to cold winter in the north and from spring to hot summer in the south.

Whereas **A.D.** refers to the years after (Jesus) Christ, and B.C. used to mean before Christ, **B.C.E.** now refers to Before the Common Era!

Teach yourself:

1. A. D. stands for Anno D_mini. When were you b_rn?

2. Research: Robert Burns' night 25th January; Valentine's Day; Guy Fawkes Night; April Fools' Day; tw_ months which have the equinox; two months which have the solstice; May Day; St Patrick's Day; Independence Day; Thanksgiving Day; Christmas Day; Shakespeare's Birthday; Oct_ber 1st.

3. 'Just a m_ment, I'll just finish this first and I'll be with you in a minute. I've already got thr_ugh quite a lot of the work.'

4. In a while = in a sh_rt time. In a little time. Wait awhile = for a time. A building project in Western Australia (W.A.), as is the case elsewhere, inv_lves many years between the idea, the planning, the commencement, the over-blowing of the c_st, a strike or two by the construction workers and completion. Thus: <u>W</u>ait <u>A</u>while.

5. At the moment, Charles is next in line to the thr_ne of England, foll_wed by his son William. In the past it was sons who had precedence, but, due to recent legislation, from now on girls will have equal rights in the line of succession to the throne.

6. I'm into the final again. I'm going thr_ugh the same emotions I had two **years ago**. The final will take place this **weekend**.

7. I won't see you t_m_rr_w; I'll see you the foll_wing day, the day after next. I won't be here next week; I'll see you the following week, two weeks from n_w, the week after next, a **f_rtnight**.

8. My mother is so _ld fashi_ned; she was born in 1978,

in the last century, the 20th century! This is the 21st century now!

9. It hasn't rained since a **fortnight** ago. We had **better not** do any planting until it rains again; surely, that won't be an_ther 2 weeks!

10. I like to drive in the daylight; we'll leave at the crack _f **dawn**.

11. Our c_untry's census is taken every **decade**. We observe births, deaths and movements in the p_pulation every ten years.

12. **Simultane_usly** c_mbining research and investment is fun.

38.

What's the Time? Do you come here often?

When at a loss for our opening words with our new partner we have just begun dancing with we might ask: "Do you come here often?" Stating the **frequency** of an event is another useful way of using **time adjuncts** to say **exactly** what is happening and we include these adverbs frequently. These words indicate the importance or relevance of what we are talking about.

There is a difference between meeting 'from time to time' or 'all the time'. How often is 'regularly'? It is amusing to discuss the fine line between: rarely, seldom, hardly ever, infrequently... until we get to the other end of the scale with: **frequently, constantly, very often, all the time, continuously** and **continually**. We may **sometimes** or **repeatedly** have trouble spelling intermittently and sporadically.

Although it is paradoxical to say we add clarity, the use of: **perhaps, sometimes, almost, approximately, occasionally** and **more or less** give indications of how exact or imprecise a time is. We guess values: 'Now is not the best time to sell. In a good market it's possibly worth....' **Rarely** are matters entirely black and white or yes or no apart from the amusing example that: we never claim to be 'slightly pregnant'.

We take our medicine **three times** a day before or after meals or get treatment **twice** a week. To run a marathon **once** in a lifetime is enough for most of us. We have our **annual** birthday and know that some plants are **biennials** and so we do not expect them to last for three years. We look forward to a lifetime of at least **three score** and **ten** and it is only a year later at 71 when we might feel we are getting old and **look forward to** getting to a **century** in the next century. The **millennium** and the predicted 'computer chaos' all passed smoothly in the year 2000, or was it 2001? We won't have to worry so much for the **next** one! A well-used philosophy of going about life is to tackle it **day by day** or enjoy it **one day at a time** as if today were our last.

Teach yourself:

1. A motivating logo is: "Focussing on the future." Rather than state the obvious, compose a different theme, e.g., 'Up-skill now.'

2. To many **g_n_rations** of n_wspaper r_aders it seems

incr_dible that their **daily** r_ading will soon be from the int_rn_t.

3. Medical and ac_demic journ_ls appear **qu_rterly,** while mag_zines _re often published **weekly, fortnightly, monthly** or **annually**.

4. The m_ _n's phases are completed in about 29 ½ days (a 'synodic month'). In each **lunar m_nth** the new moon is like a crescent and the full moon circular. The moon takes about 27 and a third days to c_mplete one _rbit and this is termed a 'sidereal m_nth'.

5. The explor_tion of space is **still** h_ppening with sp_cecraft continu_lly being sent into orbit _round the Earth and even l_nding on Mars. However, the sending of any m_nned sp_cecraft to the moon seems to have been h_lted **indefinitely** at the moment.

6. Spa_e stations enable **long-term** exploration of space and provide the benefits of medi_al, te_hnological and scientifi_ research.

7. **Per_anent** co_ _unications satellites have enhanced telephonic reception and allowed us to see worldwide pictures on television.

8. When the first R_ssian space satellite was la_nched in the late 1950s hardly anyone could predict the benefits

of the development from this technology. When the first airflight took place in the early 20th century hardly anyone could predict the scope of airline travel a cent_ry later. The rate of progress develops exponentially from the very limited to the _nimaginable.

9. **From time to ti_e** it is worth reflecting on how just a few **decades ago** we had a li_ited range of ideas about what is possible now.

10. Our mind has a **contin_ous** sense of c_riosity and pioneers **contin_ally** go ahead with daring beneficial projects.

11. The **ra_id rate of _rogress** seems to be **constant** or **non-stop**.

39.

In the Right Place at the Right Time: There are 3 reasons:

We may write or speak with passion or want to explain cause and effect. However, not only do we want to know **when** events are happening we clarify the scene by saying **where** they happen. Whether as writers or as readers, speakers or listeners, we like to have and to be guided by a planned **direction**. As the writer or speaker we know what we are talking about. However, we must keep reminding our reader or listener what is taking place, who is involved and when and **where**. What is obvious to us may not be so to our reader!

Very often we experience an element of apparent luck, either good or bad. We gain promotion and modestly claim we were in the **right place at the right time** or we know of a dreadful piece of bad luck when the person was in the wrong place at the wrong time. We always try to give a logical explanation, despite the role of 'fortune'.

A basic example of a word which makes our writing seem to be of an advanced level is to use the word '**there**' fairly often. "There are three main reasons for this situation." However, for location we say 'in that place' by using '**over there**' or 'there it is'. "I lost some money. I asked the room cleaner if I had dropped it **there** yesterday, but he told me there was nothing there." **Here, there** and **everywhere**.

After a while we have and keep developing an awareness regarding how we locate times and places and allocate reasons. **There is no doubt** that we should make our explanation clearer and remember to stop our reader feeling lost. We need look no further than being told how to use the computer. 'Step 9 is easy (if we recall steps 2 and 3).'

We notice: 'There is some evidence to suggest…': 'There is every likelihood that…'; 'There used to be'; 'D'you know the clock tower? I'll wait for you there.' '**There** once was a young lady from Leeds, Who swallowed a packet of seeds, It soon came to pass She was covered in grass, But has all the tomatoes she needs!'

Teach yourself:

1. "There will be widespread rain in the m_rning with f_g on l_w gr_und. There is the likeliho_d of hailst_rms in southern regi_ns."

2. Everyone is agreed that we _an _ut down on pollution

in many **areas**, yet whether **global** warming is o_ _urring we are unsure.

3. A life in the great outdoors with fresh air and the wind blowing in our face is reco_ _ended for our physical and _ental health.

4. Sun Yat Sen (or Sun Zhong Shan) was born in Guang_ong in southern China in 1866 and _ied of cancer on 12th March 1925 in Beijing. He was the first Presi_ent and the foun_ing father of the Republic of China. At the age of 13 he went to live with his el_er brother in Honolulu where he picke_ up some English. In 1886 Sun studied Me_icine in Guangzhou and gra_uated as a _octor from Hong Kong College of Medicine in 1892. After helping to organise several uprisings he went into exile in various countries inclu_ing Japan, Englan_, Cana_a and the USA. In 1905 Sun joine_ forces with Chinese students living in Tokyo and organise_ four uprisings between 1907 and 1909. He raised funds in Singapore and Malaysia to promote the Revolution in 1911 in Guangzhou. January 1st 1912 was _eclared the first Year of the Republic.

5. Although mainly con_erned with lo_al domestic politi_s, Sun Zhong Shan travelled worldwide and is known of internationally.

6. Useful words include: overseas, _ome, abroad, inside, throug_out.

7. We get on or travel **a_oard** a _oat, train, aircraft, yacht, _us, ferry.

8. Directions and locations incl_de, left, right, middle, centre, in between, north, south-west, and it is useful to know the latit_de and longit_de of our hometown, capital city or place of st_dy.

9. We have a holi_ay at the seaside; at a funeral we stand at the gravesi_e; at a boxing contest we want a ringsi_e seat.

10. To be pre_ise use exact: times, dates, positions and **lo_ations**.

Xi An station, platform 3.

Xi An is the famous city at the eastern end of the silk road in China. Its translated name is simply West Peace. The character for 'peace' is 'An' and is on the right: a lady under a roof which signifies calmness. Xi An is the home of the Terracotta Warriors. Think in threes while waiting on platform three.

40.

When and How Things Happen

Changes happen constantly and we may as well employ words which describe how and at what rate these take place. They may happen suddenly and abruptly or, as in **evolutionary processes**, gradually.

Political change might occur speedily yet we observe that, actually, the more things change the more they stay the same. In Egypt in 2011 Hosni Mubarak was relatively suddenly deposed after 30 years of his Presidency. Almost a year later, in June 2012, Mohammed Morsy was eventually elected and apparently many Egyptians "finally, are delighted to have a democratically elected President." We are **still** wondering what the difference is going to be.

We use the French word 'coup' to describe a **sudden** overthrow of a government. Meanwhile/at the same time/ while this is happening, very often the military power of the army is involved. Although the generals promise their influence will only be **temporary,** they often **remain** as a significant factor in ensuring the changes are not too revolutionary. Subsequently, a **smooth** transition of power may take place or the army will be a '**presence**' for many months to come.

In business when buying goods we **first** pay a deposit for our purchase **beforehand**. We either repay the total sum **gradually** month by month on hire purchase terms and only take possession of the goods **after** the **final** settlement; or we **pay it off** in one go.

Originally and **traditionally**, marriage was **normally** and **mainly** intended between a man and a woman. **Nowadays/in this day and age/in modern times/currently** there is the question of gay marriage to consider. **Presently,** some countries permit marriage between two men **or** two women while some countries oppose such a union. If a marriage is **permanent/forever**, the change is a huge long-term step.

Teach yourself:

1. On land we measure **speed** in **miles** or **kil_metres per h_ur**, while at sea we measure speed in **kn_ts**, which is not **quite** the same.

2. A handy tip is to explain by using **se_uences** of three. Although we want to learn English **_uickly** it still takes

years to do so. How many years it takes depends **first,** on attitude; **second** on the amount of practice and **third**: the level of immersion in English.

3. If the govern_ent owes us _oney then we expect them to **take their time**; however, when we owe them money we are expected to _ake pay_ent **i_ _ediately**.

4. **Whenever** there are grey skies we know that _lue skies are not **far _ehind** and optimists o_serve that every cloud has a silver lining.

5. **Subse_uent** to the pollution by radiation of the seas the **conse_uence** is that many fish are **now** contaminated.

6. The business world **is changing,** my English **is impro_ing** and my _ocabulary **is increasing.** I **never** expected to go o_erseas.

7. This is the **era** of communication. I **hardly ever** thought I _ould travel **beyond** the borders of my country or **around** the _orld or be **situated in** a job overseas.

8. We often notice that when there is a **_irth** there is a **death** just before or soon after. My friend's _aby was _orn on June 21st and her grandfather died on June 22nd, the day after.

9. Our essay **beg_ns** with an introduction; the main body paragraphs come **next** and, **f_nally,** our conclusion. It matters not in which order we wr_te them, as long as we get them r_ght eventually.

10. I'm sorry I'm **late**. I'm not very **pu_ctual**. Have I kept you lo_g? Have I held you up? Have I delayed you?

11. Farmers, _arents and teachers spend much of their **time** being _atient. Although it is best for a _regnancy to go **full term**, it is of little consequence if a baby is born slightly **_rematurely**. Farmers **wait** for cro_s to **ripen** and teachers wait for students to **mature**.

41.

Conditional Sentences and Situations

When we speculate on what might occur in the event of a prediction coming true we often use **'if'** sentences. This situation may be highly likely or virtually **impossibly imaginative**. "If I **was** to borrow fifty cents from you and if the world **were** to end tomorrow then I **would**n't have to pay it back!" We use **modal verbs** frequently.

There are many times when we know that if something happens then there is a **usual** or **expected** consequence. 'If that cyclone comes in this direction we **will** get heavy rain.' 'When we heat that water to 100 degrees C it **will** boil.' 'If we don't cook it properly we'll get food poisoning.' 'If anyone phones then tell them I'll call back.'

We wish for an outcome: 'If you **could** possibly get here for our wedding we **would** be delighted.' 'If we went by train it **would** be cheaper than paying for parking.' 'If those refugees hadn't gone by boat they would still be alive.' 'If we don't take action now the problem **will** be worse later.' 'If we looked at whole sentences rather than just an item of grammar we **would** get the whole picture.' 'If you take IELTS then you **will** get all the headaches you deserve.'

We then find **unlikely situations**: 'If you **were** driving at 190kph in the fog you **would** scare your passengers.' 'If we **were** attacked by another planet we **could** hide in the cellar.' We sometimes use 'might': 'If she had gone straight back to work after having her baby she might have become the head of department or even the head teacher.' 'If he had scored from that penalty we **would** have won and not lost.' 'If we make an alliance with the USA we **might** upset our relations with other countries, many of whom are trading partners.'

We can talk about the good old days: 'If we had had a fridge in those days we **would** have been rich, but we didn't because we weren't.'

Teach yourself:

1. If st_dents **were** to do far more many research projects they wo_ld improve their English very rapidly.

2. If young people behave like delinq_ents and look for ways to cheat 80% of the time they would do better to work sincerely for 20% of the time in order to show themselves they can s_cceed.

3. If students learnt two or three sentences by heart each week they would notice both the str_ctures as well as the vocab_lary. They would then be able to repeat these sentence styles in whatever way they wanted to express themselves in each new context.

4. If we get the wrong point of foc_s or have a fearful attit_de then we will get the wrong view and lose confidence.

5. If students think that writing academic English is diffic_lt then they would be correct in this ass_mption.

6. If students were to cond_ct research from several so_rces and amalgamate what they find, then that would be original work.

7. If students were to stop and observe how other people write academic English, then they wo_ld realise that we all have the same diffic_lties. We all copy, follow and adopt the same style.

8. If st_dents would to do research and find pathways safely explored already in academic writing then they wo_ld find their own ways of expressing themselves are as good as anyone else's.

9. Our life is intrig_ing because it is full of complications and complexities. When expressing a most _nlikely or

impossible situation we use 'were' instead of 'was'. '**If I were you, I would....**'

10. If anyone ever took notice of what I said I wo_ld feel flattered.

11. If students fo_nd many examples of the types of grammar sentences in each chapter they would soon see they would be writing very correct English. They **would** grad_ally be able to write their own tho_ghts down in correctly formed sentences.

42.

'If' Sentences and Living in Dream Land

We all have phases of living in dreamland. We find it easier to give advice rather than accept it or we do less than half of what we suggest others should do. We use 'if' sentences all the time when dreaming or giving advice. This implies that we use modal verbs frequently: **'you ought to …', 'you should…', 'you must/have to**…' and when dreaming we start with **'If I were rich**…' 'If I **were** an Olympic athlete… ', 'If only I lived on the beach in Australia…' Other modal verbs include: **may, will, can, would, could, shall**.

The impossible conditional to recall is: **'If I were you**, I would…' Instead of using 'was' **we use 'were' for these most unlikely of situations**. 'If I **were** the richest person in the world, I would…'

When giving advice it seems so logical to say, 'Oh, **if I were you** I **would** leave him and find a new guy.' This is the best example of when we want to reply, 'Well, you're not me, so how do you know how much I am in love?' Teachers in the classroom are paid to **advise** and to give advice. Once beyond the classroom it applies to each of us that we do not fully understand someone else's situation and how complex and complicated it all is. It is best to restrain ourselves from advising and to keep reasonably quiet. Giving **advice** is vital when we are informative and hint: 'I assume you know your interview is in Kingston and not here in Epsom?' Or we confirm what the person wants to do anyway, 'Yes, I agree. It's time you should move on.'

We may have some fun playing with **modal verbs** and **conditional situations**. University work often expects speculation even though it is impossible to say what is going to happen. However, we can be a fortune teller and use our foresight: "We are all doomed unless we act now" is a sentence we have heard on the radio daily year after year for the past fifty years. People constantly create many needless fears.

Tip: Because the grammar is so difficult, **avoid** using the conditional!

Teach yourself:

billion, survive, tallest, yacht, future, purpose, teenagers, karaoke, good, life, mature, roots.

1. If we intensively fish the sea and farm the land in order to feed 7 _____ people we will soon be very short of fish and fertile soil.

2. If only some well-meaning countries would stop interfering in the politics of other countries they would realise they do more harm than ____.

3. If I were the richest person in the world I would make sure that everyone sang _____ every day and thus kept the peace.

4. It's never my fault! If my family ____ were not so complicated I would be very successful by now.

5. If I owned the best _____ someone would probably push me off it.

6. If I owned the _____ building a cyclone would blow it down!

7. If we lose our focus on one purpose of life then we should focus on our new aim and enjoy that new _____ and journey.

8. I suggest that if you want improve your English then you should specialise in reading intermediate or advanced level grammar and vocabulary books. At first they are difficult; on the third reading they are

easier to follow. Also allow that you will _____ and improve and you will then widen your reading and viewing.

9. We will grow healthy plants and bake good cakes as long as we respectively don't pull out the plants to inspect their _____ and we do not keep opening the oven to check their progress.

10. If _____ realised they will one day be a mature 30 year old and still having fun, they wouldn't be so anxious to be in a hurry.

11. If you feel this project has a bright _____ then you should go ahead and do it. The attitude should be: "I will make it a success."

12. If people _____ to a good age with a good sense of humour then it is be clear they must be intelligent and deserve respect.

43.

Reporting Words that help us Avoid Misinterpretation

When newspaper reporters are sent out on assignments they have to report what happened or what was said. Feature writers of newspaper and magazine articles may have to **give an opinion,** but must be <u>careful</u> about what they say. They are not the judge and jury in court and do not decide what happened. They do not want to say completely the wrong thing such as making a false accusation.

For legal reasons too, we have to be guarded in our choice of words. We must not report that "she had blood stains all over her shoes which obviously showed she had just murdered her lover." We do not know who committed the murder or whose blood it was, if indeed a murder actually took place at all. We may say what **seemed** or **appeared** or is **alleged** to have happened. Even if we witness the event we do not say who was responsible; we **report** either that the male is deceased or that the police will <u>allege</u> that Lucy murdered Tom as long as that is what the police have actually said. **Denials** usually happen next and we leave the verdict to the court of law.

The police wait for the results of the autopsy for the cause of death. They might say that foul play was involved or even that the person **appears** to have committed suicide. We need <u>**EVIDENCE**</u> and the reporting of the facts and not opinionated prejudice. We do not say: "Yes, it's terrible what men are like! It's just the same as when my boyfriend asked for his engagement ring back and I nearly stabbed him to death." We must 'hedge' and be **careful with our words**.

Rumour and 'there's no smoke without fire' are clear signs of bias, prejudice and usually, **false assumption**. Even witnesses of the same event give different versions of what occurred. 'Hedging' **implies** being careful about stating even what might have happened. We cannot be definite. There is room for the cautious use of '**possibly**' and '**probably**'. We must not give our opinion of what we think happened. When uncertain, we keep quiet or hedge and '**allege.**'

Teach yourself:

1. We do not give advi_e because we do not know our listener's cir_umstances. Similarly, we do not say "what I think happened."

   We have to know exactly what happened and then we can speak.

2. Thus, s_ientific research has to deal with measuring and statistics.

3. Many of these verbs are followed by another verb with the use of 'to', such as: **forget to, de_ide to, promise to, fail to, learn to, tend to, afford to, refuse to, seem to, appear to, aim to, agree to, plan to, remember to, obje_t to, alleged to, hope to, deserve to.**

4. When reporting we say: **it appears/seems that, she believed that, said that, con_eded that, estimated that, _onsidered that, told us that, explained that, argued that, discovered that, held that, alleged that, implied that, a_knowledged that, understood that, confirmed that, guaranteed that, thought that, concluded that.**

5. These verbs are useful in university style research essays and are usually followed by 'that': **note, assert, conclude, reveal, assume, state, agree, mention, predi_t, _laim, observe.**

6. Use these words in the sentences below: **liable; presume; fire; evidence; suggest; recommendation; appears; Apparently.**

7. _____, those who get ahead in early childhood stay ahead.

8. The results of our research _____ there is little difference between the ability of left and right-handers.

9. We can _____ that people's attitudes correspond closely with the beliefs of their cultural heritage.

10. Anecdotal evidence is ____ to prejudice and misinterpretation.

11. It _____ there is room for improvement in teaching methods.

12. Our study's e_____ shows that previous reports are unreliable.

13. Thus, our _____ is that swimming lessons should be available to all primary school children.

14. There is no smoke without ____ is a foolish expression. Our neighbours came running when they actually only saw rain water vapour evaporating like steam off our fence in the hot sun.

44.

Verbs used in the way we Say Something to our Listener

Although a confession is not always accepted, a person may **confess** to the police to a crime, or we **say** something to someone. We **tell** a child; **whisper** to our companion; **confide** in/to a friend; **propose** to our soul mate; **announce** to the world; **report** to our supervisor.

We **admit** and **explain** to someone our reason for being late or **explain** how a machine works, **emphasise** the most important features and **insist** on the proper method being adopted. We might even **boast, brag** or **broadcast** to everyone about our achievements.

We <u>declare</u> an interest in or even a **vested interest** in a business proposal or **declare** at the end of the wedding vows that 'they are husband and wife'. We **highlight** the virtues of the happy couple and **stress** the need not to **argue** over petty matters such as the toothpaste. Fifty years later they **teach, point out** and **demonstrate** how to get on with each other: "**Patience!** Turn off your hearing aid."

As scientific theorists we **advance** or **put forward** or **propose** new theories or hypotheses with regard to, say, the significance of music as a part of our daily life. We **describe** our research methodology and **prove** beyond doubt the invaluable contribution singing plays in reducing the risk of heart attacks and reducing stress. In fact, we **suggest** or **stress** that it reduces stress. We **hint** that music is vital.

We prefer to **reason** or **agree** with people that there is no need to **shout, shriek** or **scream** at each other. We **gather, learn, infer, see** and **hear** from what they say that it is better to 'jaw jaw' (talk) rather than to 'war war'; or, it is better to make love than to make war. They **plead with** and **confirm** that **confess**ion is good for the soul and that **yelling** at each other is hard to forgive and forget. We **apologise** to a friend and **promise** them we will make a new start. The worst journalist will ask, "Do you **deny**…" whatever. The stain remains.

Teach yourself:

1. Do you promise to tell the truth, the whole truth and nothing but the truth? How do you respond to my question?

2. Choose "you" "to" or "at" to follow these: **e.g. bark at,**

urge you: remind ___ , admit __ , bellow , shout , yell , promise , mention , explain , tell , say , howl , decide , pretend , permit , encourage , order , allow , scream , boast , announce , reveal , command, forbid , roar __ .

3. Write short sentences or questions using the keyword and 'with': e.g. I agree with you.

    Discuss: I want to…
    Reason
    Confirm

4. Write short sentences or questions using the keyword and 'from': e.g. I've **gathered from** several sources that you have good news.

    Discover
    Heard
    We can infer
    Learn
    See

5. Write short sentences or questions using the keyword and 'about': e.g. He's always grumbling about something or other.

    Mutter
    Complain
    Wonder

Write

Dream

Explain

6. Now use 'of': You never **think of** me.

Hear

Remind

45.

When one Verb follows another: 'to' and '-ing'

Especially when reporting, we use one verb after another. Often, the **second verb has the '–ing' ending** or we can use both the verbs and **add 'to' in between**. 'I remember clean**ing** my teeth' or 'I remember**ed** to clean my teeth.' A famous song by Elvis Presley is: "*I can't help falling in love with you.*"

These are actions that happen continuously; or likes and dislikes: we keep try**ing**. The plates need wash**ing**, the garden needs weed**ing**, the clean**ing** needs do**ing**. When giving instructions we suggest: 'try press**ing** the red button;' 'try keep**ing** your mouth shut for a minute;' try focuss**ing** on the job in front of you.' 'I like cook**ing** noodles, but I can't stand wash**ing** the dishes afterwards.'

We **regret doing** a foolish thing, especially for say**ing** something cruel. We can't **bear being** heartless when we are usually **keen to please** with our kindness. We **intend making** a fresh start tomorrow. We **mean to start** our diet next year. We intend **putting it off** until then. We **want to**

211

cut down on what we eat and we can't **keep putting** it off. We won't **bother dieting** until after the festive season. Some kleptomaniacs can't **stop stealing** or **wanting to steal**. 'We can't **go on meeting** like this or **hurting** each other.' 'It's time for action, I can't stand it when we **go on talking** about it; it's time to **start doing** something about it.'

When people are **accused of doing** something they may, often most justifiably, **deny doing it or having done it**. The worst reporters ask, "Do you deny…" Whatever the truth, the damning stain sticks.

Key words for this double verb –ing or 'to' are: **go on (talking), keep (trying), regret (saying), regret to say, decide to, enjoy/like doing, need (mending) to mend, can't help laughing, stop moving, hate (saying)/to say this, love (dancing) to dance, continue (washing) to wash/ playing/to play**. I can't stand talking about it. Let's do it.

Teach yourself:

1. I must do something. I'll learn _ _ dance and start playing chess.

2. When did you begin danc_ _ _? When did you learn _ _ dance?

3. Is it dangerous to attempt _ _ tightrope walk across Niagara Falls?

4. Don't bother complain_ _ _, they won't stop playing cards.

5. I hate wasting my time like this. I'd like _ _ go to bed instead.

6. Try be_ _ _ punctual next time; I don't want to be kept waiting.

7. I remember promis_ _ _ you, so don't go on complain_ _ _.

8. Shall we go fishing next week? Yes, I'd love _ _ go.

9. I like to exercise, to go fishing and _ _ get some fresh air.

10. You needn't straighten my tie, it doesn't need straighten_ _ _.

11. I can't help be_ _ _ nervous on my wedding day.

12. I love framing photographs and then I try hang_ _ _ them in the right place in my hall. I don't like _ _ buy expensive works of art.

13. I couldn't bear to hear her get_ _ _ angry with me. I stopped seeing her which was preferable _ _ jumping off a cliff!

14. I prefer my new friend. She doesn't try _ _ impress me with her good looks. I love her sense of humour and she likes hav_ _ _ fun.

15. We just need _ _ graduate; then we'll enjoy work_ _ _ abroad.

16. She doesn't mind sunbath_ _ _ on the beach all day but I can't stand gett_ _ _ burnt under a hot sun.

17. We can't stand paying rent, so we're choos_ _ _ _ _ buy a flat.

18. We began sav_ _ _ money two years ago. We still try _ _ save.

19. We don't want _ _ put off marry_ _ _ in June but we will have to remember _ _ check if the church is available.

20. I'm **beginning** _ _ lose my nerve. I must start _ _ believe in myself. I **dread** _ _ **think** what will happen if I don't.

21. I sometimes imagine runn_ _ _ in the Olympic Games and I'm in the lead in a long race, but I always fail _ _ finish my dream.

22. I choose _ _ admire myself as well as enjoy admir_ _ _ others.

46.

Our Good Grammar has its Uses: Pioneers do Research

We express ourselves in a range of ways, language being one of them. It pays dividends to treat these grammar exercises as an **integral** part of concentrating on the **whole range** of everything associated with English. This **integrated** approach includes **sentence constructions, cultural aspects** and **vocabulary**. By discussing topics, reading passages and using visual images we regard English as a means of communication and a language in which we are **immersed**.

Through making **positive choices** while we are young we **enrich our life forever**. Our ways of passing on information by the use of our ever-widening list of vocabulary and reasonably correct grammar enable us to enjoy and encompass at least two cultures. Our work **will be improved upon** either by us or by other more worthy experts. We allow for this present deficiency. The next person, the new broom always knows and does better. However, **we are the brave pioneer**.

The natural occurrence is for us to have a strong desire to **express ourselves**. We do so effectively by using **various tones of voice**: gentle softness, moderately or loudly and through using correctly formed sentences. Our duty is to make the effort to **do research**. We want to be accurate; in turn, it pays to do our homework.

As we write down our thoughts we **enrich our life** considerably. Our correct use of grammar allows us to be precise in what we wish to say and want our listener to know. We have a wide range interests and hobbies. We go to photography classes or enjoy growing plants or we want to improve our tennis. There is a possibility that we hardly need take lessons because these hobbies come to us naturally. However, as every sports-player, photographer and gardener will testify, we **gain some useful tips by reading what others claim** has worked for them. We also never forget the pioneer: the creative person brave enough to be the first to go ahead and to try something new.

<u>Teach yourself</u>:

1. The standard sentence must include a v_rb; this does **not include participle forms** such as: 'The orchestra playing music.' i.e. **<u>not</u>** '-ing' verb forms; 'playing' is not a verb.

2.   The simplest pattern order to follow is: **subject, verb, object.** 'Cats chase mice.' 'Ca_s' is the **subjec_** (the doer), chase is the **verb** or ac_ion and the **direc_ objec_** is 'mice', the noun. In 'Jane passed the ball to me' 'Jane' is the **subject**, 'passed' is the **verb**, 'the ball' is the **direct object** and 'to me' is the **indirec_ object.**

3.   The **predicate** includes most of the sentence apart from the subject. It includes the v_rb and the subs_qu_nt d_scriptors.

4.   Pronouns take various forms: **p_rsonal pronouns** include: **I, you, he, she, we, they** and **it. D_monstrative pronouns** include **this** and **that** and **these** and **those. Ind_finite pronouns** include: **any, some, every** and **no.** Also: **many, none, few, several, another.**

5.   Interr_gative pron_uns help us to ask questions and include: who, what and which. We als_ use when, where, why, h_w.

6.   In theory we dislike splitt_ng infinitives. But, on many occasions we do so! The rule says: 'Every year he confesses **to forget completely** our ann_versary'. However, we prefer '**to completely forget**'. We prefer: '**to strongly des_re**'; '**to gladly award**'; '**to thoroughly research**' To effectively split an infinitive sounds good sometimes.

7. A gerund is a verbal n_un formed by adding –ing to the main verb as in 'I enjoy **skiing**' or 'I'm vegetarian and s_ I dislike **fishing**.'

8. Clauses usually include a subject and a verb. They are important to ident_fy and when comb_ned they form complex sentences: 'Although our garden is small, _t is the most colourful in our road.'

    It is worthwhile collect_ng examples of **conditional, reason, time, place, purpose, result, noun, adverb** and **adject_val clauses.**

9. Relative clauses often st_rt with a rel_tive pronoun such as **'who', 'that' 'which'**. 'She's the girl **who won the r_ce**.' 'There's the cat **that looked at the king**.' 'I arrived late, **which w_s silly of me**.'

47.

Syntax and Relative Clauses

By 'syntax' we refer to the order and arrangement of words in our phrases, clauses and sentences, and each sentence must have **meaning** and **make sense**. Just as prepositions usually precede nouns so the verb and the object go together. The term 'syntax' is actually the study of the arrangement of words in sentences, but here we are concentrating on **word order**.

The constant advice to those studying the English language, whether they are at intermediate or even advanced levels, is to **keep it simple**. Keep It Simple Sweetheart, K.I.S.S., is the useful acronym which tells us not to experiment too much. For example, a student may ask **how to write an introduction. Tip**: Wait. First, **read the question**, state in the introduction **what you are talking about** and your **viewpoint**.

Likewise, we have to be careful about relative clauses, but not get over-anxious until we meet or need to include them.

Relative clauses give **extra information** and are sometimes defining relative clauses. They usually follow the subject of the sentence:

The Chinese restaurants *that exist in most suburbs of English speaking countries* cater for 'western' tastes.

Good sea food, *which is very hard to come by these days*, was what we were brought up on as children when we lived on the coast.

The customs officer, *who was able to speak German*, explained the situation to the immigrant.

We also use 'the one who' or similar phrases to help us define who or what we are describing: 'My little sister, **the one who** lives in Paris, teaches English. My other sister, **the one who** lives in Chelsea and who has twin baby daughters, is too busy to work.' Two points of advice emerge: be **clear** and **extend by adding detail**, detail, detail. We **develop** and **add to** and **extend.** We even state the obvious.

Teach yourself:

1. The woman, **to whom** he was introduced on a blind date, later became his wife.

    We use '**whom**' when it is the object of the sentence:

2. The man **whom** I wanted to speak to was on annual holiday.

    And after the preposition:

3. She was grateful to her teacher without **whom** she would never have passed her examination.

Try these: who/that/which/when/where/whose

4. The swimmers, neither of who/whom had any clothes on, emerged from the sea and ran as quickly as they could to their car.

5. The couple who/whom live next door to us are both teachers.

6. The population of Perth, which/who was less than 2 million five years ago, is expected to be more than 3 million in ten years.

7. Jill, who/that speaks French very well, works in Avignon.

8. The manager, who/whose secretary left last week, is very busy.

9. Friday 13th is a day when/where people try to avoid bad luck.

10. Can you return the money that/whom I lent you last week?

11. Spain, who/where my sister lives, has a most interesting culture. The Prado, what/which is in

Madrid, is a famous art gallery. Bullfighting is a sport that/which is on the decline.

12. The police have caught the girls who/that stole my car.

13. The monsoon rains, when/where they eventually arrive, cause floods.

14. This is the house that/who Jack built.

15. It is interesting that/who there is little wrong with the economy now, which/what is not what the situation was like a decade ago.

15. The Great White Shark, whose/which presence caused the beach to be closed, has moved further along the coast. The shark, who/which has been tagged, was detected further south.

48.

Open-ended Questions Encourage Extended Speaking

An excellent way of extending conversations when engaging in social discourse is to ask open-ended questions. Closed questions require the briefest of answers, 'yes' or 'no'. **Open-ended** questions allow the speaker to give an opinion or an informative or emotional answer.

If we asked the winner of the 800 metres track event in the Olympic games who had just broken the world record, "Is this your fastest ever time for this event?", then the answer would probably be very short! Rather, interviewers are trained to ask, "**How do you feel**?"

Some open-ended suggestions ask for too much information and prompt a ridiculously long answer, such as, "Tell me about your country" or "What is the history of this castle?" Better questions are, "Which five places should I visit in your country?" or "Originally, why was this castle built?" We ask the athlete, "What sort of training do you do?" rather than, "Do you do any training?" We might use the **infinitive or the –ing** form: "What do you plan on doing? What do you plan to do? When are you going to start? Are you starting soon? Is there anything to stop you? What or who is stopping you?"

Question tags are provocative; **tags provoke answers**. The positive start has a negative ending: "There are two things holding you up, aren't there?" or "There's a secret you haven't told me, isn't there?" A negative start has a positive ending: "You aren't sure, are you?"

As usual, we are either **asking** a question or **checking** we are correct. "The weather forecast for today is bad, isn't it?" Some question tags are meant to create conversation: "I expect you are a great believer in climate change, aren't you?" "Well, I don't know who told you that because I believe quite the opposite. In fact, for a start...." Especially when talking with astrologers, we find that **expressing** ourselves is cathartic and more important than being scientific, isn't it? Or is it?

Teach yourself:

1. Yes/no questions allow no room to explain: "Answer yes or no. Have you stopped beat_ng your w_fe yet?"

2. Some pr_sent t_nse qu_stions take a lif_time to answer: "Where is h_aven?" or "How long does it take to fall in love?"

3. Olde_ people have the wisdom to ask **<u>echo</u>** questions. These invite the speake_ to tell us even more: "I've just come back from **Thailand**." "Oh, _eally. You've been to **Thailand** have you?"

4. "I travelled al_ng **the Silk Road**." "Oh, really, y_u've been along **the Silk Road have you**? What are s_me of the places you saw?"

5. Other present _erfect questions include: "Have you ever....?" We ask about their travels "Oh, yes, what was it like?" or ask if they have ever done something naughty "...cheated in a test" or "...taken something?" We invite the _ast tense: "What hap_ened?" We want them to tell us their history and what they have done.

6. There are times when we g_ess, ass_me or pres_me: "When did you first realise you were attractive/handsome?" Followed by, "How did you know?" "How did you feel?" "What happened?"

7. Some questi_ns invite superlatives: "What was/Tell me ab_ut the best/w_rst m_ment/day in your life?"

8. The use of "_hy" questions invite and encourage an opinion to be given: "Why do you prefer your home town?" _e ask for one reason, but actually we are looking for three reasons and _anting the person to

speak for more than a minute, even two. We might infer they are either homesick or want to get away from it. We make general conversation; we merely listen and then dig deeper.

9. The factual **'where'** and **'what'** and **'who'** questions are f_llowed by '**why**' and '**how**' questions: these invite the words to fl_w. We share experiences and devel_p trust. Explanati_ns come after the introduct_ry facts. Some of these may be intimately personal. We have to be sure we can handle m_st, if not all of the truth.

49.

Complex Sentences

Once we know of ways of answering questions by using relative clauses and words such as 'because' we readily **combine** our short statements and compose complex sentences. The words used as relative pronouns we also use as conjunctions to help us combine simple sentences; these include: **which, who, when** and **where**.

We know of relative pronouns and clauses which are related to, among others, **time, comparison, purpose** and **reason**. There are many conjunctions which relate to **time** such as: **after, before, as soon as, immediately when, whenever, until, since, while**. For example, in the following sentence we can include several time conjunctions in various sentence formations in order to say more or less the same thing. "I shall stay in hospital for a few days **before** I have my baby and **after, as soon as** I'm well enough, I'll be home."

Using the same sentence we could arrange to give reasons using: **as, because, due to, owing to, since**. "As/Since I'm having a baby I'll be in hospital for about a week **because** I'll need time to recover."

Conjunctions and verbs associated with **comparison** include: **more or less than, prefer to, would rather, better/worse than, -er, -est.** "This is the **longest** pregnancy I've **ever** had. However, I **prefer** to go full term, **which** is what I will do this time. I'm not sure if it's **cheaper** or **more expensive, as long as** it's **better** than before. **The reason why** it is better to go full term is due to/because…"

Conjunctions of purpose include: **so as to, in order to**. We juggle **'come'** and **'go', modal verbs.** We use **'in case'** far more often than **lest** (hardly ever). "I won't say when I'm coming home **in case** (lest) the delivery is earlier or later than expected. The baby's head is pointing down **so as to** have an uncomplicated birth." **In order to** create complex sentences we **should** notice how others write, copy their words or connecting words until we become independent.

Teach yourself:

Join two sentences: You peel the potatoes wh_le I wash the rice.

Use these words or **choose your own** to make <u>one sentence</u>: **while; at the same time; while; when; so that; so that; so that; which/better/than/when; as; because; When/immediately; whenever/and; which; since; cheaper than; when; as soon as.**

Someone broke into our house. We were asleep.

I need a corkscrew. I can open this bottle of wine.

Tom graduated from university. He was 22 years old.

Jane arrived at 2 p.m. Tom arrived at 2 p.m.

We were waiting for the train. We saw David.

Xixi is learning English. She wants to study in Canada.

We did not want to be accused of shoplifting. We allowed the security guards to check our bags.

I got 73% in my exam. Last time I got 69%.

My boss was annoyed. We were late.

We heard the good news. We opened a bottle of champagne.

I feel afraid. I hold my head up high. I whistle a happy tune.

Mark always looks tidy. It is more than can be said for Jane.

They have changed addresses twice. They were married 5 years ago.

This dress is cheap; it cost $79. This dress is cheap; it cost $77.

I will fall in love. It will be forever.

You can have some tea. Give me your cup.

50.

Academic Writing using: however, because, although

All young students should realise that they will eventually mature into being responsible adults who will take on responsible jobs and high status positions. Everyone wants to learn through 'let's have games and some fun'. **However,** the time will come when both academic reading and writing become our **serious obligation**. Think about it!

To be practical, it is highly likely that we will follow what has been written before and virtually copy a few of those scripts. We will probably make adjustments so that accusations of plagiarism are avoided. Consider the following anatomical description regarding the wrist and hand: ...*Muscles of the posterior compartment extend the wrist and fingers.... Most muscles of the posterior compartment arise from a common tendon on the humerus;* ***however,*** *the location on the posterior humerus* ***differs from*** *that on the anterior.* ***Although*** *the hand performs many different movements,* *it contains* ***relatively few*** *of the muscles that control those movements.*

The above description is eventually what we have to comprehend. It contains the facts, yet also has the conjunctions '**however**' and '**although**', as well as **comparisons**. Once we are familiar with the anatomical terms we find that **all writers use the same range of connecting conjunctions** that we are familiar with too. In fact, because anatomy books are so long and descriptive these writers are obliged to **extend their range of linking words**; we can do likewise.

Thus, although at first academic writing seems to be a daunting task, it is in fact composed of **connecting issues** of debate; we **compare and contrast** the various components. It includes **examples** and there is an account of the results of varied procedures, processes and actions. Clearly, it is a big step to be just as precise in our use of descriptive English. All writers: do **research, focus and adapt. The professional does research.** We do not wish to lose ground.

<u>Teach yourself:</u> Use the following words in the sentences below: **because; also, because; as, causes, resulting; but; which; because; whether or not; by contrast; and; because; when; since; biggest; smallest; which; almost entirely; although; most; but; because.**

1. The big__t muscle is the gluteus maximus in the buttock. The small__t is the stapedius wh__h is inside the ear.

2. B_____ its force is exerted far from the fulcrum, the brachioradialis is a weak forearm flexor.

3. S____ the elbow is a hinge joint movements promoted by these muscles are limited a_____ e_____ to flexion and extension.

4. The ball and socket shoulder joint is the most flexible joint in the body, b__ pays the price of instability.

5. W___ a nerve impulse reaches the axon terminal it sets into motion a chain of events that triggers neurotransmitter release.

6. A_ the receptor proteins bind neurotransmitter molecules, their three dimensional shape changes. This c_____ ion channels to open. The r_____ current flows produce local changes.

7. The myocardial cells are weakened by the temporary lack of oxygen, b__ they do not die. Far more serious is prolonged coronary blockage, w____ can lead to a myocardial infarction (MI) commonly called a heart attack. B_____ adult cardiac muscle is amitotic any areas of cell death are repaired with non-contractile

scar tissue. W_____ or n__ the tissue or the patient survive an MI depends on the extent and location of the damage.

8. A_____ irises come in different colours (iris=rainbow), they contain only brown pigment. M___ newborn babies' eyes are grey or blue b_____ their iris pigment is not fully developed yet.

9. Rods are our dim-light and peripheral vision receptors. Cones, by contrast, operate in bright light a__ provide colour vision.

10. The inner ear is a___ called the labyrinth (maze) b_____ it ….

51.

Further Academic English

In addition to the complex and complicated academic English already covered here, there are many directions in which our descriptions and discussions may proceed. There are **alternatives, consequences, results and concessions** to state and to make. **Therefore**, once we know how to use the **connecting** words we have a range of pathways to choose from so as to show our expertise in our specialised subject. We gradually comprehend and appreciate the expert knowledge and ability of **academic writers**. We all use functional linking words!

Assembling the theory is difficult because the combinations of facts, variations and possibilities are endless. **Nevertheless, even so, in spite of this**, even in an Accountancy text-book the author follows our rules of short paragraphs, which include examples. We see that **academic writing** is the **best way** of consolidating our grammar as well a good way to absorb English. **Likewise, in the same way, similarly**, we should imitate good styles of writing. **On the other hand, then again, alternatively, conversely, instead, in contrast to this**, we might give up!

However, nevertheless, we want to mature.

Thus, an excellent tip is to keep most of our sentences fairly simple and not too extensive. We want to **get into a statement**, yet we also want to **get out of** or **finish it** without losing ourselves or our reader in complexities beyond our understanding or **control**. In many academic studies non-native English speakers write long sentences which take more than one breath to read out loud and a good deal of additional time to comprehend. Thus: K.I.S.S. or keep it short!

While we are discussing academic writing some practical advice to the student is to copy <u>exactly</u> what is written. The writer has taken a lot of trouble to write a perfect sentence, yet some students copy a 'version' of what is written, thus there are glaring errors of grammar or spelling mistakes. Dear student, please copy correctly!

<u>Teach yourself:</u>

There is no doubt that the writer of *'Contemporary Accountancy'* is not only competent, he is confident about what he is saying. After each of these paragraph openings will come either the detail or examples. The accountancy student pleads: "<u>**Please, tell me more**</u>!"

Fill the blanks in these paragraph openings and notice that we are certain about the theme of the paragraph. We read on to find out:

1. Accounting can have unint_nded eff_cts, **such as**....

2. Managers **need t_ make** specific decisi_ns.

3. Accounting informati_n can be placed in tw_ br_ad **categ_ries**.

4. It ha_ to be stre_ _ed that accounting i_ **only** one of a number of _ource_ of information available to deci_ion maker_.

5. **In additi_n**, banks n_rmally require security, which can take vari_us f_rms.

6. **There** are more sop_isticated regression analysis tec_niques.

7. Organisations _re const_ntly faced with decisions **rel_ting** to products and services they sell.

8. **When** firms m_nuf_cture only one product, the process of product costing is rel_tively str_ightforw_rd.

9. **On the one h_nd**, we do not know which debtors will p_y and, **on the other h_nd**, we h_ve to _llow for incre_sing b_d debts.

10. A **f_rther** arg_ment s_ggests that incentives exist for some types of b_sinesses.

11. **Therefore**, politi_al _osts _reate in_entives for managers.

12. **Although** co_pliance is not _andatory, _embers of the profession _ust co_ply.

13. The **differen_e between** the definitions of assets and liabilities _entres on who _ontrols the e_onomi_ resour_es.

14. **However**, many _actors a_ _ect the _requency and _ormat.

15. **Keep calm and make a plan; write the essay following the plan; read it through because we want to correct any errors.**

52.

Recipe for success: -ing, noun phrases, an activity or result

In today's newspaper is the well-known advice that 'manag**ing** risk is the key to success.' We all have suggestions or a philosophy of life about how to make progress or what we should do. We can concentrate on **build**ing up our tips and advice and then we have a theme for each paragraph or even for an essay or a book.

We have to combine **research** with the use of our **accurate grammar**. One theme to be found in this book is that by **research**ing and writ**ing** academic English we make **rapid progress**. We must be factual, show purpose, take advice or copy what others say and present our distinct personal point of view early and clearly.

A teacher will suggest to 17 year old students that they have to concentrate when they go to university. One student may say that they are not going to university, but making curtains instead. In fact, the same rule applies to all of us: at about the age of 18, whether in university or not, we are going to **specialise in acquiring a skill**. We do this apprenticeship for four years or so and then we want to go on to even higher and innovative standards of work in our mid-twenties. Whichever direction we take, both **improving** ourselves and being more comfortable with English are practical and realistic ambitions.

Actively advanc**ing** to higher standards or reach**ing** out is natural, whether in university or not. To paraphrase our title: 'Going on to refined standards of work is the key to success.' '**Cooking a meal** for twelve people is the way to learn management.' 'Doing an hour's housework daily is the doorway to health.' '**Working is the way to wealth.**' '**Helping others** is the gateway to happiness.' '**Saving the best till last** is the way to enjoy our meals.' 'Being active is the key to sanity.' We can be busy find**ing** the right words to suit as our guidelines, adapt**ing** our adages, adopt**ing** worthy maxims, and, in doing so, we are **paving the way** to success.

Teach yourself:

Turning; direction; course; culture; attitude; realistic; citizen; foolish; effectively; hatched; lethal; immersion; obstacles; hobby; hair, sense.

1. Managing risk is the key to success. Setting _____ targets helps us to get through each day, week and year.

2. Experiencing i_____ in English when in an English speaking country or culture forces us to learn.

3. Studying another language helps us to learn to use our own more eff_____. Opening and broadening our mind is refreshing.

4. Discovering a door to another _____ is similar to starting a completely new journey in our life.

5. _____ over a new leaf is one way of making a fresh start in life.

6. Is being a _____ of the world preferable to being patriotic?

7. Counting our chickens before the eggs are _____ is optimism.

8. Following a faith helps us review our a_____ day by day.

9. Losing d_____ by behaving like a delinquent is a hard lesson.

10. Overcoming _____ allows us to continue towards our aim.

11. Believing that failure is not an option is better than doing a business _____ at university.

12. Having a passion about our h____ is the biggest incentive to become a knowledgeable and competent expert.

13. Having a _____ of humour is a certain sign of high intelligence.

14. Massaging the scalp promotes ____ growth.

15. Handling dangerous chemicals may be _____.

16. Being over-optimistic is _____. We need caution too.

Make up sentences by using an –ing word and adding some of these words or phrases: the best; the worst; the doorway to; the beginning; the first thing I ever learnt; the start; the last.

E.g. Tying my shoelaces was the ….. Getting married was/will be….

53.

Adjectives

When we go to today's newspaper we find examples **right in front of us** of virtually each aspect of grammar covered in these chapters. The photograph on today's front page is "**Two spear** fishermen came **face to face** with a **white** pointer shark." Colours and numbers are often **adjectives**. On the newspaper's back page regarding the Olympic Games there is a claim that "Australia's swimmers are **underpaid**."

Adjectives add more to the description of objects, things and people. They are **descriptive of nouns** and **pronouns**. **Adverbs** usually add more information about a **verb**, though they are descriptive too of adjectives. In 'The brave rescuer' 'brave' is the adjective, while in 'the incredibly brave rescuer' 'incredibly' is the adverb. Adverbs are usually recognisable by their '-ly' suffix. Not all adverbs end in '-ly', and so we experiment by substituting a word that has an '-ly' ending to see if it still makes grammatical sense. She sings well: 'well' is an adverb and we can substitute 'beautifully' to check that the statement still makes sense. 'She sings well/beautifully enough to be in opera.'

Adjectives are not always necessary. If we find them difficult to place then we **may very readily omit them**. We include them in order to make our writing more descriptive or, to be practical in an exam we add them so that we get nearer to our set word target! Adjectives add information about **size, shape, colour, number, taste, attitude, direction, age, weight** and **sound**. Among their endings are '-ed' and '-ing'. "The investor lost his money and was asked to do some work. He was **terrified** and **frightened** by/at the **frightening** thought."

<u>Adjectival forms</u>: **Demonstrative**: this, that, these, those. **Distributive**: each, every, either, neither. **Quantitative**: some, any, no, little, few, many, much, two, thirty-three. **Interrogative**: which, whose, what. **Possessive**: my, your, his, her, its, our, their.

Teach yourself:

Qualitative adjectives: these tell us more about things (objects) but are especially helpful when describing a person: slim, healthy, dead, alive, happy, tall, short, cheerful, trustworthy, generous, loyal.

1. Both men and women are 'g_ _d l_ _king', but generally speaking, a w_man is regarded as beautiful while a man is hands_me.

2. As a team or individually, a great attr_bute is to be conf_dent.

3. We are n_ less w_rthy than any_ne else.

4. Some c_reless people t_lk behind people's b_cks and s_y how b_d others are; gr_ndparents openly say how good people are.

5. Major qualifications in life are to be s_nsitive and ch_ _rful.

6. Are you all right? What's wr_ng? How d_ y_u feel?

7. That's most k_nd of you to ask. I'm f_ne thank you.

8. Describe vario_s types of m_sic.

9. Descriptions of nat_ral life are us_ally colourf_l.

10. The princip_l _ctor in a dr_m_ is c_lled the st_r of the show.

11. Let's c_mpare: wh_se feet are the biggest?

12. Don't buy a n_w car. It's ch_aper to buy a s_cond-hand one.

13. The interesting th_ng in life is that we don't have to be brilliant; we just f_nd that other people drop out, make excuses or g_ve up.

14. Anoth_r factor is that w_ak-h_arted people make **more** _rrors.

15. There is h_rdly ever _ny need to be envious of others.

16. Our m_st preci_us asset is our inner self-c_nfidence.

17. Those who play ins_ruments or spor_s in which in_ense concentra_ion is required seem to acquire the abili_y to concentrate deeply on most other matters, e.g. languages.

18. As family life can be very co_plex and co_plicated it is someti_es opportune to take advantage of overseas travel.

19. Each da_, look for adjectives and where the_ are placed.

20. L_ _k for adjectives, but _bserve the wh_le sentence t_ _.

21. Is it far from here? Use 'near', 'close' and superalitives.

54.

More Adjectives

Most **native speakers** have hardly any idea how to identify a noun, adverb, adjective, verb or preposition. Thus, we do not have to know either. However, when embarking on an English course the more sensitive we are to what is in front of us **the more <u>aware</u> we are** about how to use **adjectives** properly. Quite literally, the advantage of using adjectives is that they make our writing **more colourful**.

We should spend two weeks or a year or two selecting our 100 favourite adjectives and then play at forming adverbs and nouns from them. It would be a changed world if everyone learned and put into practice: 'appreciation', 'appreciate' and **'appreciative'**. That quality of appreciation would be a major advance in our thinking. When we take too much for granted, then trouble is looming. Words affect the way we think; our ideas become meaningfully **vivid** and **bright**.

Which sex is the most **'attractive'**? If men realised they are as attractive to females as females are to men then men might stand up straighter and have more self-confidence.

We could even play with the words 'beautiful' and 'mature thoughts' in the same context.

It is permissible to be a fairly ambitious person if only to have the aim of improving ourselves day by day rather than rotting in bed till noon. Learning a language **opens up a wider world** to us; we have the urge to travel and to make our one and only life as interesting as possible.

Combining **beautiful music** with learning a language through songs is like making a discovery equivalent to winning the Nobel Prize. Music loosely labelled as 'pop' has been recorded for over seventy years. Our **favourite** songs, especially those with **clearly** spoken words inspire us to practise enunciation and phrasing as we sing along. Words or **song lyrics** emerge from our **deepest** feelings; they are a **hidden** and **inspiring** way of learning. Knowing the parts of speech is important, but **singing songs feels better**!

Teach yourself:

safe; long; closed; behind; limited; new; simple; cold; free; diverted.

1. Merely by considering adjectives we are _____into wondering about how to make life interesting. We want to open doors.

2. Those who have a _____ mind to what is natural, musical or wonderful enclose themselves in a prison of their own making.

3. Why lead a life that is _____? Be Superman or Superwoman!

4. Try a different culture; leave our ____ home and explore. As the poem says: 'If you can meet triumph and disaster and treat those two imposters just the same'. Today and tomorrow: start again.

5. Life is a journey, short or long. Get on a boat; leave that complex situation _____ or see the simple in what seems complicated.

6. It isn't as bad as we think and our bright ___ world keeps turning.

7. Are you happy? What is important? Are you being reasonable? Have you been waiting ____? Are you being sensible? Are you sitting up straight? Am I heavy? Compose adjectival questions.

8. There's something you're not telling me isn't there? Is it a dark secret? An open secret? A personal secret? A family secret? Tell me what it is. I expect it isn't half as terrible as you imagine. There's no need to be nervous; be brave; or are you determined not to tell me? I won't

be shocked. You're still a great person. We say keep it s_m___ but, actually, some things are best kept secret.

9. Be different. To what extent are we prisoners? Or are you ____? Which country do you want to visit? Somewhere tropical or ____? Old or new? Obvious or obscure? Is your journey dangerous?

10. Some things in life are imp_rtant, s_me m_re s_ than _thers. Most people I meet are not fam_us. However, their lives are far more fascinating than th_se of supp_sed 'stars'. It's amazing!

11. Wond_rful news. Use adj_ctives. Write s_ntences in _nglish.

12. W_rds lead to ideas: Hardly anything in biol_gy is **disgusting**.

55.

Adverbs

As with adjectives, it is worth knowing how to identify **adverbs** because when we use them they make our writing more colourful. However, the same advice applies of not overusing them when we have a doubt about the correct grammatical forms in sentences.

It is worth **noticing** and collecting adverbs. For instance, we can have fun composing sentences so as to practise modifying adjectives. "You are important. You are **terribly** important!" "You will grow up. You'll be mature; **unbelievably** mature!" We can add to verbs: "You dance well. You dance beautifully." We can mix adjectives and adverbs: "Your visions will become clear only when you think **clearly**." By creating sentences which contain vivid or plain adverbs we will know "how to learn English **quickly**."

We want to learn English both for fun and for serious reasons; we have to take it **seriously**. By listening to songs often rather than **occasionally** we find that we have a basis for our more serious academic writing. By **regularly** reading the parts of the newspaper that are of interest we can **underline** adverbs and adjectives. Actually, by focussing on whole sentences we see the parts fall into place together more **frequently, naturally, repeatedly** and **constantly**.

Finally, the limit of our collection of adjectives and adverbs may seem endless. Therefore, it is as well to find other people's lists and select our favourite top twenty or one hundred. We need not do this **hurriedly**. Everyone likes to start out having fun and **eventually** most people want to take things **seriously** so as to find fulfilment in expressing themselves **personally** or **academically**.

We may collect **adverbs** under the headings of: time; place; position; directional; manner; degree; linking words; comparatives; comment.

Teach yourself:

1. Luckily and fortunately we can list 'l_ckily' and 'fort_nately' _nder the "**Attitude/Comment**" category in our vocab_lary book.

2. Also: adverbs such as 'predict_bly', 'interestingly', 'incredibly', 'coincidentally', 'mir_culously', 'unexpectedly', 'responsibly' 'typically', 'al_s', 's_dly', come in this group. Add 30 or 40 more!

3. Adverbs of **time** indicate wh_n or how oft_n: **WHEN**: today, tomorrow, y_sterday, last w_ _k, now, th_n, yet.

4. How often (definite): weekly; d_ily; annu_lly; nightly; fortnightly; hourly; monthly; qu_rterly; ye_rly.

5. How often (indefinite): so_etimes; always; nor_ally; since; never; repeatedly; hardly ever; often; seldo_; forever; frequently; usually; regularly; constantly; rarely; continually; continuously.

6. Relationships in time: **Find at least ten indefinite <u>time</u> adverbs**:

    Have you seen Mark **recently**? He hasn't been here early **lately**.

    Formerly Tom **always** arrived punctually, but he's always been late since he's been using his bicycle. He's usually here already but earlier than this though. Previously he was the first to be here, so I expect he'll be here soon. Ah, at last, finally, eventually you've got here. The meeting still hasn't started yet because we couldn't begin before you arrived anyway. Prior to starting, there is another speaker and you will give your talk after her.

7. <u>Linking</u> words are incredibly useful. Some students gamble that they are going to start the third or fourth paragraph in their essay with one of the following: first, h_wever, alth_ugh, on the _ne hand, _n the other hand, c_ntrary to expectati_ns, in additi_n.

8. If we are adding further points we use: in addit_on, furthermore, moreover, bes_des, apart from 'x' there is also 'y' to cons_der.

9. If we are saying what the res_lt is of, say, 'climate change' we use conseq_ently, as a result, therefore (avoid 'so') hence, th_s.

10. "Have you ever….?" "Yes, twice. The first time was…."

254

Grand temple standing in front of us in the snow. Climbing: There are various temples halfway up the hill or at the summit and climbing the mountain is a popular form of exercise in China, especially at festival times. Temples are being built in profusion and these augment those from ancient past days. Beyond the road at the foot of the mountain is a huge complex of temples. The architecture is formidable and gives a sense of awe. There has been some snow but this will quickly melt and the appearance will change. We talk about the past, the present and future and even eternal spiritual beliefs.

56.

Adverbs of Manner

When we want to describe **the way** in which an event took place then we say what sorts of feelings are involved or **how** an event took place. Did they live **happily** ever after or did she speak **angrily**? Will the world carry on in more or less the same <u>manner</u> or will things happen **differently**? We continue to approach most matters **confidently**.

Useful verbs are: 'walk' or 'dance' or 'spoke/speak' as our activities: **danced well**, gracefully, beautifully, properly; **walked silently**, hurriedly, sensibly, quietly, correctly, casually. She **spoke** warmly, softly, **pleasantly**, frankly, politely, sincerely, freely, wonderfully. There are two or three hundred adverbs of **manner** and we can collect a hundred within a week and a very long list within a month.

It is always good for our attitude if we remind ourselves once a week that we are truthful and therefore **speak truthfully**. We loyally stay with a partner and **wait patiently**. When we are hopelessly or helplessly in love; then we **love passionately, spontaneously, deeply,**

sincerely, devotedly, tenderly, honestly and always **faithfully**.

When writing emails our intentions might be misunderstood which is why we use a few emoticons to go with our words such as a rose or a smiling face. In our writing we add to our description by the use of adverbs or adjectives to show we are happy and greet **happily**, we are cheerful and speak **cheerfully**, in love and **lovingly** write **tenderly**.

We like to work carefully, neatly, diligently, thoroughly and meticulously. We discuss matters **smoothly, willingly, discreetly** and **peacefully**. In science we investigate and measure **systematically, specifically, accurately, scientifically, rigorously** and **precisely**.

The words we avoid are 'nice' and 'nicely', apart from, "Oh, yes, that's nice dear", or "Oh, **nicely** done!"

Teach yourself:

1. I asked for my money b_ck but was told **sh_rply** to go away!

2. Cl_mbing to a temple on the hilltop is sp_r_tually upl_fting.

3. _ddly enough, I met some_ne who looked exactly like y_u.

4. I've seen you bef_re, but we haven't been f_rmally introduced.

5. I f_intly remember meeting you at a conference five ye_rs ago.

6. My guide dog h_s served me f_ithfully every day for ten years.

7. When he scored the goal he took his opport_nity s_perbly.

8. Please list_n to my instructions car_fully this time.

9. I sp_cifically told you to go to the mark_t, not the supermarket.

10. Don't look _t me so s_dly, as if you're going to cry.

11. L_t's face each day **ch_ _rfully**.

12. Pardon my abrupt manner. Let me put this d_licately, if you go to univ_rsity without improving your English you'll struggle.

13. M_st of us prefer to be treated gently rather than r_ughly.

14. Your great grandmother has di_d. She passed away p_acefully.

15. I'll _ut this sim_ly: you get out of bed now or I'll _ull you out!

16. Some people grow old **gr_cefully**, others do so disgr_cefully!

17. Our n_w manager has a r_fr_shingly different approach.

18. For ex_mple, he doesn't jump to conclusions h_stily.

19. The bus _s leaving now. Hold on t_ghtly please.

20. On our holiday it rained stead_ly and cont_nuously nonstop.

21. He is c_ntinually phoning me every h_ur or two all day.

22. I d_st_nctly remember tell_ng him last Monday not to phone.

23. Quite _rankly, I want him to stand on his own two _eet.

24. Ec_n_mically speaking, some Eur_pean countries are in stress.

25. When people c_nsistently evade paying tax, trouble foll_ws.

26. Why are you looking _t me so str_ngely? Is something wrong?

27. Is it better to act sp_ntaneously rather than th_ughtfully?

28. It sounds dull, but survival is more lik_ly if we behave **s_nsibly**.

29. The best ways to study are eff_ctively and effici_ntly.

30. Honestly and sincer_ly, you won't r_gret studying English.

57.

Adverbs of Degree

It matters little how we categorise adverbs as long as we know how use them to make our writing more descriptive. Grammar books make a distinction between adverbs of 'degree', 'manner' and 'time'. It is sufficient to acknowledge there are many and varied kinds of adverbs. However, we should observe and recognise them and have experience of their **position in a sentence.**

Adverbs of degree tell us to what extent an action had an effect. "How did you do in the exam?" "I did very badly/well!"

"Can you feel that?" "No, **hardly** at all." "Ouch! That **really** hurts!"

There is a difference between '**qualitative**' adverbs: feel **deeply** moved; **highly** successful; **strongly** motivated; AND '**classifying**' adverbs such as **utterly** disgusted; **absolutely** sure; **perfectly** aware.

Most adverbs in this group come before or after the main verb: "I admire him intensely.' However, 'almost', 'virtually', 'nearly' and 'largely' come before the verb. "He **virtually** gave all his money away." "He **almost** drowned!" "We **nearly** crashed several times."

> We can be **dreadfully/awfully/extremely/terribly/truly** sorry.

> We are **deeply/enormously/exceedingly/powerfully/profoundly** moved and

> **wonderfully/incredibly/unbelievably/entirely/perfectly** happy.

> **Utterly/absolutely/tremendously** astonished/amazed/disgusted!

It is usually too easy to opt for **'very'** good and so we should look for alternatives such as **quite, most, exceedingly, wonderfully, jolly, incalculably, overwhelmingly, extremely** good of you to help us.

We appreciated (verb) his appreciative (adj.) words of thanks and his appreciation (noun) was most appreciatively (adv.) received. Next, say how much progress we are making and how **confident** we are. We are **significantly** more mature at age 26 than at 18. Consider.

Teach yourself:

1. "I'm abs_lutely certain. Do you agree?" "Oh absolutely sir!"

2. When we make a mistake we can sometimes pay d_arly for it.

3. There has been an am_zingly bad accident. The road is blocked.

4. In order to pass the exam I must do **c_nsiderably** better this time.

5. I'll be en_rmously pleased to pass the exam this time.

6. I'll be perf_ctly happy to lend you some money. I trust you.

7. The topic of climate change has been ext_nsively debated.

8. The extent of ice covering Antarctica has been dr_stically reduced.

9. I am imm_nsely grateful for your assistance.

10. I had my doubts. I wasn't ent_rely happy about it.

11. Good shot! That's sl_ghtly off-centre but close enough.

12. Oh, I'm dr_adfully sorry. Did I hurt you?

13. Significantly, the twins look rem_rkably similar to their father.

14. I would be et_rnally grateful if you would be my teacher.

15. Although it pays to be cautious I advise you to think pos_t_vely.

16. "Are we there yet?" "Yes, we're n_arly there. Two hours to go!"

17. Doing a job perf_ctly well is better than doing moderately well.

18. The result is clear; the outr_ght winner is Miss Mexico!

19. It is a prof_undly moving honour to receive the award.

20. Your version of the event is signif_cantly different from hers.

21. Six of us girls lived together and bec_me pr_ctically like sisters.

22. The attitude of those who dress well and those who don't is n_ticeably different. However, this is purely my opini_n.

23. Envir_nmental c_ncerns are supremely imp_rtant n_w.

24. The desire to be by the seaside comes to us q_ite nat_rally.

25. Some people swim r_gardless of the threat of shark attacks.

26. Sports fans like to collect p_rsonally signed autographs.

27. I _ant one of you to answer **truthfully**. _hether done accidentally or deliberately, who broke the _indow?

28. How well we do depends on which one of us turns up, i.e. if it's the one who constantly apologises or the one who acts confidently.

58.

Adverbs of Place

"The girl of my dreams is coming **here**." Later, "**There** goes the girl of my dreams." The positioning of adverbs is variable. It is a matter of emphasis where and how we place them and to know how to do so is a matter of experience. As with giving dates and times, telling our reader **where** someone is or is not helps to make the picture very clear rather than keeping the situation vague. We should **state the obvious**. When shopkeepers do not tell us where they are then there is no sale. It is obvious they know where they are, but they should tell us too!

Usually adverbs of place come after the verb, though we might actually begin our sentence with, "**Above** and **beyond** the orchard lies the Buddhist Temple on the hilltop and the long, winding pathway leading to it." In this unusual case the subject goes after the verb.

When there is no object then the adverb is placed after the verb as in "They went **overseas**." "They went **abroad** for their honeymoon." "He's gone **away** for a week." "She's **upstairs**." "She's not **here**."

Somewhere is usually positive while **anywhere** is usually negative. "I'm sure I've seen her somewhere." "I can't see my keys anywhere."

Some of us have a startling awakening when we go **overseas**. We discover it is not our own country that everyone is talking about worldwide and globally. In fact, the newspaper headlines usually refer solely to their own situation, that is, **locally** and **domestically**. For each of us, we assume we are well-known **widely**, not only **nationally** but **internationally** too; but, we discover, not to any great extent. We are neither the centre of the world nor as important as we assume.

We use 'Adverb particles' as prepositions: **in, out, over, behind, in between, throughout, beside, near, by, aboard, opposite. Where? Meet halfway, upstairs, downstairs, indoors, there, out of doors, northward, underfoot, downwind, away, ashore, upstream, downtown, ahead, overhead, offshore, next door, inland.**

Teach yourself:

1. A situation or a place? (a) Meet someone halfway. (b) A teacher stands in loco parentis. (c) First, it's all uphill and then it's all downhill. (d) We can't always bend over backwards to help. We have limits.

2. Ar_und Elm Park Farm may be seen bats, buzzards and badgers.

3. Adj_ining the farm stands Woodland View Cottage with views acr_ss open countryside to Dartmoor and Bodmin Moor.

4. The Farm is nestled beside Pancrasweek Church, with land that runs d_wn to woodland which contains bluebells and deer.

5. Thr_ugh the southern border of the pasture runs the River Tamar.

6. Other attractions are a stone's throw aw_y in all directions.

7. Located three miles from Holsworthy and six miles from Bude, the self-catering home sits **with_n** the main farmhouse buildings and the easily accessible pathway leads stra_ght from the parking space to the visitor's own garden and separate entrance.

8. Without d_scriptors of 'place' in our writing we could be anywh_re. 'Som_where' is not _nough; we must be more pr_cise.

9. Througho_t our story or description of our jo_rney through life or _pstream or downstream on a river we can name locations.

10. Even though I walk thr_ugh valley of the shad_w of death, I fear no evil for you are with me.

11. **Find Wordsworth's poem**: I wandered lonely as a cloud that floats on high o'er vales and hills, when all at once I saw a crowd, a host, of golden daffodils; **b_side** the lake, **b_n_ath** the trees fluttering and dancing in the breeze.

12. Clock hands turn cl_ckwise while the sun appears to turn in an anticl_ckwise direction to th_se in the s_uthern hemisphere.

13. I looked for you th_re, but you were n_where to be seen.

14. Where is lone sailor Jessica Watson? She is h_meward bound after rounding Cape Horn on her r_und the world sailing trip.

15. Plan your essay; write it; read it **through**.

59.

Complex Sentences

One of the main reasons for studying grammar and working towards getting it closer and closer to being correct is that we are more willing to write **complex sentences**. We express approval or disapproval with our facial expressions, yet we use complex sentences in order to state what we approve or disapprove of and **why**. Then, eventually, we are gladly relieved to read, write or listen to a simple and short sentence.

Some of us live in a situation in our own country in which we are satisfied with what we have. However, we usually wish for improved conditions, especially when we compare how complacent our way of life is compared with the progress being made elsewhere. We state our view, give reasons fluently and **communicate with confidence**.

We express a viewpoint: Theorists readily express what should happen in schools, **yet** in actual situations their ideal is as remote as asking a cyclone to be gentle with us. The person speaking 'hot air' uses complex sentences in order to justify why they themselves are not in the thick of the action. **However,** most issues are too complex and complicated for idealists to face. Idealists think we have schools, **while** realists know some schools serve partly as detention centres. Teachers want their students to grow; experts far away want results.

Because we are generous we may use, '**Although** your point is reasonable, I think we should….' Some people take on the role of being the exceedingly good person or expert. They should combine their complex sentences with practical work in the thick of the action beyond radio talkback programmes. In order to justify and explain our actions we **merge our good command of language** with managing the day by day and month by month reality of actual tough situations.

When we call upon our inner strength we combine our instinctive and nurtured senses of direction. Sentences take longer to master because we have to consider both practical **reasons** as well as grammar.

Teach yourself:

1. Even if we knew _ost of the answers to the _ysteries of the universe we would have to overco_e other people's sense of co_placency and self-i_portance in order to gain their interest and to get our _essage across in long and complex sentences.

2. H_wever, a sh_rt sentence may get to the p_int quickly.

3. Very often, we use c_nnecting or linking words to j_in sentences.

4. We say wh_t we usu_lly do, **where** it happens and at what time.

5. There are colo_rs to incl_de and we say what our senses tell us.

6. It is essenti_l for us to get a person's attention. On the one h_nd, we have long, complex sentences while on the other hand, for the s_ke of variety we use short and simple sentences.

7. In university life, res_arch is nec_ssary and in our r_port or thesis we have to justify our conclusions using evid_nce from research.

8. Noneth_less, although we need not have to grasp at rel_vant research conducted at, say, Stanford University, in order to show that an active life leads to a longer life, we still have to combine sev_ral short sentences into one extend_d complex sentence.

9. When m_king comp_risons and correl_tions we use a longer sentence.

10. This means that we must either use our c_mmon sense or p_int out ass_ciations between _ne set of data and an_ther.

11. A _ood starting point is to include some back_round or historical setting re_arding our study topic and say why it be_an.

12. As a beginner, we should copy what other researchers ha_e alluded to in their research **so that** we become familiar **not only** with the _ocabulary, **but also** how authors handle long sentences.

13. Obvio_sly, we m_st not plagiarise what other writers have said.

14. **On the contrary**, while we adapt their words and let the_ provide us with a fra_ework of our own, we must reme_ber that even published authors have struggled to _aster their sentences!

Bamboo

Bamboo in the snow. The flexible bamboo is long-living because it is flexible, resilient and hardy. It can be put to so many uses and we describe it by using a myriad of adjectives.

60.

Sentence and Paragraph Building

Just like native speakers, we do not have to know the difference between an adverb and an adjective. However, while identifying these parts of speech we absorb ways of constructing a sentence. The more exercises we do the more naturally we focus on **one theme** and make these complex **connections** appear to be straightforward and orderly.

We like to be told information or something new and we also like easy-to-read sentences. A book which explains anatomy is apposite. The writer has to **join** sentences which explain as simply as possible how various complex parts of our body are **linked to** each other.

To paraphrase: *"The stalk of the pituitary gland **connects** it to the hypothalamus, while the veins leaving the pituitary drain into the cavernous sinus and other dural sinuses. The posterior lobe is actually a part of the brain. It derives from a downgrowth of hypothalamic tissue and maintains its neural connection with the hypothalamus via a nerve bundle called the hypothalamic-hypophyseal tract, which runs through the infundibulum."*

Both 'anatomical life' and English sentences are pathways apparently held together by a series of **links** or **connections**. By explaining these connections in a fairly simplistic manner we then help to make the complicated almost comprehensible! We should expose that part of the brain or use a picture to clarify what we are describing. The words complement the picture: we know where it is and what it is linked to!

We constantly attempt to answer questions such as: **where, what, when** and **how** things happen. When this information is given **clearly** then we read on with ease and we know **where** we are. What **may be clear** to us, as the expert author, may not at all be obvious to our reader. We politely and gently explain clearly using connections, ties, links and attachments: 'a chain is as strong as its weakest link.' **Linking words** give us direction and our ideas flow more cohesively.

Teach yourself: More Adverbs:

1. The m_vie, *"Desperately Seeking Susan"* came _ut in 1985.

2. Susan accident_lly gets hit on the head and, due to her amnesia, is **dr_matically** involved in a series of misunderstandings.

3. Some people are **app_llingly** bad-mannered while, **on the other hand**, others are ple_santly well-m_nnered.

4. He relied h_avily upon his benefactor to fund his expens_s.

5. The woman in the wheelchair was f_tally injured in the fall.

6. When on parade soldiers must be pr_perly and c_rrectly dressed.

7. We _mpress our boss _f we will_ngly and eagerly work hard.

8. Scottish and Irish accents are d_st_nctly d_fferent.

9. Top tennis players m_rcilessly and ruthl_ssly set about winning.

10. Authoritarians impose rules rig_dly, but not upon themselves.

11. Good business adverbs: get it done eff_ctively and effici_ntly.

12. Our business must r_n like a smoothly and finely t_ned engine.

13. We will perform our service pr_fessionally and h_nestly.

14. We should gr_ _t our custom_rs warmly and courteously.

15. Custom_rs want consist_ntly good s_rvice.

16. Your smile must sh_ne as br_ghtly as the sun and stars.

17. Listen to our clients att_ntively and speak cl_arly to th_m.

18. We want to be sol_dly in profit and not be heav_ly in debt.

19. Last year's result was m_serably low and pla_nly not good enough. I c_nfidently expect we will comf_rtably improve.

20. We can sell our goods br_skly by being f_ercely compet_tive.

21. We will work well coll_ctively as a t_am or ind_pendently.

22. We automat_cally th_nk and bel_eve we will do well every day.

23. Every transaction must be made leg_lly rather than ill_gally.

24. I will gladly pay a b_nus to th_se who should be richly rewarded. That does not include those who work p_ _rly.

25. Our new plan is working brill_antly. We can work full-t_me.

61.

Reasons, Comparisons and Causes, Result and Effect

"There's a reason for everything!" That will have been said to virtually everyone either by their parents or teachers in virtually every country. This is immediately followed up by realising that the question '**why?**' is also asked in every country and culture.

"We did it for several **reasons**." "The **advantages** and disadvantages of doing it this way are as follows:…" "The **solution** to the problem is to …. **because** …." "The increase in the number of … is **due to** …." "The author of '*One Flew Over the Cuckoo's Nest*' introduces and creates conflict **as a means** of discussing institutions and choices…"

Another way of answering a 'why' question is to explain that "**the cause of** (say) the friction in the dormitory is/was due to…" "**Owing to** the stationary anti-cyclonic high pressure zone in the Australian Bight, the easterly winds will be very warm. **Because** no movement is expected any time soon, Perth's hot weather will persist."

Preferably, we do not look to **blame** someone or allot fault, at least not falsely. After all, the act is done and we move on. However, blaming is another way of saying 'why.' Many people set themselves up as being very important; they sit on committees and have wonderful ideas. However, they leave to others the job of putting their ideals into practice and then **blame** them for **why** things went wrong. With foolish hindsight they quickly compose **reasons** or **excuses**.

Success often depends not so much being creative; it is more a case of making the fewest errors. When management err they reply instantly with sound **reasons** by letting the words roll fluently from their tongue as if that was their original intention all the time! The result is that **people soon learn to become inventive**. We are led to believe any **reasons** given by a professional in a white coat and wearing glasses who looks terribly serious saying, "I firmly believe it is important that we should...." **Idealising usually ignores realities**.

Teach yourself:

1. IELTS examiners like to see the use of c_nnecting or linking w_rds. We can demonstrate their use in almost every paragraph.

2. One m_rk of a good student is the effective use of complex sentences intermixed with the occ_sional short one.

3. **To put it s_mply,** th_s means being able to seamlessly comb_ne two or more apparently simple sentences into one.

4. Th_s sk_ll involves being famil_ar with adverb_al and adject_val clauses **as if** it was natural for the fluent wr_ter to do so.

5. Good writers show they have extens_ve exper_ence of study_ng Engl_sh **and** they have presumably made s_gn_f_cant progress.

6. Their comp_tence indicates they have had y_ars of practic_.

7. It is **also** fair to ass_me that the writer is a mat_re person whose ideas seem to show intelligent and reasoned tho_ght.

8. **Futhermore,** they appear to sh_w b_th care and a g_ _d attitude.

9. A simple sentence us_ally comprises a s_bject, verb and object.

10. A good exercise is to find the difference between transitive and intr_nsitive verbs **bec_use** we will notice how we form sentences.

11. **Alth_ugh** we need not even c_nsider this as we write, the mere practice of these sentence constructions will extend our fluency.

12. **Another** worthwhile pr_ctice is to consider the position of adjectives and _dverbs in sentences **bec_use** fluency develops from our concentr_ted observation and by doing the exercises.

13. **However,** we do not absorb our lessons i_ _ediately; we take weeks, _onths and years in order to learn through our experience.

14. **Eventually,** we notice what we have lea_ned in the classroom is actually everywhe_e and we lea_n to string our thoughts togethe_.

15. Good topics include: (a) my fa_ourite recipe (b) my tra_els (c) my best/worst day (d) fi_e (?) ways to be likeable, e.g. …

16. Go ahead; find so_ething you can talk about auto_atically.

17. A proficient wri_er's abili_y will be apparent and shine through.

62.

Diversity in our writing style, e.g. when Comparing

It is best to find it easy to combine extending our vocabulary by doing grammatical exercises. These features and activities are **integrated** into or **integral to** each of our sentences. Realising this, we make a further leap forward by being able to use **various** styles of sentences. Our readers and listeners want us to introduce some **variety**.

When we talk about **differences** and **similarities** we are **comparing** and **making contrasts**. We notice differences and classify by looking for variations. When we want a new direction in our business or ways of writing sentences we want to **diversify**. Writers and businesses acquire a variety of diverse skills in order to extend their abilities.

We are strongly advised that one way to keep our writing interesting is to avoid, for some reason, **using the passive tenses**. We **are advised** to say, '**They did it**,' rather than say '**it was done**.' The '**active voice**' is apparently deemed to be more dynamic! However, especially in scientific reporting, it is **necessary to use the passive**.

Novelists like to introduce **conflict** or misunderstanding because we are keen to know what the characters choose to do. We come to a bridge or crossroads where we have to **decide** which way to go. Our sense of curiosity opens up pathways to choose between. Whenever there are <u>choices</u> to be made we hope the main players choose sensibly. We identify with them and hope they do the right thing.

There are many chances to make our writing varied by using **various** tenses. Thus, we state fairly precisely **when** things happened or what is happening now and we also guess **where** we will be as we make our plans for next week or next year. We are proud of what we have done. When writing about a new interest then we know we still employ similar linking words. It is safe to explore. The world will not end tonight. Therefore, we may as well make life interesting by enjoying lots of **variety** and **diversification**....whatever this entails!

<u>Teach yourself:</u>

1. <u>Linking words</u> assist us. Having the ability to write complex sentences of a diversified range _eeds time to develop. It is only achieved through lots of experience **a_d** by having a wish to do so.

2. We have to reach for the grammar book_ **and** find they **al_o** contain the correct guidance for u_ to write accurate English.

3. **In a_ _ition**, we realise we are making life interesting for ourselves too by using varie_ ways of writing sentences and paragraphs.

4. It is not so much the grammar that is us_ful; the main ass_t is the range of **div_rsity** we introduce into our writing.

5. We look at the grammar closely, _**et** we stand back and realise we have found alternatives in the wa_s we can express ourselves.

6. **We wan_ _o hold the a_ _ention of our lis_ener or reader**.

7. We are an interesting person, **b_t** we have to <u>sell</u> o_r story too.

8. People are mostly interested only in their own lives; **ther_fore**, we have to arouse their int_rest and continue to **engage** th_m.

9. **W_en** we are trying to sell a product we have to make it a wort_w_ile buy for t_e customer.

10. **Theref_re**, we talk mainly ab_ut what is of **interest to them**.

11. Our listener or reader will s_ _n lose interest **if** we only talk about _urselves _r if we keep saying things in the same way.

12. **Nat_rally**, we are also inspired to contin_e writing if we introd_ce a diversity of interesting long and short sentences.

13. A business will lose money if it tries something new **but** doesn't have the s_ills or _nowledge or secrets to mar_eting.

14. Whether we are writin_ a love letter or an exam assi_nment, we are looking to impress or to get a _ood grade from our reader.

15. In the s_ng it is said, "I would d_ anything for l_ve."

16. We k_ _p our reader's inter_st **by** using variations and reflect that, along with linking words, **div_rsification** is a key word.

63.

Being Spontaneous Requires Skilled Craftsmanship

We wish to be doing something **purposeful** in life. For safety's sake, whenever we have an overwhelming desire to have fun and to be spontaneous it makes sense to use our skills as well as our common sense. **Controlling** our spontaneity leads to things going better.

Ask any teacher, we spend much of our life filling up time. Actually, we prefer to spend our time doing **purposeful** work or following **enterprising pursuits** either for fun or as a challenge. In our writing an achievement is to persuade our reader to read on by making our comments intelligible and easy to read. Thus, using planned and grammatically correct sentences is essential as well as sensible.

First, we must be **available**; second: sensible. It is said that in war a soldier's time is 1% hell in battle and 99% waiting in boredom. We are **available**. If we took our crying baby to see the doctor we would expect a professional opinion and not a spontaneous suggestion of, "Oh, why don't we go ten-pin bowling?" Being sensible is vital!

We have a desire to express ourselves and we are blessed with an ability to do so in a way that **makes sense** both to us and to others. Perhaps it is best to write an email but not send it; it is enough to write and **express** our feeling or point of view; we get it out of us. However, we prefer to let it be known what we want or would like to happen. We like to say it. Therefore, both what we say and how we say it need considerable consideration and a high level of fluency.

Spontaneous writing flows forth from us easily. However, **perfection is difficult to achieve**. Although we should express ourselves in the best way possible, some people are so contrary that anything less than perfection is unacceptable. This is like saying that "problem families shouldn't have children." There is a compulsion placed upon us to be near to perfection rather than be spontaneous! Being fairly correct in our grammar is preferable, but not an absolute necessity. Just write!

Teach yourself:

Falling in love is natural. Being spont_neous, such as when laughing or making a sudden decision to go off on a holid_y for a weekend or more, is good fun. On the other h_nd, we are glad we have had some education about sexu_l activity; otherwise our spontaneity might lead us into huge responsibilities at a f_irly young age.

We must consider. When writing ess_ys or embarking on extended academic writing it is hardly ever likely that we will le_ve our first draft to stand as it is. We are careful about what we s_y; we add details and h_ve to create coherent and logical sense. The br_in surgeon or motor mechanic may as well follow correct and c_refully thought out instructions. Ac_demic writing involves the hidden mess_ge of, 'Be careful; be c_utious. Get it right. Make it clear. Keep it simple.'

Fairly s_fe advice to essay writers is to "think in threes". We spontaneously want to stand up and express ourselves reg_rding an important point. However, we soon find ourselves _dding: "And for _nother thing, I also think we should….." eventually, "and before I forget, last but not le_st, it is imperative that we should ….., and furthermore, just one more point th_t I must…. " The implication is that we did not think properly when st_rting off spontaneously.

On a different tack: In spontaneous speech we use **<u>ELLIPSIS</u>** fairly often. For ex_mple, we m_ke a comparison and shorten our sentence by **omitting** words: "You may think th_t is funny, but I don't!" (think it is funny). We use 'too': "I'm glad you say the situ_tion is serious because I do too." Or we might use a mod_l: "Oh, come on Roger." "No Angela, I want to, but we mustn't!" It is very good fun to start a spontaneous dr_matic dialogue with the one line: "It's not a secret _ny more. Your friend told me everything. You know." "What? Everything! Even _bout ...?" Then we see what arises from wh_tever 'omission' (ellipsis) might be discussed! Secrets are not examples of **ellipsis**, but they are similar: they are the things that are left unsaid.

64.

Defining and Non-defining Clauses

Most English language and grammar classes spend quite a while identifying 'defining clauses' and 'non-definable' relative clauses. We need not take this so seriously, apart from enjoying the exercise like we would a game. While we are hunting for these clauses which add more and identify who and where and what we are talking about, we absorb another variation in the way we can construct sentences. Simply: these clauses clarify or add to what we are talking about.

'**Defining clauses**' add <u>essential information</u>. We use 'who', 'whom' and 'whose' when referring to people and 'which', 'whose' and 'of which' when talking about things. We use 'that' for both. **We give EXTRA INORMATION**. The sentence usually stands up well enough without this clause, but it clarifies or adds interesting detail:

The woman <u>who I met at the concert</u> knows you very well. Those things <u>which you thought were secret</u> are now known to many. Other people <u>that were standing next to her</u> found out as well.

Of course, those people <u>whom you know well</u> were not surprised though. Thus, the woman <u>whom I used to admire</u> is now someone I distrust.

Defining*:* "Accidents *which occur in heavy fog* happen suddenly." "The policeman *who ordered me to get out of the car* played the bad cop; the one *who offered me a drink* played the good cop." "Roses *which are attacked by black spot fungus* are difficult to have success with." "Research *which is unreliable* should be ignored; for example, is it true that babies *which are breastfed* become smarter adults?"

Non-Defining*:* Non-Defining relative clauses give non-essential information and are surrounded by commas: *"My son, who married a Belgian, is good at flower arranging. My other son, who has six toes, supplies the flowers from his greenhouse. My sister, who's 22, knows about floristry and runs a floristry shop, a florist's."*

Teach yourself: Identify the clauses:

1. People **wh_ live in glass houses** shouldn't thr_w stones.

2. Research the nursery rhyme: 'This is the h_use **that Jack built**.'

3. The girl **wh_ is talking to T_m** is my sister.

4. The man **wh_se wife wants a div_rce** now lives overseas.

5. That cat, **the _ne which is best at catching mice**, bel_ngs to Julia.

6. The cat **which is a bit _verweight** is mine.

7. The player **wh_se g_al-sc_ring could be better** was n_t selected.

8. It's best not to kill the g_ _se **that lays the g_lden eggs**.

9. The runner **wh_se w_rld record was just broken** has retired.

10. The girl **to wh_m he is engaged** d_esn't want to marry yet.

11. The w_rd **that she used t_ describe him** is unrepeatable.

12. The man **wh_m she used bad language ab_ut** I'll tell you about later.

13. At last, the letter **that I sent nine d_ys ag_** has finally arrived.

14. The view **that we ch_ _se to ad_pt** should be one of optimism.

15. We _ften use relative clauses **which c_me after the _bject**.

16. A sh_wer **which is shared** is better than having n_ne at all.

17. We shared the sh_wer, **which is better than having n_ne at all**.

18. The angel of death passes over h_uses **which have red d_ _rs**.

19. I have the strength to ign_re those **wh_se opini_ns are unfair**.

20. The newspaper **that I get _n Saturdays** has _ver 300 pages.

21. A woman **wh_ is scorned** has a fury h_tter than 1,000 fires!

22. 80% of children **wh_ are allergic to peanuts** gr_w out this.

23. In m_nths **which have no 'r' in them** we sh_uldn't eat _ysters.

24. Those **wh_ haven't washed their hands** need to d_ so n_w.

25. People wh_ **do a lot of research** usually gain the m_st profit.

26. H_wever, beware _f research which states, "Babies that are breastfed are smarter." Research **which is biased** is unreliable.

27. Swimmers **who train early in the m_rning** need m_ther's taxi.

28. Opinions **which are unfair** are alm_st always p_ _rly grounded.

65.

The Present Perfect Tense and Time

For the present perfect tense we use the verb '**have**' followed by the next verb being the **past participle**. *"I have made my bed"*. *"She has built her career on a very solid foundation."* *"They have created the most wonderful garden."* This construction allows us to add details, extend our statements and to keep talking. We answer questions such as: "Where have you been? What have you been doing these days?"

We add adjuncts of time: *"I've been waiting for hours!"* *"She hasn't arrived yet."* *"We've been married for a long time."* *"In total, she's been a teacher for ten years. But, she's only taught here since 2012."* *"How do you know I've been wearing these socks for a week?"*

Some actions are over with: *"A Treaty has been signed. Peace has broken out."* *"The President has been shot!"* *"I've finished with my travelling days."* *"I've retired."* *"They are the champions. That assessment has been made on performance rather than promise."*

We find it comfortable to make conversation by using sentences of between seven and seventeen words. We usually need more than five words to get our message across and we risk running out of breath if we talk for longer than twenty-five words. As the present perfect refers to both the past and present we are able to construct sentences which include further information; in this case, about time. To *"I've been having a lot of trouble starting my car"* we can add *"**since** we've been having these frosty mornings."*

We build, add to and lengthen our sentences by providing the simplest of information. To say **when** things happened or what is happening now seems to follow fairly naturally and helps us to speak as fluently as a native speaker. **Time adjuncts** let us be **obviously clear** when things happened at any time up until now. Adding reasons is difficult. We also make appointments and plans for the next five years, when we are getting married and about how long we can stand this job!

Teach yourself:

1. Add your own endings to these:

a. Have you ever seen ………

b. I've never seen ……..

c. I think I've seen ………… before, a long time ago.

d. I have already been ……….

e. Have you been …….. yet?

f. We've just been ……

2. We have been ……-ing (indicates the present perfect continuous).

steal intend disappear watch sleep sell

a. I've been _____ing this television programme for many years.

b. He's been _____ing to lose weight since January 1st.

c. My money's been _____ing, because she's been ____ing it.

d. That man has been ____ing newspapers there for years.

e. Tell her to get up. She's been _____ing in bed all morning.

3. The present perfect is especially used for describing trends observed from statistics, graphs and tables: *We can see from the chart that …* or *Research shows that…*

a. The n_mber of women in f_lltime work has been rising.

b. While sales of cars have been d_cr_asing the number of people taking overseas holidays has been r_s_ng steadily.

c. In some countries the outbreak of contagious diseases has been d_clining; in other countries it has been showing signs of incr_ase.

d. There has been gr_wing concern that there are too many theoreticians and not en_ugh people doing the practical work. They have j_st p_blished their findings. They h_ve rese_rched this topic for 12 years and have been cond_cting investigations for a decade. There have been too many chiefs and not enough Indians. There have been too many Admirals and not enough sailors.

66.

The Past Perfect with the Past Simple

We use the past perfect to give a brief or extended history of what happened prior to another event that we then go on to talk about some more. The past simple tells of one event. Using the past perfect helps us to relate two or more events, with the past perfect part usually stating what had happened first. We use **'had + past participle verb'** and often we use **'had already'** and **'had just'** done something.

When we are able to use the past perfect then we quite readily **extend our sentences**. We will find memorable examples:

*"We __had__ only **just __finished__** having our fun when his mother **arrived**."*

*"She **had phoned** to check first __before__ she **drove** to the airport."*

We also use **'when'**, **'after'** and **'as soon as'** as conjunctions:

"No sooner __had__ he __written__ his report __when__ a new crisis erupted."

*"**After** the volcano **had erupted** we **ran** as fast as we could go!"*

*"**As soon as** the 'all clear' siren **had sounded** we came back."*

We also use 'till/until' and 'before':

*"She said we **couldn't** eat ice-cream **until** we **had eaten** our rice."*

*"**Before** we **had ridden** for two minutes the rain **began** in earnest."*

When unsure of how to start an essay then a **short history** of what led up to today's events is a good place to begin. For example: the school camp: "Years ago, before you arrived, it had been unthinkable to take a mixed group camping. Thus, appreciate how difficult this is."

We also use the **past perfect** for our job application when saying what we **have** just **done** and **had done** before. Our sentences look impressive if we use two connecting verb tenses.

Teach yourself: Time and the use of the past perfect:
(Use: **before, after, as soon as, then, when, till, until, just, already, since**)

1. It had taken four hours to cross the moor b_ _ _ _ _ we arrived at the halfway house. A_ _ _ _ we had rested and had had lunch we walked for 4 more hours.

301

2. Some of us had never been camping u_ _ _ _ the day we set out!

3. We were told that we couldn't go in the canoes u_ _ _ _ we had learned the safety precautions.

4. Thus, as s_ _ _ as we had read the rules we went canoeing.

5. Because we had heard of making our writing more interesting by using a mixture of long and short sentences and we had practised the past perfect b_ _ _ _ _, t_ _ _ the exercise became fairly easy.

6. The agent selling the house phoned j_ _ _ after he had received the photographs we had sent of the sea views from our house.

7. Mitt Romney had already criticised the British readiness for the Olympic Games a few hours b_ _ _ _e he met the Prime Minister.

8. The P.M. asked Mitt Romney if he had accumulated his millions of dollars b_ _ _ _e or _f_ _ _ he had avoided paying tax.

9. The organisers of the Olympic Games had planned for the opening ceremony to be held on July 27th and that took place t_ _n.

10. We saw that the Olympic Games had changed a lot s_ _ _ _ the days they started in ancient Greece, over 2,000 years ago.

11. In fact, it wasn't u_ _ _ _ the marathon runner had heard the crowd that he found his inner strength to regain the lead and win.

12. Athletes from over 200 countries began competing the day

    a_ _ _r the opening ceremony had been seen by 1 billion viewers.

13. Although he had j_ _t broken the record, on his next jump he jumped even farther.

14. Many _eo_le had already arranged to take two weeks off work to watch the s_orting events on television; and others did so t_ _.

67.

The Past Perfect and Past Continuous

It is worth repeating the point that, when explaining a situation, we usually want to give some **background history**. In fact, to give some history gives us a starting point. We use extended sentences as well as short ones. These parts of speech are commonly used about our own personal story. We often use two parts: **we were doing something when something else happened**, usually an interruption such as "We were having a shower when there was a knock at the door."

The past continuous: I/he/you/we(to be)was/were(doing something).

Because they can be used in any essay we are told not to use phrases such as *'the birds were singing'*, *'the sun was shining'* in exams. However, we remember that the past continuous refers to **temporary events while something else was happening**. We use the participle '–ing' preceded by the verb 'to be' as we extend our statement by adding what else happened at the same time. "*I was reading a ghost story when someone knocked on the window.*"

The past perfect is formed with *"had"*. Whereas the present perfect is used for an **action in the past** and **is still continuing,** we use the **past perfect for events which are finished**. There is often a **relationship between two events** and these tenses allow the **connection** when reporting. To quote: *"Within minutes, whereas our men's team **had** just come fifth in the previous race, our girls' team **was winning** gold in the relay."* We can use the **past perfect continuous with the past perfect**: *'Van Gogh **had been suffering** from illness for some time, but he **had worked/was still working** right up until his last days.'*

When we need this account of what happened in the past we find that we can **connect** two short sentences without too much difficulty using the perfect, past continuous, present perfect and past perfect.

Teach yourself: *There is a mixture of past tenses in these sentences:*

1. I was s_rprised to see her do so well because she had s_ffered from ja_ndice and gland_lar fever as a child.

2. The driver in the car accident had b_ _n killed in a collision and had been d_ad for ten minutes before the police arrived.

3. The footballer h_d been doing up his bootl_ces when

an opposition pl_yer pushed him off bal_nce and stood on his h_nd.

4. Her b_yfriend had fl_wn all the way from Los Angeles to see her, but she didn't tell him that she had just flown to L.A. to see him.

5. They had met when he kn_cked at her door asking for help after he had just dr_pped his keys when he had been getting _ut of the car.

6. He told her that he had always had a problem re_embering people's names, but he had had no proble_ reme_bering hers.

7. It was only aft_r buying her an exp_nsive computer that she had told him she pr_ferred the latest mobile phone to do m_ssaging.

8. She told him that she was gl_d he was an English teacher as most English people she h_d met before knew hardly any gr_mmar.

9. She w_nted to speak well because she had h_d dreams of becoming a doctor which w_s why she was le_rning English.

10. She had also fou_d out when she was writi_g about human anatomy that once she had learnt the _ames of the different parts she had also lear_t how to write longer sentences by describing the parts and by explaini_g what happens. It's all about connections.

11. She had le_rned through using the gr_mmar books and then using those lessons in pr_ctical expl_nations.

12. She had been forced into learning in this w_y and thought th_t her an_tomy books had been of even more use than grammar books.

13. She was now racing ahead in b_th her surgical studies and her English. She t_ld him how her concentration had impr_ved. She had learnt by example, by c_pying and now by writing. She uses linking words in anatomy contexts and when connecting sentences.

68.

Modal Verbs

These bearers are carrying this old lady up the
mountain in a bamboo chair.

*Must get to the top while there is time: Some older folk refuse to
settle for anything less than getting to the top while they still
find it possible. This elder is being carried to the temple at the
summit. Meanwhile we discuss: heavy, heavier, heaviest; fit,
fitter, fittest.*

Although the current 'hot air' fashion is to urge us to be
positive and have a positive attitude, we hardly ever enter
into a venture with the intention of failing. We already
believe, 'I know I **can** do it' without being told a positive
thinker's assumption that: 'I earn a living by telling you to
think positive(ly). I am a positive thinker, you are not.'

Modal auxiliary verbs include: **can, may, might, must,
should, dare, ought, need, will** and **shall**. The past tenses
include: would, could. "I **would** have done it if I had
known how I **could** do it." In a slightly different context,
talking of ability, "I would if I could, but I can't so I won't."
On many occasions we use the past and the modal when
talking about our duty or an obligation or a wise decision.
Many conclusions are made in hindsight: "I was going to
do it but I didn't. If I had done it then I **would** be rich now
and for evermore."

We can talk and speculate about the future: "Someone told

me I mustn't, so I won't listen to them again. Things might be different next time. I think I should listen to my own inner voice in future."

'Must' usually means it is a necessity as does 'need to'. When we say 'have to' we usually imply that someone else or the law decided what we must do. "In Hong Kong we have to drive on the left" or "Mother said you need to put your dirty clothes out to be washed." "I had to."

When talking about past tense situations we say what might or could have happened. We talk of **possibility and probability** or **certainty**: 'He **might possibly** have won the race if he had been fit, but I **would**n't have bet on it. Anything **could** have happened and **probably** would have!' We are readily offered advice by those least qualified. When advised, "Oh, you **must** think positively," we inwardly say, "I already quite naturally think positively; however, when engaging in speculation I **need caution rather than be impulsive**. That's why I'm doing it and you are only advising."

Teach yourself: **Self-improvement is our Focus**:

Each one of us has known circumstances when it is reasonably prudent, wise and acceptable to bend the rules or even to cheat. The layers of bureaucracy which create rules and regulations h_ve to or are obliged to state the procedures that sh_uld be followed. The rules m_y then be seen to possess some practical flexibility because the principles m_st allow for the practicalities that w_ll surely occur.

There are two sides to most regulations. For example, a University administrator is oblig_d to restrict the degree of fraternising that can be permitted between lovers on campus; after all, the administrator has to or n_ _ds to act in the role of loco parentis. However, it is virtually unnatural for there not to be close relationships. Common sense m_st prevail. Likewise applies when doing assignments.

It is wise for students to appreciate that overt cheating is foolishly distracting. It c_n be self-detrimental and cause those so engaged to lose focus. Instead of gaining confidence, people who cheat or constantly complain and criticise w_ll find themselves falling far behind. Cheating changes what o_ght to be the gaining of a sense of self-reliance and confidence to being a form of self-deprecation.

As a requirement of doing research, all overseas students m_st plagiarise to some extent. However, even when leaving morality to one side, it is foolish to lose focus on the ultimate objective of self-improvement. After all, university is but the first step in our progress. Especially as it is impossible for any of us to be 100% perfect, every university wi_l permit some flexibility. When we are beginners then copying is to be expected and even a requirement when learning. Outright cheating is a foolish aim. We have a desire to be a more mature person as a result of our course of study. Our **focus** sh_uld be on imitating our role models, yet with the ultimate intention of becoming self-reliant. We choose to develop our better qualities. 'You don't have to be perfect; just prove that you c_n study fairly well.'

69.

Modal Verbs are Implied in Imperatives: We should...

"Hold fast what you have" is a biblical saying which we would today usually add 'hold fast to what you have' and as a short motto is "Hold Fast". This imperative urges us to abide by our ethical principles and to stay strong when under pressure in the ups and downs of life. We try not to regress. Change can be directed as progress for the power of good rather than allowing change to produce a chaotic situation.

An imperative is usually a short saying, direction or command regarding what is essential, urgent or necessary to do. Usually, an imperative is an order, but it is sometimes an obligation that we **should**, for example, **'maintain discipline, establish trust** and **be persistent'**. It might be a desire: 'Fiat Lux', 'Let there be light.'

As many mottos are derived from their Latin roots we discern that just like the orderliness of Latin, our life is enriched by the guideline of **order**. For example, a 'caveat emptor' warns the potential purchaser when, for example, buying a house to **'let the buyer beware'**.

We are interested in imperative instructions or an invitation such as "Don't worry. Have a cup of tea." We **instruct** or **make suggestions** about how to mend a puncture or how to ride a bicycle. We follow the instructions in a chemistry experiment or when cooking. When we want to be spontaneous we hear "you should..." or "you shouldn't."

We have our own mottos such as: 'Give'. 'I am important, but so too is the community important.' 'Reach out.' 'Teach through example.' It is when we highlight what is implied or what we mean that we use modal verbs. We **should, we ought to, must, have to....be responsible**. Cheating is attractive, but such a distraction! How well the proverb is maintained that 'cheats never prosper.'

The golden rule is to "Treat others as you would prefer to be treated." However, we are interested in finding short phrases or pairs of words which may serve as our guide. Without being obstinate: '**Hold Fast!**'

Teach yourself:

1. The Naval _____ ord_red the first fl_ _t to sail w_stwards.

2. Altho_gh the swimmer sho_ld have been disq_alified the other competitors made passionate pleas to the _____ to be lenient.

3. Advice/Advise: We adv_se someone. We _____ the adv_ce.

4. On various occasions we can use Elvis's words: "T_ke my ____."

5. Every winter we are adv_sed to get immunised against ___.

6. When learning to pl_y the pi_no we learn that if we play flat-fingered we will h_ve to move our wrists for every note we play. _____, keep your wrists just _bove the level of the keys.

7. We should s_t comfortably enough on the front of the p_ano stool so as to be _____ and able to move our legs.

8. Enjoy music; enjoy a hobby; enj_y languages. By _____ and being passi_nate ab_ut playing music and learning languages we _pen up the full range of life's em_tions.

9. Martha Graham said: "Gre_t d_ncers are not great bec_use of their _____; they are great because of their p_ssion."

10. "So go and make your _assions come alive! _ick interesting ideas as your to_ic. Start off with a dynamite first sentence. Add necessary details or

those of interest. Add _____ descri_tions. Conclude with a sentence that shows why you are _assionate."

11. **Warning** from Scott Gerber: Before you get _____ about a hobby becoming a business proposition ask yourself 9 questions. First, is your idea a profitable business or just a hobby? Elsewhere are eight other questions which will help you be realistic. Don't let your passion blind you into being a foolish idealist and bankrupt. Be a pessimist, and your business will be better as a result.

Commander; Therefore; accept; flu; passionate; technique; vivid; concentrating; comfortable; hand; judge.

Rock at Albany

The granite rocks at Albany, W. Australia, are either igneous and volcanic or metamorphic and changed under pressure. This one looks as if it has not undergone too much change in over a million years. In our writing we are very much involved with discussing changes: what used to be; is now; will be. It has resisted rapid erosion and has stood up straight and strong for millennia. It will do so for many thousands of years yet to come. "I am strong."

70.

The Conditional and Modal Verbs

Another occasion when we meet modal verbs is when we use the **'if'** word and conditional tenses. We have to use and study conditional sentence constructions, yet they are best avoided as they can be a little complicated. Also, as we are often speculating, these ideas are hardly worth bothering with as no one is able to foresee the future.

Conditional ideas are close to being dreams: 'If you won a million dollars what **would** you do?' 'If my great grandfather were still alive he would be amazed.' 'If he were still alive, I would be amazed too!'

Some situations are real: *'If any more first-footers knock at the door don't open it.' 'If you want to immerse yourself in using the English language then you **should** go to an English speaking country.'* Some people like to find fault: *'If you had carried those plates properly, like I told you, you wouldn't have dropped them!'* Finding someone or something else to blame is a foolish yet common human trait: *'If we're late we can blame it on the car and say it wouldn't start. We won't mention you taking an hour to do your make-up.'*

In a real situation we use present or past tenses: *'If you don't turn off the heat the water in that kettle will boil dry.' 'Ann, if I have said the wrong thing I'm sorry. Why didn't you tell me?'*

In unreal situations or when speculating we are talking about the present or future, but we use past tenses: *'If I had known you were coming I would have baked you a cake.' 'If I had known a pair of scissors was going to fly across the room I wouldn't have turned round would I?' 'If you could choose seven places to visit anywhere which ones would you choose?' 'If we had sold this house three years ago we could now afford anything we wanted.'*

In **impossible** situations we use **'were'** instead of 'was': 'If I were you, I would....' 'If you were the Emperor, what would you request?' 'If I were on Mars, would you send me a love letter every week?'

Teach yourself:

1. People like to b____ hospitals. They like to say that if they had done more they m_ght have saved her life.

2. People like to blame the _____. If there were more police on the streets they c_ _ld reduce crime by their mere presence.

3. In a perfect world the students w_ _ld be interested in everything I attempted to teach them, but it's not a _____ world.

4. Some people are refined, but if you tried to pass on your words of _____ to this class it would be like casting pearls before swine.

5. If I had the cash you need I would ____ it to you. I haven't got it.

6. If pigs c_uld fly! If I had h_d 200,000 dollars in my pocket to ____ you out of gaol I w_uld have given it to you, but I d_dn't h_ve it.

7. If I had known how bad the _____ was going to be I would have walked. In fact, I could walk faster. Let's get off and walk!

8. If it st_ps raining you m_y go out. If it st_rts again ____ come in.

9. If Ann phones, could you tell her to get lost because I'm not going. If she had warned me last ____ I could have gone.

10. No, I'm not blaming you. I'm just saying that if you could read a ___ then we might know where we are and which way to go.

11. If anyone's to blame it should be you and not me. I was here on time and you were ____. You should have been here to supervise.

12. There! I told you that if you kept on trying you _____ do it.

13. If you don't bring your bike inside someone ____ steal it.

14. It's strange. If I get criticism from 12 different people they will say 12 different things and half of them don't even know me. I wonder if they are identifying what is ____ with them and not me.

15. I m_ght have known he had gone to watch the ____ volleyball.

16. If the _____ had been quicker she w_uld have been saved.

Blame, ambulance, could, give, will, traffic, then, late, bail, wisdom, police, week, perfect, wrong, map, beach.

Deer (in Richmond Park discussing matters).

Deer: Interlocking antlers: When writing, think in threes. There are three things we always consider as our reasons or motivations. We want money or rewards. Second, we are involved in relationships near and far. Third, we willingly or reluctantly have to accept that our status will or must change. These deer have three matters to settle while we use modal verbs regarding what has to or might or must or could happen.

71.

Discourse Markers: Excepting, Apart from:

Another way of extending our sentences as well as using modal verbs is to use **'as well as', 'besides', 'apart from', 'but for'** and **'except for'**. This allows us to compare two things or people. One item is preferable to or not as **preferable** as the other. There are **advantages**. **Apart from** learning English, when we concentrate on and study a topic we learn new techniques and other ways of doing things. 'Apart from learning to ski you'll also make some useful contacts.'

There are many discourse markers and these allow us to make wise comments and extend our sentences. Sometimes there are two advantages to point out: *'If you do this course, **apart from** finding it useful you'll **also** have a chance to be in the same class as Jane.'* At other times we can state advantages and disadvantages: *'Except for having to do statistics, which, anyway, we can twist around to mean anything we want them to, you'll find this degree course very useful.'*

We use **'As well as'** when we make a list of items in which the options are all favourable or unfavourable. *'As well as helping you sleep, this drink is quite nutritional.'* *'As well as giving me a headache I dislike that choice of music.'* We use 'Besides' similarly: *'I like Sundays because **besides** sleeping all morning I also like the roast dinners.'* Most of us fluently make instant excuses. 'If it hadn't been for' is used in a similar way to 'but for'. We include something negative: *'But for the fact that we spent so much money, we would have enjoyed a beautiful day at the boat racing regatta.'* *'If it hadn't been for you I would be rich by now.'* We can often give **examples**.

The discourse markers included here give us reasons to extend our statements. They are particularly useful when answering questions regarding advantages and disadvantages. '**Apart from**' is far easier to use than: 'except (for)' 'but for' and 'besides'. After our paragraph's opening sentences we almost **automatically** expect, "For example,"

Teach yourself:

1. B_t for the arrival of the _____ there was the threat of violence.

2. Ap_rt fr_m tasting better, if you grow your own vegetables you will ____ money.

3. Exc_pt for the delay at the _____ we enjoyed our holiday.

4. Apart from improving my tactics when playing table tennis, I find that reading about the ____ is helpful for learning English.

5. _____ learning the grammar aspect of using *'apart from'*, I am continually improving and finding more examples each day.

6. Except for those who live there, you will have to show your ____ when you arrive and go through customs.

7. Our hotel ____ was wonderful, exc_pt f_r the occasional mosquito waking us up in the middle of the night.

8. I'm sorry to say everyone failed the ____, except you Mark

9. Besides the constant _____ in water supplies, the worldwide problem for the next decade is going to be food supplies.

10. The house is in good condition, _____ from that fence which was blown down in last night's storm.

11. B_sides sunbathing on the boat trip we also did some fishing and ap_rt from being a good angler Mark is good at cooking ____.

12. As well as being good at sailing Mark seems to excel in most physical activities. For example, he's an _____ swimmer.

13. As well as being a tour guide I think he sh_ _ld train to be a sports _____. Apart from being fit, his classes would love him.

14. Except for a few things, I _____ nothing, apart from my books and a good house to keep both them and me in comfort.

15. Besides a bit of love, people only wish for _____, praise and appreciation, exc_pt that it's too much to expect. It's too hard.

16. There are many ways in which we can improve our English. ___ _____, we can immerse ourselves in the language by going to…

Besides, For example, teacher, exam, fish, apart, police, airport, crisis, respect, save, game, room, visa, excellent, desire.

72.

More Discourse Markers

Apart from giving examples, making lists and making exceptions there are many other discourse markers. It is uncertain how many, but just accept that many people use: 'well', **'anyway'**, 'as I said', 'by the way', 'I mean', **'you know what I mean'**. Some of these are helpful in keeping us as the main speaker and some, like the irritating 'you know', are best forgotten and only used when being hesitant!

In reply to Scarlett's "What shall I do?" in *'Gone with the Wind'* we could reply, "Honestly, I don't know." Rhett Butler replied rather more bluntly, "**Frankly**, my dear, I don't give a damn!"

Here we are trying to extend our sentences and be as familiar as possible with modal verbs as a way of observing what is said every day. 'It wasn't my fault, David told me to do it!' **'Well, honestly**, if David told you to jump in front of a bus **would** you do it?'

Discourse markers prepare us for a point of view or a change of direction in the dialogue: 'Well, **anyway**, I must be going now.'

When we speak generally we say '**Well, on the whole, generally speaking, all in all, in most cases, as a rule, to some extent or even a large extent**, your class did well in the exam, **apart from** Sam.'

"I **suppose** he will have to do it again. He should, he ought to." "Oh, must I? I **suppose** you couldn't overlook it could you?" "No, **I'm afraid** I can't this time, I **mean**, it's **more or less** a disaster! **Well**, I **suppose** I could turn a blind eye to it actually; **after all**, you did turn up to most of the lessons. **Anyhow**, this subject is not so important. Oh, **by the way, incidentally**, my car has broken down. Could you **by any chance** give me a lift to the station?" "Well, I **sort of** think I could. No **doubt** you'll make it worth my while?" "**As a matter of fact**, yes, I could **actually**." "**All the same**, I must act professionally."

Teach yourself:

1. Mum, is it okay if Jane and I, **you know**, go away on h_liday? You trust us don't you? Anyh_w, I've already bought the tickets.

2. Well, for one th_ng, I know you're old enough to act responsibly and for another thing I th_nk, **in my opinion**, it's good for you. And, talk_ng of Jane, regarding her parents, is it all r_ght as far as they're concerned? You've asked me and yet, d_d you ask them?

As well as that, you ought to ask your father, oughtn't you?

3. As a m_tter of fact, I've already asked him and, bro_dly speaking, he said it was fine with him, in other words, as long _s it's fine you. I'm afr_id he left the decision up to you as he **gener_lly** does.

4. Well, **to tell the truth** your f_ther and I didn't even bother to ask our p_rents if we could go aw_y. Don't tell anyone; we just went!

5. I didn't think you would o_ject, **still**, I thought you might have _een, **so to speak**, old-fashioned about it. **In other w_rds**, we can?

6. **Actually**, in my opinion, you young people today aren't _alf as adventurous as we were in our day. In fact, to **tell you the trut_**, we did far more than you and that's w_y we tell you to be careful. We know what we did at your age. You s_ould enjoy yourselves!

7. **Well**, I'm g_ad you approve. **In fact**, we're both old and wise enough to be married. **After a_ _**, Jane's not exact_y a chi_d.

8. Well, **actually**, I've n_ticed that! I w_uld hate to think that b_th of you are g_ing to gr_w up yet stay naïve. The s_ _ner you get on with it the better **as far as I'm c_ncerned**. I mean, **after all**, it's a pretty t_ugh life out

there and **the sooner** you two get realistic about it **the sooner** you'll realise! On the _ne hand, we don't want to stand in your way of enj_ying the best years of your life, but **on the _ther hand, you see**, we don't want you to make a mess of it.

9. **Act_ally**, we think we're old eno_gh to look after o_rselves.

10. Do you, **now**? **Anyway**, come here. All the best and, better **still**, don't tell an_one about what _our father and I did at your age! It's nothing new actuall_; for example, have _ou talked to grandma?

73.

Although and Though as Useful Contrast Linking Words

A good strategy is always to consider **balance** and two sides to a debate. We should keep many connecting words as our best friends. **Although** it is unwise for us to have a preconceived strategy of starting our second paragraph with 'Although', our third paragraph with 'However' and our fourth paragraph with 'Nevertheless', there is a lot of sense in having these key words in mind. We are going to argue; thus, we have to introduce a fairly broad basis of discussion.

Some successful students go into exams with the fixed idea of using a sentence beginning with, for example, '**Although**.' They should know though that the sentence has an opening statement which has a pause using a comma, followed by some allowance or other which gives another side to the argument. Thus, it is wise to **OBSERVE** many examples of the **construction** of 'although' sentences.

Although we might adopt this tactic of predetermining the use of linking words before we have even read the topic

question, this policy is extremely risky. Clearly, **though,** there are going to be many instances when we can use 'although.' **Therefore,** we have to observe essays which include this sort of framework. We may be advised about the overuse of 'first, 'second', 'third' as our support, **though** we see that this structure is a good friend to many essay writers. **Despite** trying to avoid this, many essay writers use this strategy. So may we.

By using 'although' we **concede** that there are other factors to take into account. This is not the only way life is. It is also helpful to us in a practical way if only for giving us more to write about, especially when, for example, we have trouble reaching the set word target. We are forced into being realists rather than idealists **though.** For the next month we can focus on 'although'. We also think of, anticipate using and **consider carefully** other **linking words,** such as, **'however,' 'furthermore', 'alternatively'** and **'also''on the contrary.'**

Teach yourself:

1. Quite often, an _____ to 'although' is 'though'.

2. 'Although' is used at the start of a _____, though not always.

3. Though is more often used when speaking and more

in mid-sentence _____ than at the beginning of a sentence.

4. There is the factor of 'rhythm' in our statements. When we make our leading statement we use 'although' and for our _____ or amendment or concession we begin our second half with 'though'.

5. 'Although' has more power and i_____ than 'though'.

6. Even though it is not so powerful, 'though' is u_____ acceptable.

7. We give _____ emphasis to 'seem', 'appear', 'look', 'sound', such as, "Odd though it may seem, the whale is in fact a mammal."

8. Alternatives to 'although' are 'in spite of' and 'despite'. "_____ her shoulder injury, she competed in the swimming."

9. We make opening statements and then we go to 'for example' and other exemplifiers such as 'f__ i_____'.

10. We use 'even though'. "_____ though the American girl broke the world record, the commentators and critics did not accuse her of taking drugs like they had the previous day with the Chinese girl."

11. Even though some countries give the i_____ they are very devoted to their religion and devoted to peace, they actually spend most of their time talking of war, defence and attack.

12. We sometimes use 'though' as a c_____ indicator at the end of a statement. "To stage the Olympics is expensive for the h_st c_untry; it's w_rth it th_ugh."

13. Despite the fact that language is important, we use body language far more in s_____ situations rather than words.

14. Although they have been told, people learn the hard way that _____ is going to be important to them at some time or other.

Despite, English, Even, alternative, usually, rather, impact, extra, impression, sentence, addition, social, contrast, for instance.

74.

Display Attitude, Likelihood and Judgement

In our essays we might say, 'In my opinion…' especially in our first or concluding paragraphs. We state our viewpoint. However, in essays which encourage us to state our idealistic view rather than what we really think, it is prudent to go along with the fashionable opinion. We have to include **research**, **use facts** and **give reasons;** by including facts we have 'structure' as well as extending our sentences.

Some of our statements include emotions such as, **'sadly'**, 'happily', 'regrettably', 'unfortunately', 'luckily'. Long ago we were taught not to say 'in my opinion' because it is obviously our writing, therefore it is our own opinion we are stating. However, we make use of using these three words to make it clear that we have a personal viewpoint. This also helps us achieve our necessary essay word count!

It is fairly advisable to present a balanced argument. If we want to say something very different from the fashionable opinion we might use 'frankly' or 'to be honest, I **disagree with this point of view**.' When our views are unbalanced, biased or show a lack of reason then we will be penalised by the examiner or scorned by our reader.

To be frank, while our exam essays may be assessed by dreamers in ivory towers in universities, some people work in the real world. As one student realistically put it, "Just plan out your 250 words, and give them the usual story!" We at least attempt to stay professional as we allow that by preparing for IELTS our English improves rapidly.

In other words, we need only give the usual arguments; examiners are assessing our overall level of English. Thus, there is good reason to get as comfortable as we can in an English speaking setting. **We are permitted to show emotions as long as our view is supported by facts.** When we claim to want a 'university life' then we have to find evidence and present each matter seriously and professionally.

<u>Teach yourself:</u>

1. Fir_t, we must make it clear what we are talking about or referring to. The age old que_tion: is it nature or nurture that makes us as we are? Thus, we might refer to: "**Physically**, he ha_ a well developed body, and **intellectually** he has improved _o much due to the diligence he shows in hi_ studies. He is an out_tanding scholar."

2. We refer to '**geogr_phically**' or 'he is (not) **politic_lly** (minded)', '**biologic_lly**', '**mor_lly**'. "Both Beijing and Kunming are in China, yet **geographic_lly** and **culturally** they are f_r apart.' '**Morally** her action is permissible, **ethically** it is deb_table.'

We c_n look out for and list adverbs associated with other topics.

3. <u>**Comment**</u> adver_s include likelihood: It is (almost/hardly) likely, definitely, o_viously, certainly, presuma_ly .... going to happen. Negative associations come with _arely/rarely/scarcely/hardly likely to occur. Fairly/rather often are moderate declarations.

4. Our <u>**attitude**</u>: when we comment 'astonishin_ly' we imply that we are astonished and reveal our possible innocent naivety. We might: be **a_reeably** surprised, **sadly** conclude that, be **seriously** concerned about, find the result to be **unbelievably** _ood. **Naturally**, I knew you would come back, you **_enerally** do.

5. <u>**Judgement**</u>: Wh_n attitude becomes judg_ment: "Oh, but Rh_tt, you're wrong, you're **t_rribly** wrong!" **Rightly** or **wrongly** I'm **deeply** happy you're back. We can **brav_ly** enter shark-infested waters, **carel_ssly** leave the kitchen floor wet, **generously** donate to a good cause, **kindly** turn off the light, **wis_ly** leave them to work it out for themselves, **stupidly** l_ave it to

them to find their own way back. Foolishly and patiently wait for you. Constantly!

6. <u>Pers nally</u>, in my _pinion, speaking for myself, I'll **pr_bably**....

7. We can 'agree absol_tely' or '**absolutely** agree'. **Apparently**, some people behave most **mat_rely** and others **immaturely**.

75.

Linking and putting Adverbs and Adjectives together

'WANTED: DEAD OR ALIVE.' This form of poster was issued by police in days of old and the wording of the urgent message contained clear adjectives. We use adjectives to describe a noun, and in our example there was usually a picture of some sort or the person's name. Probably the wanted person was **extremely dangerous** and armed, that is, with a gun, knife or sword. The description adds to the urgency of the matter: **really serious; extraordinarily urgent**!

We combine adverbs and adjectives in order to emphasise our heart-felt descriptions. In **formal** examinations we have to remember to keep our wordings formal rather than use bad language or swear words. Some of us when new to a country may believe from what we hear said daily that a combination of profanities or swear words is acceptable. These words are not acceptable in exams, but they give us a chance to substitute other words when we feel strongly.

If we are ill and asked, "How do you feel?" we have to say

something like "Really awful!" instead of swearing. From this simple example we can build other descriptions. *"How do you feel?" "Really bad! Utterly dreadful! Absolutely terrible!"* We recall that colours are adjectives most of the time and when we have been doing exercise we say our face is as deeply red as a beetroot; when ill: *'I'm off colour.'*

When we are content with life we are "very happy", "immensely proud", "highly delighted", "absolutely wonderful", "just great". "How do you feel about your exam results?" "Absolutely thrilled!"

While 'wonderful' can be placed before the noun as in "She's a wonderful singer" we use the adverb 'wonderfully' after the noun as in "She sings wonderfully." Thus, we have to observe the positioning of adverbs and adjectives and remember the priority of adjectives as in opinion: **size/physical quality/shape/age**.

<u>**Teach yourself**</u>:

1. Using 'threes' is effective: He is t_ll, d_rk and h_ndsome.

2. He is incr_dibly tall, dark and handsom_.

3. Here comes the br_de, short, fat and w_de.

4. She's wonderfully warm-h_ _rted and absolutely down-to-_ _rth.

5. Be careful of using some adverbs in formal writing when they are best used informally, such as 'pretty' when meaning 'quite' or 'fairly' is used often: "Oh, yes, that's a pre_ _y g_ _d shot!"

6. Avoid people who find that giving out h_rsh criticism comes to them r_ther easily. They tell us we are **completely** useless, or we've made an **utterly** _wful mess of it all, and that we (not they) are a **totally** dre_dful rogue. They feel **deeply** hurt, yet proudly comfortable being **terribly** indign_nt and _**bsolutely** furious.

7. Prefer to feel absol_tely inval_able, **extremely** important, totally tr_stworthy, inwardly **stoically** strong and **immensely** pro_d.

8. When we discover a friend we feel dee_ly ha_ _y to see them. They light up the room with their certain and calming _resence.

9. Some people are _**rilliantly** inspiring for a day, while the rest of us hold the esta_lishment together with our **outstandingly** good staying power, enduring stamina and **long-lasting** sustaina_ility.

10. A person in an occupati_n of responsibility who d_es wr_ng may be seen to behave in a **m_rally** reprehensible manner.

11. If we w_nt to be a he_d te_cher we will get and keep the job if we s_y: "I **firmly** believe…" or "It is **extremely** import_nt to…."

12. An attractive word to use is 'attractive'. We _ind a person to be magnetic, **awfully** attractive or o_ great attraction. In business we are attracted by an **immensely** attractive _inancial proposition.

13. To most, bullfighting seems to be terribly unfair and m_rally wrong. However, in Spanish culture it is an **em_tionally** m_ving spectacle for the audience. Views can be **c_mpletely** the opposite.

76.

Adverbs come from Adjectives by adding –ly

It is a general rule that adverbs end in ' **–ly**' but worth remembering that this simple rule by no means **strictly** applies. It is possible to speak or make our message **loud and clear** as well as **loudly and clearly**. By the time we have made a long list of adverbs formed from an adjective we will have observed the construction of hundreds of sentences. Our aim is to be versatile and fluent as well as read English and be comfortable in adding adverbs and lengthening our sentences.

Many great writers keep their sentences short and also use monosyllabic words, thus we do not have to strain too much to add detail. We remember our KISS maxim of **keep it simple sweetheart**. Simple becomes simply, short becomes shortly and great, greatly.

It is good to remember that we can sell **cheap or cheaply** with the connotations of cheap inferring that the quality is not so high. We thus remember that saying cheap is usually informal and not formal. "I guess you got that dress cheap" is not exactly complimentary!

We notice that **many adverbs of time go before the main verb or start our sentence**: (We) **occasionally, frequently, scarcely, usually, periodically, immediately** go/went to the cinema. We can start an imperative sentence with 'always': '**Always** clean your teeth'. But it is usually before the verb: 'I always signal when I turn left.' The important point is that the positioning of words in a sentence is variable and it pays to observe the variations. We **quickly turn** the page or **turn the page quickly**.

Me may quickly learn English and learn English quickly. We focus and do homework or make our hobby one which we spend **a lot of time** at. This advice should only need to be said **once**. Poor students **complain** about their teacher; others in the very same class take their hobby **seriously** and find their **teacher is great**. What's the problem?

Teach yourself:

1. The_e was a na_ _ow defeat for the Japanese swimmers. They **narrowly** lost the _elay to the world record holde_s.

2. There have been many s_preme moments in the Olympic Games, with many co_ntries doing supremely well recently.

3. When h_rses jump fences at the Olympics we say they had a fault-free clear r_und and that they jumped faultlessly.

4. The two swimmers who made f_lse starts were mercifully not disqu_lified because they h_d obviously been distr_cted by noise.

5. Some pe_ple (usually the ladies) suppose it is fashi_nable to arrive late and we f_rgive them by all_wing them t_ be **fashionably** late.

6. In fact, some people are **frequently** late and arrive late fre_uently.

7. Instead of scolding latecome_s we might say in a kind(ly) and fatherly way, "Ah, you're here. (At last!) We were wo_ _ied."

8. When we come to our concluding p_r_graph or make our final point in _n ess_y we say, "Lastly, …." (Not "At last….")

9. As it rained **continually** we _alked between sho_ers, but when it rained **continuously** _e didn't even get the chance to go out.

10. Even_ually, i_ stopped raining comple_ely and we could go on.

11. The movies, "High Noon", "Casablanca" and "The Graduate" are si_ply _arvellous. In all, the dialogue is very clearly spoken.

12. Inter_stingly enough, the stud_nts are **quite** absorb_d by the storylines and they totally forg_t they ar_ absorbing English too.

13. It is truly wonderful to see students mature and make _ood use of their English. They deservedly and _reatly enjoy their travels.

14. F_nnily eno_gh, they willingly benefit from the experience of being able to travel freely. Any restrictions they have are not d_e to any limitations in their English. Travel repeatedly opens up considerably more opport_nities, especially for those who want f_n and willingly want to see people from afar from a new perspective.

77.

Transitive and Intransitive Verbs

For the sake of our health it is useful to do some exercise without us necessarily having to know the anatomy of our body. Being aware of **transitive** verbs is another instance of when it is best to experience the theory regarding these parts of speech without needing to be an expert on them. We benefit from doing the exercises, and if we remember the details then that is occasionally an advantage.

Transitive verbs take a direct object and **intransitive** verbs do not. We ask 'who?' or 'what?' or 'where?' after the verb to see if there is an object. "The bird spread its wings and flew." "its wings" is the object of "spread" and so "spread" is **transitive** here, whereas "flew" does not have or doesn't take an object and is **intransitive**. "The bird" received the action of the verb "flew".

It is easy to remember, "We must go!" with 'go' being **intransitive** and not taking an object. Many **intransitive verbs describe a sound** or a **movement**. "First, she **smiled** and **yawned**; then she **slept** and **snored**." "The earth **shook**; the volcano **erupted**; the lava **flowed**."

An extension of our observations is to notice when we look up words in our dictionary if a verb is intransitive. Most dictionaries will have the indication of 'verb, intransitive (*v.i.*)'. We can look up 'dive', 'swim', 'arrive', 'persist', 'sneeze' 'accelerate' and 'economise'. These are clearly intransitive in the past tense. 'She sneezed.'

Some transitive verbs **omit** the object **(ellipsis)**: 'The party went well. Let's do the washing-up. You **wash** (the dishes); I'll **dry** (them)."

Some verbs are followed by completion of place and are transitive: "He **escorted** her **to the train station** to see her off. She dragged herself away from him and was directed to the right platform."

The exercise for us is to notice how we use verbs and also to discover that some verbs of <u>change</u> are both transitive and intransitive!

Teach yourself:

<u>Use these words</u>:

Informed, chased, bought, avoided, had, shot, told, cornered, shocked, get, release, killed, wanted, helped, discovered, found, drew, married, escaped.

Bonnie and Clyde, 'The Barrow Gang', gained fame as robbers of banks, shops and stores in the USA in the 1930s and were urgently sought after because they sometimes s___ anyone who stood in their way. Bonnie Parker had **m_____** Roy Thornton at the age 16, but ran off with Clyde Barrow four years later. They had fallen in love at first sight. Clyde already **h__** several convictions and was wanted for both robbery and murder. He **w_____** money for his plan to break into a jail and **r_____** some prisoners. In the early 1930s there was an economic crisis and they **f____** employment hard to come by. Because they had **k_____** many people they had **s_____** a nation. They **a_____** the police, but it was difficult to **g__** accommodation. They became desperate and discontented as the police **c_____** them across several states. Eventually, the police **c_____** the gang, which had become five by now. But Clyde **h_____** them to shoot their way out of trouble. However, some photos were found in their rooms and their faces were seen in every newspaper. In 1933 the gang **d___** attention to themselves when the owner of their rented property **t__** the police. When Clyde **b_____** medical supplies for Bonnie the pharmacy owner also **i_____** the Sheriff. However, in a gunfight some members of the gang were arrested, but yet again the wounded Bonnie and Clyde **e_____**. By 1934, following several more murders, there was a reward on their heads and they were ambushed and shot 50 times. The police d_____ an arsenal of firearms, and artefacts from their clothing remain on view in the local museum. Their gravestone reads: 'Gone but not forgotten.'

78.

Verbs followed by the Gerund and other –ing words

The purpose of looking at gerunds is to enjoy extending our sentences. There is a point in **widening** our range of expressions if only for having a better grasp of English than others in our exams.

A gerund is a cross between a noun and a verb and is similar in form to the participle. **Gerunds are verbs in noun form**. A gerund can be the subject of a sentence, "**Smoking** is bad for our health." "**Sneezing** is the first sign of flu." Whereas in "*The student is writing*" 'writing' is the present participle, in "*Writing is a job*" 'writing' is the gerund.

A good way to start when making a fairly long list is to contrast what we like and loathe. "I **enjoy watching** movies" "I **detest waiting** in long queues". What do we do? "**Practising** daily is essential when **playing** in a concert." "I do **swimming** every morning and go **cycling** every afternoon." "**Mountain climbing** is my favourite pastime in summer and **skiing** is a favourite pursuit in winter." "I suggested **marrying** in the spring whereas Jane anticipated

living in France for a bit longer." We also go: camping, skate-boarding, boating and fishing. We enjoy: cooking, bell ringing, sightseeing, cinema-going, driving, snorkelling, riding, drawing and doing lots of other **hobbies**.

We can **prevent, avoid** and **resist attempting** dangerous activities by **thinking** carefully before **acting** on impulse. Other favourite words which are often followed by **gerunds** include: **appreciate, consider,** and **understand**. Words such as "I **appreciate** your coming"; also **forgive, stop, mind** and **prevent** are often followed by a pronoun: "Forgive me for saying,..." "I want to prevent them killing dolphins." "They **stopped me drinking** too much." "You don't **mind me sleeping** here do you?" Some –ing nouns are countable such as: beginning, feeling, drawing, warning, painting, meaning, suffering, meeting. Gerunds such as teaching, planning, singing and doing I.T. **are jobs or hobbies**.

<u>Teach yourself</u>:

1. I'm not sure if he's earning a living or l_v_ng off his earn_ngs.

2. A form of c_pit_l punishment is h_nging.

3. A bit of d_ydre_ming is permissible or is it just w_sting time?

4. Your dr_v_ng makes me nervous. I'm looking forward to arriving.

5. The trainer's _nject_ng of enthus_asm insp_red the team.

6. B_eath-holding is a requi_ement for pea_l divers.

7. Sh_plifting is an _ccupation to s_me and theft to _thers.

8. In order to see the countryside we can go long distance tre_ _ing or ask a truc_ driver if we can go truc_ing from coast to coast.

9. When ph_t_graphing people or plants we need g_ _d lighting.

10. Finding eno_gh f_nding is a major problem for sports teams.

11. St_dying and researching _s_ally result(s) in us feeling deeply satisfied about observing and discovering more about a s_bject.

12. Improving our list_ning usually l_ads to d_ _p_r thinking.

13. I c_n't underst_nd you beh_ving b_dly when I told you not to.

14. In spite of st_nding in the r_in he w_ited without c_tching cold.

15. We're g_ing _ut, s_ d_ing the c_ _king is unnecessary.

16. Being g_ _d at ph_t_c_pying is the first thing a student must d_.

17. Instead of d_aling in stol_n goods, in prison he sp_nt his time dealing cards and gambling; som_times winning, usually losing.

18. Taking pot luck m_ans acc_pting what_v_r comes along.

19. Many don't mind w_rking in any j_b. S_me like status-seeking.

20. _sk him if p_rking here is leg_l. I'm fed up with p_ying fines.

21. Your l_ _king out for them won't make them arrive earlier.

22. Emigrating usually m_ans leaving what's not so good and the s_ttling in a country and city w_ think will b_ b_tter for us.

23. I int_nd phoning as soon as we g_t th_re, not y_t.

24. It's the st_rting that is h_rd for us when t_ckling an _ssignment.

25. It was so f_nny, I couldn't help la_ghing.

79.

Alternative Sentence Constructions: Gerunds and Infinitives

The most important aspect about learning a language is that we arrive at a time when **we feel very comfortable when reading, listening** and **attempting <u>to speak</u> it**. We listen attentively and understand most of what is said or written. Eventually, we also find alternative ways of stating, writing or uttering our own words.

For the sake of variety we use a variety of vocabulary and synonyms and different styles of sentence, especially when trying to please our reader or listener. We might say, 'I began **smoking** at the age of 14.' or 'I began **to smoke** at the age of 14, but I forced myself **to give** it up.' By using the infinitive 'to...' or the '–ing' form makes no odds.

We can also have the –ing or infinitive after can/could: 'I can't stand **seeing** people smoke' or 'I can't stand **to see** people smoke.'

We can regret or be sorry. 'I regret meet**ing** you.' Or we can change our mind and use the infinitive 'I'm happy **to meet** you.' For 'remember' we all have the trouble of 'I remember com**ing** into this room for something' as well as 'I'm always **forgetting** names.' But 'I always remember an event of long ago as if it were yesterday.' We all 'intend **to do** something but we never get around **to doing** it.'

We always <u>**agree**</u> <u>**to do**</u> something or agree with someone or **refuse to agree** or to do it. We can try experiment**ing** with a new way of doing things or if we want some coins we can try look**ing** under the chair cushions. "I might be **ashamed of ever thinking** of such a thing, but I refuse **to be** ashamed of help**ing** you pay for a taxi."

We are 'afraid' of many things: 'I'm **afraid** <u>**to say**</u> I blame you'. 'I'm afraid to jump/of jumping and hurting myself.' 'I'm afraid we forgot.'

'I'm **sorry for** breaking the eggs.' 'I'm **sorry to** interrupt you while you are doing your exam and for interrupt**ing** your conversation.'

Teach yourself:

1. I remember thinking my days at _____ were important; I now see them as only the starting point.

2. Don't bother to phone me! Are you ____? Don't bother phoning!

3. I encourage you to reach out for higher _____ as soon as you can possibly get them. I encourage you to study.

4. In fact, never stop studying, sometimes _____ and sometimes as if it is just a way of loving a useful hobby.

5. _____ you study also includes extending your language. The vocabulary is specific and so you can't help absorbing new words.

6. Why don't you try doing the history of ___? You'll always continue liking art and continue your own drawing and painting.

7. I'm not going to persuade you to do it. My job isn't advising. I advise you not to listen to what sounds like any _____ from me.

8. Begin by contacting a few places of higher _____. What they say in their brochure is what they begin to teach you to do.

9. I won't force you to do _____. You may love doing medicine when you're 18 but later you might love to do something else.

10. I'll just warn you to take it _____. A few students give up trying; they insist on missing classes or outwitting the teacher.

11. It's worth thinking about. There's no point wasting ____.

12. A good strategy is to prefer making less noise. Contrary to what people think, teachers choose to notice the _____ ones far more.

13. Imagine being 25 and _____. I suggest: keep thinking about it.

14. I don't ____ helping you for as long as you prefer to keep going.

15. Do some planning. I assume you want to _____ .

16. What's ___ point of worrying?

Whatever, quiet, anything, university, advice, seriously, deaf, mind, graduate, qualifications, art, mature, education, seriously, time, the.

80.

Prepositions

We at least look for various grammar points and in most instances it matters little whether we know our parts of speech and grammar well or not. The main thing is to use our words in their proper order and to be grammatically accurate. We want to avoid **solecisms**!

By investigating **prepositions** we notice that as they are used in such a wide variety of ways then it is mostly through experience and by noticing and observing them we will then go on to make fewer errors.

What are you searching **for**/looking **at**? What are we talking **about**? There's nothing to worry **about** if we know what we're looking **for**! 'It's ok, we're not talking about you.' **Prepositions**, such as 'for', 'by', 'about' and 'at' usually come **before a noun or are associated with '–ing' verb forms:** 'with', 'between', 'in', 'from', 'of', 'on', 'out', 'to'.

We can choose a theme of <u>change</u>, e.g. changing **into** something else and subject **to** change. There is a change **in** temperature or things die **out**. New life comes **into** being and someone passes **on**. If we don't like it then we change it **over**, or exchange it **with** someone else or move **on to** another place. To start **off with** it is difficult to say if we are using an adverb or a preposition. To wrap it **up**, we will look **out for** phrasal verbs in the next chapter. Life goes **on**, day **by** day.

Verbs and a preposition include: talk, think, care, hear, laugh, **about;** shout, point, shoot, laugh and fire **at**. Play, deal, go, stay **with**. Learn, stop, and prevent **from**. Differentiate, decide, distinguish, choose **between**. Apply, apologise, forgive, hope, long, prepare **for**. Convinced and assured **of**. Concentrate, count, depend, insist and rely **on**. **Adjective + preposition**: anxious **about**, amazed **at**, annoyed **by**, responsible **for**, interested **in**, frightened **of**, aware **of**, kind **to**, fed **up with**. **Noun + preposition**: information **about**, need **for**.

Teach yourself:

1. We used to write letters, but now we keep in touch b_ email.

2. We want to change fr_ _ expensive electricity to cheap gas.

3. Acquiring new energy resources is vital f_ _ many countries.

4. We all have to adapt _ _ new circumstances.

5. There has been a transition f_ _m agricultural to industrial work.

6. Village life has been abandoned b_ migrant workers.

7. The impact o_ technology has altered the way we think _f our relationship w_ _h nature. There has been a shift away from self-sufficiency t_ dependence _n wide-scale co-operation.

8. There has been the elimination o_ many diseases.

9. There has been an expansion o_ health care.

10. There has been enormous expansion i_ air travel.

11. There has been a fundamental change i_ family size.

12. The price of _ood _luctuates _rom one season to another.

13. People are c_nverting t_ having s_lar panels on their house.

14. We are not complacent about or satisfied w_ _h what we have.

15. We are worried and anxious ab_ _t keeping up with innovation.

16. Nicola is different f_ _m most women. She's a boxer. Two years ago, due to her back injury, she could hardly get out o_ bed and was unable even to sit up. Now, when she puts o_ her gloves and enters the ring she

changes _rom the ordinary t_ the extraordinary! In the fight yesterday her feat _f daring and bravery was crowned b_ her smile. The crowd rose not f_r a female boxer, but f_r a champion. She showed steadfast resolve fro_ the first second. The crowd chanted her name as she walked into the arena until the moment her victory was confirmed a_ the end o_ the last round. We are proud _f her. She was the best fighter i_ the tournament.

17. These days we are no longer shocked b_ what women can do.

18. They no longer just talk ab_ _t it, they care _ _out it and do it.

Eucalyptus tree growing into blue sky.

Reaching for the sky. This eucalyptus tree is reaching for the dark blue skies. We can talk poetically or be scientific and describe the many species using academic writing. Enjoy reaching out.

81.

Phrasal Verbs

There are certain parts of speech in English such as the three aspects of the subjunctive (**'if'** sentences) and **phrasal verbs** where it is simpler to identify what is actually said rather than be pedantic and categorise items. There is merit in doing so if that makes life easier. Otherwise, in this chapter we are looking for **verbs** which **take a preposition or two**. We <u>look</u> them <u>up</u> or <u>read</u> <u>about</u> them.

Although we need not be too concerned about it, in informal speech and writing it is acceptable to say 'let's **pick up** some general knowledge'. However, in <u>academic writing</u> it might be better to say, 'We must **acquire** some general knowledge.' We write **'<u>postpone</u>'** rather than **'put it off'**. Yet phrasal verbs also allow us variety and **flexibility** in our expressions. In academic writing we are allowed to use 'comprises' or 'consists of' and even 'is **made up of'**.

The good point to emerge from this observation is that our academic writing has to show a **refined use of English**. At other times, we use phrasal verbs very willingly because most of us have to deal with practical matters while theorists indulge in what 'should happen.' Most of us are not lost in principles only; we have to **'get on with** it!'

There are **hundreds of phrasal verbs.** The point here is to suggest that we make notes when we observe a particular point. We **look at** it, **write** it **down** and **think** it **over**. We may not **reckon on** listing them all, but when we **come across** them we may as well be amused and **interested in** them. We might **get around** to doing it. While we are laughing we are learning: absorbing it and **soaking** it **up!**

There are (a) **transitive**, (b) **intransitive** and (c) **ergative** phrasal verbs to name but a few: verbs with prepositions to accompany them. Respectively: (a) **hand in** our essay, (b) **carry on** and (c) **hurry up!**

Teach yourself:

1. _hen someone tries to state their idea we ask, 'What are you **getting at**?' _hereas, in academic _riting we ask: '_hat are you inferring?' ('**conjuring up**', 'summoning **into** existence.')

2. In 'university speak' we do not **knock off** an e_ _ay. We discuss, write, research meticulou_ly and present our _cientific findings.

3. Belonging t_ academic life is as if we belong to an exclusive arist_cratic s_ciety. The rest of us forge ahead as we **buck up** our ideas, **get down to** work, **clear up** misunderstandings, **get our act together, muddle through, scrape through, stand _ut, break with** convention, **gr_w up, speak up, wise up, skill up** and **live it up**. We must **toughen up** as we ask, 'What are you **made of**?'

4. Some phr_sal verbs do not need synonyms: **meet with,** encounter; **cast aside,** dismiss; **bring about,** c_use; **h_nd down,** bequeath; **piece together,** assemble; **go into,** discuss; **set out,** describe; **made up of,** comprises.

5. We come **acro_ _ ideas** or we di_cover and encounter them.

6. A good way to **br_sh _p** on phrasal verbs is to have a game of seeing how many **turn _p** in a few pages of writing. We notice that text books **leave** them **out** or **c_t down** on them; they are **hard to come by** and we have to **h_nt** them **down**. In an article about e-books the a_thor wonders if they can **co-exist with** the paperback. She grew up with paperbacks and they are now hard to **cast aside**. She wants to **pore over** them forever. The physical presence of the book on the shelf reminds us of what **passed thro_gh** our mind when we first picked it _p and **read** it **through**.

7. We meet strange terms: "L_ _k what the cat dragged in." (We greet someone as if they look terrible!) "_h, please, don't drag that up again!" (We wish they would f_rget our time of mistakes.) "Oh, we've got a l_ng time to go. I'll have to drag out this less_n for as much as they can stand." (More or less waste time.) Try the same with: 'hand', 'set', 'c_me' and 'look'. How did this **come about**?

82.

What do you Want? Would you Like to....? I'd Love to

Many of us indulge in selling something at one time or other; or we ask what someone wants. Thus, if only for the sake of marketing, advertising, requesting or saying what we **feel** we may as well spend time considering properly: **like, prefer, want, wish for, hate** and, especially, **love**. Advertisers love to use the word '**love**'; we can too!

We **love** to be creative, but may have a fear of being harshly judged and the fear of criticism stops us. We use a step by step process; we want less and less worries and wish to build our **confidence**. We work on what we most **want** to do as we **wish** to restore and maintain our certainty. If we had to survive in the worst of conditions we would be forced to be creative and eventually be inspired or forced to do so.

We should use the word 'hate' only when we want to break off a relationship, but we can use it as a contrast to '**love**' or when stating what we '**prefer**'. We notice the word order with 'I love to draw pictures.' **Subject, verb, to,**

<u>infinitive</u> or perhaps verb-ing. 'I can't **bear to** see you looking unhappy. Would you prefer going sailing?'

We apply the same construction with: **need, bear, prefer, hate, like, wish, want, care, help**. 'If you can bear to, would you care to dance?' 'Thank you, I'd love to dance. I hate to tell you this, but I prefer to walk around the dance floor.' After the main verb we can insert a pronoun/object. 'Do you care to go for a walk?' 'I'd prefer **us** to stay in.' 'I'll help **you** to clean up your room.' 'If you want **us** to I will.'

While on this topic we show what we prefer: '**rather**'or '**sooner**'. 'Would you like to dance with Mark?' 'No, I would not! I'd **sooner** go to the moon than to dance with him. I'd **rather** dance with you.' We have feelings and preferences and after this exercise we **prefer to** find **positive things** to say **rather than** talk about hate and dislikes. The word 'hate' is too strong. Avoid it. We **prefer to talk about love**.

<u>Teach yourself</u>:

1. I would like to _____ you to my party. Do you wish to come?

2. I'll agree to __ to your party if you consent to marry me.

369

3. I would ____ to be your wife, but I want to think it over first.

4. I won't make you promise to do anything you don't ____ to do.

5. I want to see the world, I want to have some ___ and I want to accumulate some money. What do you wish to do?

6. I'd rather you didn't say you wanted to have fun before getting married. I prefer to say we can have more fun and money when we are married. Have time and take care to ____ about it.

7. "I wish to make a complaint." "Do you wish to see the manager?" "Would you care to have a similar product?" "No thanks. I prefer to have my money ____." "We refuse to refund your money!"

8. When we want too much we create frustration. We can live without envying others. It is best to prefer not to want too ____.

9. It is exhilarating to watch the Olympic Games. Would you ____ to see my photos of Usain 'Lightning' Bolt?

10. I would have liked our country to have ___ more gold medals.

11. Oh, I prefer not to look __ the medals table. Everyone's good.

12. I ____ to think the medals table is taken seriously by anyone.

13. I ____ want to say that I really enjoyed London and Sydney and Athens and Beijing and I want Rio to be another success.

14. Do you prefer to fly there or to go by ship? I'd _____ go by ship.

15. Would you like to _____ a DVD or to have a normal lesson?

16. At the start of a lesson the class wants to watch a movie. At the end of the class I'm warned to teach them next time. No matter how much you try to please your class you can't please them all about anything. Would someone _____ to clean the board?

Go, think, want, watch, fun, won, at, care, just, volunteer, much, invite, back, love, hate, rather.

83.

The Passive: Revision

We prefer the passive tense to the active voice when 'who' or 'what' caused the action is unknown or not too important. **Active**: "**I received** a letter this morning." **Passive**: "This morning this letter **was received** by me." We have a **different emphasis** and we use the verb '**be**': 'is', 'are', 'was', 'were', 'have/has **been**' and other variations using the verb to 'be', followed by the **past participle**.

Another clue about using the passive voice is: we often use, or are tempted to use the preposition '**by**' someone often unknown. Active: 'Somebody threw three eggs last night.' **Passive**: 'Three eggs were thrown (by someone) last night.' (the 'be' part is 'were' and the **past participle** follows: '**thrown**') 'This charitable donation, **by** someone unknown, has just **been** received.' 'This note was written by Jim.'

A most important sentence to include in almost any essay, along with the clause 'good communication is vital' is: "The situation is serious; something must **be done** about it before it is too late." The infinitive 'be' follows the modal 'must' followed by the past participle, 'done'. We could readily insert 'by someone' into that sentence after the word 'done'. The work must be done. The train station must be built.

Academic writing and scientific reports **are renowned** for using the passive. However, we **are told** that if we want to avoid our writing being uninteresting then we should avoid the passive as much as possible. Apparently, the active voice is more forceful and striking.

What **has been done** about it? What **is being done**? What **will be done**? We particularly use the passive when describing a process. Thus, describing how to cook something makes use of the passive voice. 'First, the rice **is washed** and the potatoes **are peeled**. Then,...' Eventually, the food will **be eaten**. The recipe book will **be written**.

Teach yourself:

Sometimes, we _re _dvised to keep our words and sentences simple and not too extended. We c_n observe th_t gre_t writers _nd books such _s the Bible use b_sic short syll_ble words _nd simple pl_in English. It is recommended th_t we do likewise.

When we _re shown wh_t to do then things _re much simpler.

Obviously, planning n_ _ds to b_ don_ b_for_ anything is writt_n. _therwise, n_thing will get d_ne. (Use 'get' for 'be'.)

We like being given g_ _d marks, but it is after _ur sch_ _l days and at w_rk when we will be pr_ud t_ be t_ld _ur English is an asset. Wherever English is spoken we will be required.

We prefer to be guided, praised and admired on our journey. Is it reciprocated? __ is worth repeating, and it has to __ repeated many times that those who use the word 'appreciation' as a sort of 'thank you' to those around them are extremely rare: one in ten thousand. Rather than utter words of praise, people prefer to complain. The person who __ appreciated will more willingly do extra work. Volunteers in the community ___ more committed to their efforts if someone appreciates their attendance, let alone their contribution. Both the giver and receiver are _____ when they are appreciated. When not appreciated volunteers are _____ and those in charge will be wondering why. We really should not only appreciate a person after they have ____ missing for a while. The appreciation should not be _____ for granted. Why should a person only be appreciated after we lose them? Winners are ____ as a result of enthusiastic encouragement. Those who are told they are invaluable will probably be counted on to reappear. People around us ___ starved of appreciation. Appreciation has to be renewed on a regular basis.

It, are, taken, made, disappointed, be, is, been, strengthened, are.

84.

Words used with Quotes and Reported Speech

A definite way of integrating the learning of both vocabulary and grammar is to include and make various uses of some quotations. We observe these in academic writing because we quote what researchers or pioneers have stated. Again, we take advantage of copying.

For academic writing we say in our research that 'Newton observed that....', 'Kepler stated that....', 'Plato maintained....', 'Moses proclaimed' 'Fleming claimed', 'the prosecution alleged that', 'Bush declared....' or 'The angered American people demanded...'

We tell someone what was said and add our impression of the way they said it. **Frankly speaking**, they **boastfully warned, shouted, cried, confessed, exclaimed, screamed, yelled, gasped, whispered.**

Some verbs stand by themselves, 'Oh, thank you!' she **smiled**.

We speak '**to**' someone or '**at**' someone. 'First, she told me the joke and then she **repeated** it to everyone else.' 'Oh, how terrible!' he **shouted at** her and then she **echoed back**, 'Oh, how terrible!' to me.

'How could you miss that? You're useless! My grandmother could have scored a goal there!' she **screamed at** the television.

A minor point: the subject, verb and quotation can be put in **virtually any order. I said to her**, "Stop that! It tickles!" or "Stop that! It tickles." **I said to her.** "Stop that!" **I said to her**, "It tickles!"

We again make use of the passive: I **am told** and **advised,** 'Never go back to places you once loved.' 'If you're going to copy then copy correctly,' is what we **were taught** long ago. It **has been** memorably **suggested** to us, 'Never use a preposition to end a sentence with.'

Usually, exclamations come first. 'Show **respect** when you talk to me!' I said. 'Don't talk while you're eating!' she warned. 'You can't learn English quickly!' he corrected, 'but you can hasten the process.'

Teach yourself:

1. 'Let's go for a drive.' He playfully pr_____d: 'Give me a hundred dollars for each minute I drive under the speed limit.'

2. 'Of course, this is only a game, but,' he a_____, 'it makes it fun to slow down and save myself from getting a fine!'

3. 'I was advised to turn learning into game and enjoy it,' he s____d.

4. 'Such as?' I d_____. 'Give me a few suggestions!' I dared him.

5. He s_____d, 'Well, for example, try turning as many adjectives as you can into adverbs by adding '-ly' to them.'

6. 'What? Like change 'patient' into patiently?' I a____.

7. 'Yes, why not?' he l_____d. He followed with, 'There are hundreds of verbs used with various prepositions.' He continued, 'It doesn't matter if they are phrasal verbs or not. Just get used to finding out which verb goes with which preposition. Just for fun!'

8. 'I'll have to look them up,' I m_____d.

9. 'Yes, of course!' he _____. 'It's no good guessing. Some idiot teachers proclaim the 'discovery method' is best when you have to do it yourself. That's useless! You never find out!' He protested.

10. 'I agree,' I ag____. 'All the students I know get together,

collude, collaborate, look up the answers and copy from books.'

11. 'Yes!' he conceded. 'What do you think our teachers did when they were at college?' he en_____. 'Everyone has such grandiose ideas about learning. The point of the exercise is doing research and if that means copying from your friends then that's how geniuses build on what others have done!' he explained.

12. He _____: 'If we did learning through idealistic discovery methods, it would be every theorist's dream coming true.'

13. 'Winners do **research**,' he conc____, 'That's it! Do it!'

suggested; smiled; added; enquired; agreed; continued; exclaimed; demanded; concluded; asked; proposed; laughed; muttered.

85.

Academic Writing and Research: the greatest leap forward

In order to graduate, students who undertake **English** as their major study area in university make their **greatest leap forward** when they tackle their **thesis**, usually in their last semester of the fourth year. While they are putting their study together they are advised to **work hard and to play hard**. They need a distraction from this intense concentration and to enjoy their few moments of refreshment.

The thesis has to have some depth to it and is disappointing if it is lightweight. Greater long-term progress is made when the study is attempted seriously. An academic study has to have an injection of thorough and proper **research** and **be written in a formal style**. At least, it has to be better than most work we have done previously.

When we hunt for a bargain, say, when choosing a suitably good restaurant we **compare** one with another. If we want to collect works of art or bargains in the antiques markets we undertake thorough **research**. When buying a car we **shop around**. Beginners pay more; those who do **research** discover the best price and quality.

Presenting a good quality research dissertation affects us by pushing us to mature. We have to be correct in what we say and how we say it. By being forced to produce a piece of work that we will remember for years to come we have to present ideas, facts and **our best English** which will not be laughably scorned at. We have to 'get serious'.

When we put forward a proposal or come to conclusions we have to back it up with a substantial amount of **supporting evidence** in order to **substantiate** our claim. Eventually, we produce an academic study we are proud of. We make the transition from submitting a flimsy essay to presenting a **praiseworthy dissertation**. We submit a piece of work which we remain proud of for many years. Our knowledge and the precision of our **academic writing** reach their peak. Our study is memorably fulfillling and we improve our English forever.

Teach yourself:

1. We may wan_ to **get rid of phrasal verbs**: we do not have to **eliminate** them totally because we use many of them frequen_ly. It is bes_ to ask a native speaker how informal some of them are.

2. Find a native speaker who has the experien_e of university writing standards and who is able to re_ognise bad taste. Their _omment may be as simple as 'You can't say it like that!' Then, further refinement is virtually certain to be ne_essary.

3. It is best to a_oid any form of 'get', especially 'got'. In fact, we ha_e **got to get** rid of it; we **eliminate** and **dispense** with it fore_er!

4. We have (got) to stop writ_ng '**got**'!! Never wr_te 'gotten'!

5. When writing for a pr_fessor we keep it formal. Okay? N_t okay! We do not ask, 'Okay, are y_u with me so far?' No text talk: 'OMG!' No!

6. Info_mally, look it up. Formally, we 'conduct/undertake resea_ch'.

7. We have to connect _ignificant specific terminology and we have to _elect **suitable linking words**, thu_ avoiding: 'so', 'but' and 'and' at the beginning of our sentence_ when making inferences.

8. Which is m_re impressive 'So' _r '**Therefore….**'?

9. **Contractions** are virtually unaccept_ble. Mostly, we use the third person, "It is believed that….' We **c_n't** write can't, nor 'It's… '

10. The rule _s, 'Don't use don't and we cannot wr_te can't.'

11. Every s_ntence must make s_nse. In order to qualify as a sentence our statem_nt has to contain a subject and a v_rb.

12. There has to be agreement between the subject and verb. 'The te_m is very successful.' Not 'are'; in **academic writing** 'team' is singular. 'China h_s won a lot of medals.' Not 'h_ve'.

13. Avoid copying. Th_s, we are not acc_sed of plagiarism.

14. Q_otations are marked with quotation marks ("sixty-six and ninety-nine"). We q_ote: Newton o b s e r v e d / m a i n t a i n e d / h e l d / claimed/insisted/asserted/concl_ded   that, "66inverted commas99."

86.

Agreement between Subject and Verb and Split Infinitives

The topic of 'agreement' provides another instance of amusement because we note how much confusion arises when aligning singulars and plurals with verbs. In formal English there are many instances of getting it wrong! We consider: "Oh, I give up!" and discover that this strict application of the rule is not worth committing 'hari kari' over.

On Australian television the commentary team have (or has) been told to say, 'The Australian team **is doing well**.' In New Zealand, just across the water, their commentary team **are** (or **is**) less pedantic or not so fussy and they continue to use, 'The New Zealand team **are doing well**.' Technically, 'is' is correct, yet, informally it feels as if the 'team' **are** eleven players, thus making 'are' the obvious choice.

Some rules are false rules, such as splitting the infinitive. Some scholars say we should not split it, yet there is no such rule. It stops the flow of natural speech if we have to say, 'the market continues to move ahead quickly' instead of the more natural flow of '**the market continues to**

quickly move ahead.' To quote Raymond Chandler, 'When I split an infinitive, my god it stays split!' The same often applies to subject/verb agreement. However: some people are fussy!

We want to be practical, realistic and pragmatic…. please! When playing sport or fighting a battle on the front line we hardly care if 'the team **is**' or '**are** going to win'; 'the army is' or 'are going over the top'. However, we must be very careful, particularly when writing an **academic** assignment. This throws up the inevitable question we want to ask universities, 'Who do you think you are?' We do not want to disillusion those of great (self-) importance. As with many, they are looked up to and therefore seen to be right, even when they are wrong. Otherwise, the earth may tremble! If they/it, our university, say/says 'the team' is singular and not plural and the verb must agree, they/it are/is clearly correct. I think!

Teach yourself:

1. Physics __ fun. In some cases statistics, politics and economics are singular as a subject to study. However, we can say 'statistics are able to show whatever we want to prove.' Politics is of interest to some, but not to me. Economics is now a fashionable subject, but the economics of the planned project are unbelievably creative.

2. We have lost a pair of scissors and a pair of trousers; where the scissors ___ I don't know, but the trousers are on you.

3. I hope the news __ good. You've got triplets. Each is doing well.

4. Measles is a worry when a pregnancy is in the _____ month.

5. _____ is difficult to cope with, but advances have been made.

6. A committee was trying to invent a horse, but the result was a camel. The committee have gone their separate ____ since then.

7. Shanghai's population __ huge; our audience is going to be big.

8. We come from a village where a crowd of 15 is immense! Our orchestra is small and so is our community. However, when we heard that the BBC w__ interested in us, then congratulations were in order. Our local school provides the facilities; from its present roll of students a new generation of musicians is highly likely.

9. Our son's 27 day vacation is in July. Our holidays are in August. The Seychelles __ his destination. The Philippines is our selection.

10. He seems to have many girlfriends, but I doubt if the whole _____ is going to accompany him at the same time.

11. On Bali rabies __ a problem. The government is dealing with it.

12. Time flies. Ten minutes is a short time, yet it is an eternity in the dentist's chair. Times ____ even tougher before anaesthetic.

13. That sheep gives __ good milk; those sheep give us good wool.

14. Gymnastics __ always my favourite viewing during every Olympic Games.

Diabetes, is, is, is, is, third, are, was, ways, is, is, harem, were, me.

87.

Spelling Rules

The **origins of English are diverse** and the spelling of many words is therefore complicated. English has a heritage of at least 2,000 years and many phrases of 800 years ago are hardly recognisable. English is still a conglomeration of mixed words and spellings from the Celtic, Latin, Anglo-Saxon, French, Anglo-Frisian, German and Norse.

With the arrival of printing the spellings became more fixed and consistently standardised. Previously, every letter in the word was pronounced, but in the 15th century words such as knight, instead of being about three syllables had one. Also an 'e' at the end of the word used to be enounced; gradually, it became and remained silent.

Because only the well-educated knew how to read and many of these scholars had learnt Latin, they preferred to keep the Latin influence and spelling. With the publication of the King James Bible in simple English in 1611 and the collection of English words into the famous **standardised** dictionary by **Samuel Johnson** in **1756**, the English language and spelling forms became recognisable to most.

Although American spellings show a marked difference with some words, there is now widespread agreement on spellings worldwide.

The word 'grammar' could be replaced by the more friendly term, 'wordcraft'. It is fascinating to delve into the history of English and such a study involves the evolution of words and their spellings. We could ask why there are 26 letters and about the origin of the alphabet. Despite being spoken around the world there remains the same basis for forming and configuring our words. Some businesses like to have a 'K' or a 'Q' or an 'X' in their name, while some like to include the aggressive 'R' sound. There is also a phonetic system used for getting sounds just right, but this is virtually only of use to non-native speakers. Even native speakers have hardly heard of it. Changes in our language have always happened or evolved slowly; however, the **electronic age** may bring more rapid changes.

Teach yourself:

S_me like to include 'y' as a sixth **vowel**, a, e, i, o, u, (y).

L_ng vowels: trade, tedium, tide, topaz, July.

Short vowels: map, mend, kittens, s_b, fun.

In words of tw_ syllables or more, one syllable is stressed: dis**liked, in**teresting, **pho**tograph, ph_**tog**rapher, Bra**zil**ian.

B is silent in bomb and d_ubt. C is silent in muscle, scene and yacht. G is silent in reign and sign. H is silent in h_ur and vehicle. K is silent in knife and knee. L is silent in palm, w_uld and half. N is silent in c_lumn, autumn. P is silent in psalm and pneum_nia. S is silent in island, and aisle. T is silent in ballet, valet, listen and rapp_rt. W is silent in drawer, dawn, answer and wr_ng.

<u>i before e:</u> as a r_ugh guide we say i before e except after c as in view, thief and receive. However, **there are many excepti_ns** such as seize. When the s_und is not ee it is spelt ei as in eight and vein.

When **adding –ing to words that end in e we dr_p the e:** creating, debating, erasing, practising, using, deleting, arriving, decreasing.

In **words of one syllable with a short v_wel** then we double the final letter: wedding, starring, barred, rotted, kn_tted, dropped, batted.

In words of **one syllable but having two vowels we do n_t double** the final letter: eating, toiling, teeming, seeming, m_aning, raided.

In words of **m_re than one syllable the final consonant is doubled:** beginning, _ccurred, preferred, forgetting, submitted, admitted.

When the **final syllable contains two vowels** we d_ not double: repeated, maintained, disappeared, concealed, esteemed.

Teach yourself:

1. When the <u>last syllable is not accented we</u> **do not double**: vomited, wander_d, murmur_d, border_d, muder_d, whisper_d (focussed??)

2. **Change the Y to ie** in: marries, accompan_es, lad_es, enem_es, arm_es, diar_es, dair_es, fair_es, abilit_es, bull_es, replies.

3. But not when ending –ey: monkeys, donk_ys, conv_ys.

4. When **adding suffixes** (to the end of words) **change y to i**: glorious, victorious, silliness, nastiness, pitiful, certificate, burial, hungrily, angrily, certify, bountiful, happiness, industrial, beautiful.

5. **Y does not change**: Hurrying, marrying, occupying, worrying.

6. When **adding '-full' then drop one 'L'**: thankful, helpful, plentiful, peaceful, dreadful, beautiful, disgraceful, handful, grateful, awful.

7. **Adding 'all'**: always, almost, although.

8. **Words ending with 'f' often end in –'ves':** calf, calves, halves, wives, leaves, loaves, elves, knives. **Be careful** with: reef, reefs, 'hoofs' is preferred to hooves, 'roofs' is now preferred to rooves.

9. **Adding –ous to words ending –our:** humour, humorous, vigorous.

10. **Sometimes a vowel is dropped: abstain, abstinence,** exclamation, explanation, proclamation, repetition, sustenance, excessive, pronounce, pronunciation, (r)enounce, (r)enunciation, procedure, disastrous, monstrous, fourteen, forty.

11. **Mis- or dis-:** dissatisfied, misspent, dissimilar, dissociation.

<u>**Difficult words:**</u> acquitted, acquire, judgement/judgment, strength, accommodation, government, lawyer, buoy, aesthetic, extraordinary, precede, proceed, psychology, pneumonia, skilful, conscience, beret, conscious, resilience, consistent, recommend, kayak, adolescent, privilege, annihilate, aneurysm, asthma, enquire, library, charisma, conceivable, courtesy, dessert, vacation, diarrhoea, circumcision, pharmaceutical, February, resistance, existence, embarrassing.

88.

Numbers

At first sight the topic of numbers seems to be of minor significance until we realise we use numerals in almost every essay and definitely in business and scientific reports. We have to know what a fortnight is and that the difference between fourteen and forty is not only twenty-six. As we check our spelling, we integrate grammar and word skills.

Cardinal numbers are, e.g. 1,578, 18,981, 5, 8, 13. **Ordinal numbers** are like the result of a race: first, fifth, eighth, twelfth (is difficult to say and to spell), twenty-ninth, 29th, ninetieth. A third of fifty-seven is nineteen. Gold: 1st, silver 2nd, bronze 3rd, forty-second, sixty-third.

There was quite a discussion about whether the last millennium ended at the end of nineteen ninety-nine or at the end of the year two thousand when two thousand and one began. Was it a mere triviality?

It is silly to give much credence to the reliability of Freudian slips or to 'there's no smoke without fire.' These are better confined to those who gossip and chatter and are selective in their views. It is also said that **statistics** can be contrived to make them prove anything we wish to prove. Likewise, 'hearsay evidence' is unreliable and not allowed in court.

However, we have to make good use of both **numerical data** and anecdotal evidence from experienced 'experts' in their specialist field. The point is that, say, a Ph.D. student will want their work to be appreciated; thus, using **numerical terms** accurately will **'enhance'** their work rather than detract from giving a good impression. "If my work is to be regarded as worthy I must include a table of statistics!"

As in most languages there are idioms which include numbers such as when confused: 'I'm at sixes and sevens today!' Valentine's Day is 14th of February in many countries and we are careful on All Fools' Day, April 1st (or 1st April). As ever, we make use of our vocabulary notebook in order to make and copy correct references and in our diary we might research why different months have varying lengths.

Teach yourself:

1. There has been m_ch debate about inclusive ed_cation. However, a lot of people don't even know what it is.

2. I've got too m_ch luggage: sev_ral cases and a f_w too m_ny bags.

3. Baggage is a synonym for luggage, but psychologically we say that we should leave all our bad thoughts behind and not still carry t_o m_ch of that useless b_gg_ge when we start afresh somewhere.

4. I see that the music_l 'Annie' is opening at the P_lace The_tre on Broadw_y (at #1564-@46) in New York City November 8th 2012.

5. Just because **more than half**/the maj_rity of pe_ple d_ or want a particular thing it d_esn't mean they are right.

6. There were a dozen road acc_dents at the weekend and a s_gn_f_cant number of dr_vers were not wear_ng their seat belts.

7. Just because Jud_th dr_nks a glass of w_ne every day as a part of her d_et, everyone th_nks she is an alcohol_c.

8. Here _re 2 lines for the advocates of being p_tient: All good things come to him who w_its; they come, but s_dly, come too l_te.

9. With 'neither' we can h_ve a singul_r or plur_l verb: neither the home nor the aw_y side h_s (h_ve) scored a go_l yet. It's nil-nil.

10. The number of refugees _llowed into _ustralia h_s just been increased to 20,000 annually. A number of refugees have drowned in recent ye_rs trying to s_il from S.E. Asi_. Everyone regrets this.

11. When cold and hungry then f_sh and ch_ps _s a f_ll_ng meal.

12. Two: _ duo, a p_ir, _ br_ce, _ couple ('those two _re _n item!').

13. A dodecahedron is a polyhedron with twelve faces and e_ch face is 5 sided or pent_gon_l.

14. All the furniture w_s swept away in the flood but plenty of photos were s_ved and each of us is alive.

15. We don't have m_ny more ye_rs to live and so with wh_t little money we have and without any worries we _re going to tr_vel.

89.

Can and Could, Have, Has and Had, Do, Does and Did

For a day or two have a look at how often the words **can** and **could** and **have**, **has** and **had** and **do, does** and **did** come to our aid. We can read a newspaper and use a highlighter marker. 'Can' as a modal verb helps us to weigh up possibilities as well as indicate ability or skills. 'Do' and 'did' help us to ask questions and 'to have' and 'had' say we possess(ed) something, while 'have' is an **auxiliary** verb which enables us to ask questions or use various tenses, past and present.

Although we should ask 'May I?' nearly everyone, apart from primary school teachers asks for permission with, "Can I go to….?" In fact, we can use other modal verbs such as 'may' and 'might'. We ask questions and state permission possibilities for the future, "When I grow up and leave home I can do whatever I like." The parent will reply, "Yes, you can, I just wish you would go ahead and do it!"

Of course, 'could' is to be considered here. "That's annoying. Could you stop it please?" or "Could you pass the salt please?" We talk about being allowed to do things: "When I was single I could do whatever I liked. Now I can only do what I'm told." '**Can**' is a readily used word and we have to make a major effort **not** to overuse it.

What the origin is of 'How do you do?' as a greeting is uncertain, unless it is an enquiry about each other's health. However, we reflect that 'do' and 'done' and 'did' appear frequently in our speech and writing. We link these words with '**can** you do….?' 'Do' and 'did' are used a great deal in getting to know someone. "Did you do it?" "Did you get lucky?" "Do you play golf?" "Does he love you?" We would do well to write a diary of what we did yesterday.

'Have' is a well-used auxiliary verb. We also show what we possess, such as "We've got two cats and a dog." We invite our friend to "Have a drink" or ask "How have you been?" We state our itinerary with, "We have to do work first, but we'll have fun later."

Teach yourself:

1. What did you say? I c_n understand you but you'll h_ve to speak up. I'll have a coffee, but could I have it weak? Don't make it too strong because I h_ve a weak heart. Did you hear me?

2. Do you have the str_ngth to do this? Have you ev_r

read the poem 'If…' by Rudyard Kipling. We can find 'can' tw_lve times.

3. D_d you do it? Have you done it? Can you find it? Have you got it?

4. What we are doing tomorrow: D_d you look at the schedule? Do you have it w_th you? We'll have breakfast at 8 o'clock, because at 9.15 we have to leave for the r_ver cruise which we're doing until 3p.m. We have to get the bus back so that we can be ready for the theatre in the even_ng. You have a packed lunch and I already have the theatre tickets. Do you have any quest_ons?

5. We're h_ving the house redecor_ted. We never did like this colour-scheme and so we're h_ving something much brighter.

6. Did you see the results? We didn't d_ as well as last time and we can _nly do better next time. We'll have to review _ur plans. We have four years in which to do s_. We couldn't do worse.

7. My p_rents are having a wonderful time and we can have a good time here too while they're aw_y. You c_n't come over can you?

8. C_uld you ask him if he's got my b_ _ks? I must have them.

9. Due to my _niversity ed_cation I can answer questions about history but I can't mend o_r fridge. Do yo_ know how to do it?

10. When I asked him he d_dn't think twice. He can be a bit impulsive and doesn't think things through. I'm sure that if we did go to F_nland on Saturday for a year there could be a lot of things he'll have to arrange to do first. I suppose he can get t_me off work. He likes to be spontaneous and so do I. I begged him, "Do come with me!" But I d_dn't expect h_m to have made his mind up immed_ately. Do you think we can have a good year together?

90.

Homonyms and Homophones

This chapter is included merely as a way of encouraging investigation with the use of our dictionary. Once again, it is debatable whether this examination of words should appear in the **grammar** book or if this a **vocabulary** exercise. We are looking at vocabulary and spelling. By now, we know we are dealing with the **idea of integrated studies**. As ever in any language there is a lot of fun to be had in the way things are said and the meaning usually depends on the context.

Homographs are written (graph) with the same (homo) spelling. What **kind** of writing it is doesn't matter much, as long as we are **kind** enough to write it legibly. Some words are used as verbs or as adjectives or nouns. 'If our Company's profits **peak** in January then I will climb to a mountain **peak** and raise the **peak** of my cap.'

Some associations have a similar context. 'The situation is **grave** and we must prepare his **grave**.' 'The **implements** we need are a spade and shovel in order to **implement** our plans.' 'The **waves** of the ocean can be similar to the **waves** in a teenager's hair as he **waves**.' 'The ladies went for a tramp in the woods but he got away.'

Homophones have the same sound (phone), but are **spelt differently**. We can attempt to create some ridiculous sentences! The words faint and feint sound the same. 'We don't feel so good when we **faint,** yet when we move deceptively and **feint** to the left but go the right we are very fit.' 'When the king dies the **heir** to the throne will breathe the same **air** as us.' 'The cat's **paws** scratching the **pores** of my skin make me **pause** when the rain **pours**.'

One of the best homonyms was used by the pop singer Sandy Shaw. Subconciously, we sang along dreaming of a sandy shore. There are some difficult spellings such as **stationary:** standing still; and **stationery:** envelopes, pens and paper. Errors over words such as these are understandable but look terrible. We must write it right!

Teach yourself:

1. Be careful with that hammer. Don't nail your nail with a nail.

2. She threw/through the ball through/threw the hoop.

3. The patients/patience waited with patients/patience with other patients/patience and played the card game of patients/patience.

4. As usual, we ate/eight a breakfast of bread/bred and serial/cereal.

5. Wait for my sun/son to arrive before playing in the sun/son.

6. Of course/coarse, we hear/here coarse/course language on the golf course/coarse as shots are missed/mist in the missed/mist.

7. It is fare/fair to pay your fare/fair even if you trip on your trip.

8. I must right/write this clause/claws before the cat's paws/pause cause me to pause/paws as the rain pours/pause into my skin's paws/pores.

9. They rode/road along the road/rowed before they put up their boat's sails/sales and then, as there was no wind they rowed/rode.

10. He liked the site/sight of this site/sight, but she was confused.

11. When we went to the zoo my dear/deer old aunt/aren't thought it was a bit dear/deer to see the dear/deer dear/deer.

12. Let's go over to their/they're/there place/plaice and see if they're/their/there there/they're/their or not/knot.

13. Steel/steal yourself for punishment if you steal/steel.

14. I know/no this principal/principle has this principal/principle.

15. Stay stationery/stationary; I'll buy some stationery/stationary.

16. You can't peel/peal your apple until the bells peel/peal and the lawn is mown/moan and then you can moan/mown or drink your wine/whine and wine/whine.

17. Her perfume and sent/scent sent/scent him crazy.

18. What did the big fire say to the little fire? You're too young to smoke. Did the cat see or hear the tree bark? What is an animal with a sore throat? A hoarse horse.

91.

Laughter

Of great delight are the early days of having a child when laughter spontaneously breaks forth and is clearly natural and instinctive behaviour. No university expert needs to tell us; we discover this fact for ourselves. No wonder laughter is a form of meditation or therapy to beat and overcome all thoughts of going to see the doctor.

However, what part it plays in our lives, especially when we are in social situations is open to discussion because its uses are varied. We laugh at jokes or embarrassing and **unexpected** situations in a comedy. We also laugh spontaneously when we are happy, especially when wanting to show we are happily carefree or we like our friend.

In **social situations** we gladly laugh when meeting people or when we know a situation might need the unspoken ambience of 'this is all fun and enjoyment and not to be taken seriously please!' The response of **laughter provides guidance** as to the atmosphere we want to create.

We might cruelly relate an incident when we remark, "It was so funny. Oh, the expression on his face, it was priceless!" Or: "Oh my little child, you were almost drowning and I should have been at the poolside to help you. You got out okay, didn't you?" "It's not funny you know. You shouldn't laugh. I don't why you're laughing!" It is an "all's well that ends well" moment. We laugh it off as 'minor'.

We like to laugh at a private thought. However, laughter can become contagious and often happens in a group setting among those (of us) when feeling good both physically and emotionally. We also show we are a part of our group and share laughter even when there is hardly anything or the weakest reason to laugh about. A worrying time to be careful of is when, once we start laughing we cannot stop; we get to a point when a 'serious' event such as a graduation ceremony turns into a farcical ridiculous joke! A giggle! We note that, literally, 'it was hysterical'. Hysteria leads on to other considerations not covered here.

Teach yourself:

The reason for including laughter here is that laughter h__ to be co-ordinated with our breath and speech patterns just as we do with p_____. Admittedly, when we start giggling uncontrollably then we lose control of every faculty. However, as sensible people we would not be seen dead giggling would we? Not much!

Laughter, like loving, is a universal **form of communication** and happens as a part of interaction and **relationships with other people**. We communicate playful intent and one of the joys of parenthood is that laughter is seen in our baby at the age of about 4 months. Thus, it seems to be one of our inborn instincts to communicate using this most contagious and magnetically a_____ response. When we hear someone else laugh then that sets us off too in an uncontrollable manner. L_____ is a social glue that _____ relationships. We continue to use it forever because we feel good and so do others.

We laugh, snigger and giggle **at** and **about** something strange and sometimes people are offended and say "This is no laughing m_____. This is s_____!" We suddenly envision a new philosophy of life and wonder if any matter at all is to be taken completely seriously, though we concede that point. After a funeral we might laugh as a way of celebrating the life of an admired person. We observe that Buddhists spend half of their time preaching and the other half laughing. Laughter indicates a viewpoint and is most therapeutic.

At times we find laughter to be p_____ exhausting: it makes our sides ache; we can't catch our breath or our eyes water. It improves our immune system, reduces blood pressure and relieves or numbs pain. We might even conclude that laughter is the best medicine. It is clearly a wonderful way of communicating. Like loving, as we are born with it, we may as well enjoy it. It is a treasured gift.

Laughter bonds punctuation matter physically attractive serious has

92.

Fortunately or Unfortunately We Reveal our Attitude

It is abundantly clear that some multi-millionaires and people in countries with far more money than most of us seem to believe they are qualified to talk endlessly and appear frequently in the media. They presume the right to offer direction and suggestions for the rest of us to adopt while assuming they are our self-appointed leader. Meanwhile, we want to respond with, "Well if I had your money I would also be able to adopt your principles. **To be frank**, your words are actually irrelevant self-seeking nonsense!" But we use restraint.

People choose to dress in a suit if only to differentiate them, their status and lifestyle from that of a farm worker or factory hand. Likewise, our opinion is detected by the words we select and use. **'Frankly'**, **'to be honest'** we hardly realise we are giving an opinion.

We make our **attitude** known. We may say that someone did something **carelessly** or **incorrectly** and **sadly, rightly or wrongly** there may be **unfortunate** consequences. It becomes **manifestly, patently, visibly** and **unmistakably** clear that although **ostensibly** a **kindly** act was initially intended, this charitable step was **presumably** or **conceivably** undertaken for motives of promoting self-interest.

We listen to experts who, **in theory** and usually with hindsight know how things should be done; however, they omit the factors which make the **reality** of their suggested pathway only possible if a superhuman effort is made. **Ironically** enough, the 'experts' are praised and lauded while those who actually achieved the objective are criticised. While some stories are credible we note that some people are too **credulous**, that is, too willing to believe what they are told. We were **definitely** not born yesterday, we **don't buy that**: we **take it with a pinch of salt**! We may seem **gullible** or compliant in order to keep our job, yet secretly and under our breath we say: "Oh yes **a likely story**! Are you **pulling my leg**? You believe it if you like. That's what you said last time and look what happened!"

Teach yourself:

Bravely and boldy; benefit of the doubt; miraculously; a pinch of salt; born yesterday; believe it when I see it; foolishly; bigot; gullible; attitude; Sadly; Strangely enough and coincidentally; Obviously.

1. Wittingly or unwittingly we express our _____ by using words such as 'sadly', 'remarkably' or 'unexpectedly' or 'predictably'.

2. Management said we are having a pay rise but I'll _____ __ ____ _ ___ __.

3. Scepticism or being sceptical is a worthy attribute in scientific research, yet in everyday life we say "I wasn't ____ _____!"

4. We won't say they played badly; let's give them the _____ __ __ _____ and just say they lost because they were tired.

5. Either f_____ or generously she lent her ATM card to a young lady who said she needed to borrow some money urgently.

6. He is quite a _____ to believe that anything that happens overseas is not as good as in his country.

7. _____ __ _____ she set sail on her single-handed round the world journey of adventure.

8. Quite _____, they scored the winning goals in the last two minutes of their final match to win the league championship.

9. I hear all the same promises just before every election. These politicians must think we are _____ and we believe them.

10. He says he has visited every country and speaks twenty-five languages fluently. Personally, I take it all with _ _____ __ ____!

11. Thank you for phoning. _____ _____ ___ _____ I was just about to phone you!

12. _____, it is impossible to prepare for IELTS in a week!

13. _____, many students underestimate the costs of being casual.

93.

Suffixes and Prefixes: Progression

We do not have to learn these suffixes or word endings, but by observing them we become more sensitive to word formation, meaning and usage:

SUFFIX	MEANING	EXAMPLES
Able, ible	Capable of being	Collectible/able, edible, suitable
Ac, an	One who can	Magician, musician, maniac
Ain, an	Connected with	guardian, chaplain, captain
-Ance, -ence	State of being	Existence, patience, compliance
-Ant, ent	One who	Assistant, competent, student
Ard, art	Habitual	Wizard, drunkard, braggart
-ary -ery	A place where a thing is kept	Mortuary, library, sanctuary, cemetery, aviary, monastery
-ative	Tending to be	Negative, secretive, attractive
-ble	Capable of being	Soluble
-craft	Skill	Handicraft, ballcraft
-dom	Rank or condition	Freedom, kingdom,
-er, eer, ier, or	Person engaged in trade/profession	Grocer, engineer, teacher, tailor, doctor, collier, miner, baker
-en	Made of	Golden, woollen, wooden
-ence	Forming nouns	Patience, resilience
-ess	Female person	Actress, goddess, princess
-ful	Full of	Thankful, helpful, thoughtful
-fy	To make so	Magnify, glorify, horrify, purify

SUFFIX	MEANING	EXAMPLES
-ice	Form abstract noun	Justice, malice, cowardice
-icle, sel	Little	Icicle, particle, morsel
-ion -tion	Indicating action	Creation, formation, deletion
-ise - ize	Treat in certain way	Organise, itemise, criticise
-ism	Form abstract noun	Heroism, baptism, Americanism
-ive	Tending towards	Attractive, perspective, active
-lent	Full of	Opulent, fraudulent,
-less	Free from	Careless, helpless, pointless,
-ling	Little	Duckling, gosling,
-ly	Having the quality	Bravely, manly, womanly
-ly	Repeated over time	Hourly, weekly, annually, daily
-ment	Result of action	Statement, enjoyment, argument, employment
-ness	Form abstract noun	Laziness, holiness, brightness
-ory, -tory	Place where/for	Laboratory, factory, dormitory
-ous	Abounding in	Famous, fabulous, glorious
-ship	Form abstract noun	Hardship, friendship, mateship
-sion	Indicate action	Incision, decision, extension
-tude	A condition of	Fortitude, solitude, gratitude
-ward	Indicate direction	Toward, inward, westward
-wise	Manner or way	Clockwise, otherwise
-y	State of	Sanity, honesty, energy

PREFIXES:

A prefix begins a word and, like an adjective, indicates meaning.

SUFFIX	MEANING	EXAMPLES
A	On, out, up	Aboard, ashore, alight
a-Ab-	Towards, away	Abscond, abort, absent, avert
Ad-ac-ar	To	Adhere, acclaim, arrive, advent
Ante-	Before	Antecedent, antenatal, antenna
anti-	Against	Antidote, anticipate, antibiotic

SUFFIX	MEANING	EXAMPLES
Arch	Chief	Archbishop, architect,
Auto	Self	Autobiography, autonomy
Bene	Well	Benefit, benevolent, benefactor
Bi-bis-bin	Two	Bisexual, binocular, biceps
Cata	Down	Catalogue, catastrophe,
Circum	Around	Circumference, circuit
Co-com-con	With, together	Communicate, compound
Contra	Against	Contrary, contrast, contract
De	Down, from, away	Descend, depart, decrease
Dia	Through or across	Diagonal, dialogue, diagram
di- dis	Apart from, not	Different, disagree, disappear
e- ex	Out of	Exclude, expel, excemption
Epi	Upon	Epidemic, epicentre, epicure
Extra-	Beyond	Extraordinary, extravagant
Fore	In front	Forearm, foresee, foregone
Homo	Same	Homogenous, homophone
Hyper	Over, too much	Hypercritical, hyperextension
Hypo	Under	Hypothesis, hypocrisy
In-im-ir-ig-il	Not	Inanimate, ignore, irregular, illegal, impossible, impasse
Im- in	Take into	Import, include,
Inter	Between	Intervene, international
Mal	Ill, bad	Maladjusted, malaria
Mis	Error	Mistake, mislead, misadventure
Non	Not	Nonstop, nonsense,
Ob-op-o	Against	Obstruct, obstinate, oppose
Para	Beside	Parallel, paragon, parasite
Peri	Around	Periscope, perimeter, period
Poly	Many	Polysemy, polygon, polygamy
Post	After	Postscript, postpone, posterior
Pre	Before	Prevent, predict, presume
Pro	Forward, before	Provide, propose, progress
Re	Go back, again	Retreat, return, refit, reflect
Semi	Half	Semi-colon, semifinal, semitone

SUFFIX	MEANING	EXAMPLES
Sub	Below	Submarine, subordinate, subdue
Super	Over, above	Supervise, superior, superb
Syn- sym-	With, same	Sympathy, synonym, syndrome
Tele	Far	Telegraph, telescope, telecast
Trans	Across	Transfer, translate, transport
Tri	Three	Triple, tripod, triangular
Ultra	Beyond	Ultrasonic, ultra-violet
Un- uni	One	Unicycle, unique, unanimous

94.

Make a Habit of Comparing Things and Stating Reasons

In most essays we talk about **changes, choices** and **communication.** We give our **reasons** as we <u>compare</u> the old with the new as we aim for making progress. We also **state our opinion** as we consider <u>cause and effect</u>. Thus, we are **always ready to use comparatives and superlatives** and observe **similarities, differences** and <u>contrasts</u>.

As ever, our **linking words** give both us and the reader our direction. When comparing we use **'whereas' 'while' (whilst) and 'although'.** Things (cities) may be approximately or almost the same, just as good as each other or **absolutely**, entirely, completely, totally **different**.

We use superlatives and note who has made more progress or the **most** progress. *One may be bigger or larger or the **biggest** or the largest or have the **best transport system** in the world. We should be fairly sure if we are going to declare the **'best'** or the **'worst'**. Perhaps one is **better** and the other **slightly worse**. *One joke might be nearly as good as the other or **significantly, considerably**, much, **a**

great deal cleaner. *One of the differences or the main difference between them is that whereas one power station uses coal the other uses hydro-electric power. The '**consequences** of this are clear to see' (to some). However, we have to **state the obvious** rather than assume it.

Pollution of the atmosphere **is caused by** one main, or three, or several complex and complicated factors. The most serious problems are caused by or are due to or are a consequence of us continuing to use fossil fuels or dispossessing people of their homes so as to build a reservoir and dams in order to generate hydro-electric power. 'One **effect** of this is' or 'the results of these actions are' that **serious** problems have been created and have to be faced. **The situation is serious and something must be done about it before it is too late**.

The reasons and causes have been given. The solutions and answers to the world's complex and complicated problems are (see page 958:)

Teach yourself:

1. The point of observing gr_mmar and extending our voc_bulary is to **<u>COMBINE</u>** these so that we express ourselves effectively. **Therefore**, noticing grammatical constructions has the **effect** of us being aware of them.

Consequently, later, we will write with flowing cohesion and coherence. We **m_ke sense** by getting our message across and by making our reader want to continue reading.

2. The **effect** of integrating the various parts of English is that they come together to form a whole and then our signific_nt mess_ge will be noticed and not hastily overlooked. **As a result**....

3. The **c_use** of being overlooked is that all people, especially others of course, regard themselves as very **important**. Thus, we have to influence them either with hearty praise or p_ss on information **which** they feel will then increase their feeling of importance.

4. The **consequence** is that we will not be dismissed, our m_ture viewpoint will be respected and our contribution appreci_ted.

5. We talk of the problems, the causes, the **re_sons**, the **effects**, the consequences and eventually the realistic_lly possible solutions.

6. We need a habit of **comp_ring** and noticing what has ch_nged. For the sake of passing exams we should make lots of **comparisons**.

7. **Therefore**, we use **comp_ratives, superl_tives** and **contr_sts**.

8. Things may be fairly **simil_r** or **immensely** or really or extremely or **rather** or totally **different**. Try comp_ring health facilities.

9. In science we are aw_re of a physical or chemical change. To **state the obvious**, one is alterable **whereas** the other is perm_nent.

10. In ess_ys we state the reasons why or talk about who, what, when and where; **communication, rel_tionships, money** (the cost). **Status** is a **significant** factor if only to heighten people's sense of self-esteem or because we want to help them to save face.

11. We h_rdly dare to mention sex, yet most people want children. This most significant aspect of life usually remains unmentioned, **although** we can discuss **health** and **educ_tion issues**.

Eucalyptus

Blossoms give rise to many topics: these are indicators of splendour, wild existence, new seasons, changes and fresh growth. Beautiful blossoms grow when given room to grow.

95.

Grammar and Statistics: The Passive and Profit

Reading and writing about statistics is an essential element in most research studies. We collect anectdotal evidence or report what experts say. We have a **hunch** or a feeling that at this time of the year something happens. However, scientific studies limit their scope by requiring numbers, diagrams, graphs and **measured data** in general.

Money and relationships are crucial parts of life and although, paradoxically, 'money' is an uncountable noun it is actually also the crucial 'bottom line.' We are wise to look at the final facts and figures for the year and to note the **changes** and **trends**.

Have sales remained steady or dropped or peaked or recovered or risen or levelled off? **Has there been** a sharp rise or fall? Strong growth rather than stagnation is wanted by businesses. They want to know what is **increasingly** important and where there is a **decline**.

We are forced to use the 'passive' voice. Decisions **have to be made** and **decided upon.** A profit **is reported, declared** and **announced** and projected sales for the coming year **are estimated.** A strategy has **to be considered, calculated** and **understood** on the basis of what **is expected** from the market trends. By referring to the graph it **can be seen** and **it is acknowledged** that sales of typewriters will still be in decline while the sales of laptop computers **have been shown** to be more in demand. In fact, **it is thought** by experts and university research teams that sales of typewriters have bottomed. **Thus,** if they say so, **it is recommended** that this line **be allowed** to wind down. **It has been discovered** and **has to be appreciated** that the typewriter is virtually deceased. It **should be indicated** and **explained** to the board that production **ought to be stopped.** The growth in the sales of laptops **is attributed to** demand from teenagers, students, mobile phone users, computer games players, experts and status seekers.

Teach yourself:

The **passive** voice uses the verb 'to be' in its various forms, followed by the past participle. The trend 'is to be seen', 'is seen', 'was seen' 'will be seen'. The trends 'were seen and predicted' some time ago.

alleged, met, declared, collected, lost, told, announced, inspected, suggested, taken, thought, launched, believed, threatened, graced, say, strengthened, promoted, committed, forbidden, shown, orbited, spoken, appreciated, mentioned, cleared, confirmed, grown, estimated, seen, broken, appreciated.

1. It is a_____d by the police that a murder had been c_____.

2. It was s_____d that as it was raining we went inside for a drink.

3. A ceasefire has been an_____ and Peace has been de_____.

4. It is t_____ that cautions were neither t___n nor s_____ about.

5. It is b_____ by anarchists that only they should be anarchists.

6. It was once f_____ to s__ that the Sun was orb___ the Earth.

7. He is the black sheep of the family and is never me_____.

8. Once your luggage has been co_____, your passport has been in_____ and you have been cl_____ by

customs you will be m__ in the arrivals lounge. We will be gr____ by your presence.

9. The popularity of the laptop has been co_____ by sales figures.

10. It can be s__ from the chart they have a greater market share.

11. Since this mobile phone was l_____ sales have risen

12. Your position as top salesperson has been st_____.

13. Your employment here has not been th_____d.

14. Sales have g____ and you have been pr_____.

15. Your successful results have s____ us how talented you are.

16. It is e_____ that we will do even better next year.

17. I hope you are glad you have been ap_____ fully now.

18. Records have been br____. Have you been unappreciated?

19. If only we had been told earlier. We weren't t___.

20. A golden treasure has been l___.

96.

More Statistics, Charts, Graphs, Columns, Rows and Axes

Nothing impresses the university teacher more than a smattering of tables and statistics in our work. Every statement is justified if a chart or table of figures is the fount of undeniable truth and veracity.

Coupled with this verification of '**therefore, according to the statistics, it is likely that**' is the wish of the collector of the numbers to be **selective** and not to have wasted his or her time. It is highly likely that not all the data was gathered using a scientifically valid method and the student will do his or her best to manipulate the figures to prove more or less what is desired to be **proved**. Another day, another dollar! They like to scare us so as to make an impact.

Furthermore, the 'experts' who want to use the statistics to prove their point are usually on a tour of the world and moving from one place to another like an unqualified doctor before their ideas are exposed as being either false or too impractical to implement. "Let the students assess their teachers." "How about the teachers assess the experts?"

However, occasionally, facts such as import or export or immigration and emigration figures persuade us to alter our mind about what we assumed to be true. For example, the **census**, which is collected every ten years, reveals a lot of facts useful for town planners or business strategists. We discover how much the population has increased or decreased and in which areas in particular.

We should be familiar with **bar charts, histograms** and **pie charts**. We present **flow charts, tables, cross-sections and line graphs** to show figures or to represent our ideas flowing from one basis point to the next. Diagrams are particularly useful for **demonstrating a process. Labelled diagrams** readily bring forth the comment that a picture is worth 10,000 words. When planning an essay and for collecting ideas, making a mind map is such a simple idea. We are creative and make everything much more obviously clear and simple.

Teach yourself:

curve, possibly, crashed, graph, axis, always, results, why, research.

1. On the stock market today, the price of ***** shares c_____d and trading had to be suspended.

2. On a g_____, the horizontal line is the 'X' **axis**; the vertical line is the 'Y' a___. These **axes** have regular gradations, steps or intervals marking the measurements used, e.g. percentages or degrees.

3. We plot various lines or bars using co-ordinates on the X and Y axes. We measure the steepness of the c_____ using gradients.

4. In research papers we use the present tense to show what is al_____ true and the past tense to discuss our particular data. Meanwhile, previous research has shown.... Our research shows or revealed. We give details of how the test or questionnaires were conducted using the past tense or reported speech.

5. When interpreting our re_____ we often use the **passive**. We use 'can be explained by' and 'are/is/was/were **due to**' very regularly.

6. We are not usually certain of why things happened or about e.g. masculinity or femininity. We use modals: can/could, may/might would/should and words such as 'po_____' or 'probably.'

7. We are fairly certain that scientific research cannot measure w__ or how we fall in love, why we recognise beauty and experience oneness with nature and the universe. Where do our emotions arise from when

listening to moving pieces of music or listening to poetry? Do we have experiences of the supernatural kind? Is belief in a God a scientifically valid way of finding meaning in life?

8. How can science and research be reliable when deciding our **moral code** or when investigating our values of what is right and wrong? Scientific re_____ may help in the decision-making regarding life and death matters such as euthanasia and abortion.

97.

There is more than one way of Interpreting Statistics

When we speculate or try to draw inferences we either **show doubt** and 'hedge' or, on the contrary say there is a degree of certainty. 'There is no/little doubt that there is strong correlation between being a good performer at both the 100 metres race and the long jump.'

We might say, 'There is evidence of global warming being caused by mankind's activities.' Alternatives are 'some evidence' or 'substantial evidence.' Hardly anyone would dare to comment that climate change is beyond our understanding and that all the recent claims are merely foolish speculation. There certainly is the **<u>selective</u>** use of evidence by those for and against blaming mankind otherwise: "Our research shows and we recommend that cars should be banned immediately."

Other useful words include 'In general,…', 'There is little likelihood…', 'There is a tendency ….' 'It would appear that…', 'There is growing evidence to support the theory that….'

What is certain is that we have to **be careful and guarded about our analysis and interpretations**. Occasionally, the proof is convincing or overwhelming. Often there is no **hard evidence**. The last thing we should do is show our bias and prejudice. It is insufficient to claim that "Manchester United is only a good football team because it has lots of money. My team would be better if we had their money." The facts may 'suggest' or 'point to' the reason why, say, many teenagers becoming pregnant is because of increased/a lack of sex education.

Useful words to employ in various contexts include: **significant, vital, distribution, complex and complicated, straightforward, simply, valid, reliable, clearly apparent, a tendency, probable, possible, seem, change, appear, conflicting, establish the facts, indicate.** We note changes and trends; we use comparatives, twice as many, four times as much, superlatives, data, percentages and fractions. "Our research shows that common sense is outdated."

Teach yourself:

In order to keep it simple, we have to imagine that the university teacher we are describing the statistics to is bl___. We have to explain what is in front of us without being over-interpretive. Time and again we are reminded to KISS: Keep it simple sweetheart.

As when describing a process, we might as well give the big picture first in our in_____and then move into the detail by using the points: first... second....third. It is preferable to find a matching but not repeated conclusion.

We note differences, **changes** and **trends.** To be honest, we rarely know why the changes or trends occurred or will occur. What has grown, jumped, declined, increased, doubled, de_____, halved, dropped by 50%, risen, recovered? Has **growth** reached a peak or peaked? Is there an average? What has seen most or least growth? The term 'rapid development' is, **relatively speaking,** very overused.

Have the rises and falls been dr_____, significant, steady, moderate, sharp, sudden or gradual? What do the statistics, figures, graph, pie ch___or the table represent, show, ill_____, indicate? What **proportion** or percentage are blue collar workers? What fraction of white collar workers are honest? Do experts use common sense?

What is the noticeable or si_____ trend or **change** during the same period? In contrast or in/by comparison what also happened in that decade or dozen years or corresponding time? The **increases** in the sales of shoes and boots in that year were **approximately, almost, about, nearly, just over** 40% and 50% respectively. However, on the contrary, compared with cars buses constituted, made up, accounted for one out of every five vehicles between M__ and July. In the same period, sales of bicycles **reached a plateau and remained steady**.

dramatic introduction significant decreased chart blind illustrate May

98.

Processes use the Passive

Expository writing shares thoughts, opinions and the expansion of ideas. **In contrast, technical writing** often aims at getting someone to follow instructions, directions or to understand a **procedure**. A description of a **process** or creation or production usually employs the **passive** tense or voice. A process is an ongoing method of operation and production and we describe the series of actions from beginning to end which bring about the resulting product.

We describe making a pot, baking a cake, riding a bicycle or growing vegetables. We have to be orderly in our instructions and state times and how or where things are **to be done**. Various types of bicycle **are designed** with specific purposes in mind. When telling someone how to ride a bicycle, follow a recipe or use the potter's wheel we have to be fairly orderly in our instructions. The making of pots goes back thousands of years and the know-how **has been passed down**.

Pots are made in potteries by forming a clay body into an object of a required shape. These are then heated in a kiln so that all the water is removed. Bone dry pots are usually glazed after heating and drying. The product can be constructed by hand. Thus, this primitive process has a list of instructions using linking words beginning with **'first'**, **'to begin with'**, **'then' 'next'**, **'after that' 'the next step'** all the way to **'finally.'** There are several ways of explaining the steps to take.

Sometimes we alert people by using a * **point by point form** of instruction. In order to avert cyber-fraud we are advised to *'visit our website', *'alert your family', *'report suspected fraud', *'hang up on unsolicited phonecalls' and *'seek independent financial advice'. However, this method **is <u>strongly disapproved</u> of in IELTS tests** and we should make our instructions or state our report clearly by using linking words in our paragraphs from 'the first step' to 'finally.'

<u>Teach yourself:</u>

Termites or bees have to work together with their respective colonies and for the good of their community as a whole. They each have a specific role to fulfil. The wasp's or bee's nest **is begun** in the spring. A 'worker' honey bee builds a nest and the first two weeks of its life **are spent** in converting pollen and nectar into honey which **is stored** in hexagonal cells to feed the larvae; thus the larvae **are fed** by the workers. Nests **are m___ up of** paper formed by the bee chewing up wood. The nest **is started** by the queen bee and after a year a new queen is **produced** which flies off to mate. New queens and fertile males **are produced** in the late summer.

Ants' nests **are** usually **f____** underground, whereas termites build air-conditioned nests above ground; the outer passages **are constructed** to keep air circulating through the home. A termite colony **is r____** by a king as well as a queen.

In the garden, in order to move ants on in a non-chemical environmentally friendly way we are advised to dust nests with talcum powder. The powder is so fine it gets between their legs and annoys them terribly. They will move pretty quickly after dusting. If they are a problem and **need to be t_____** chemically then we use an effective ant-killer. For custard apple trees we should not kill the ants because they play an important and **critical** role in flower p_____.

In p_____ aboriginal societies a process of using fire **was e_____** which, at first sight **was thought** to be destructive. However, in the next year, by using fire to clear the land the regeneration of trees, plants and vegetation from which food **was s_____ was seen**.

pollination; ruled; treated; employed; primitive; made; supplied; found

99.

Writing a Letter

Writing a letter may seem a bit outdated since emails have become so popular. However, for the sake of passing exams we have to stay familiar with this discipline. There are certain details to include; thus assessing an exam candidate's letter content and correctness is a way of grading their **thorough consideration**. For a start, the letter must flow, make sense and include a **purpose** and a **suggestion** for action.

Apart from the opening salutation and closing, it is highly likely that the letter-writer draws to their reader's attention: **who** they are; **why** they are writing; **when** an event occurred; **what** they want and would like to happen. Letter writing involves using all the tenses, a wide range of relevant vocabulary and a variety of lexical abilities, i.e. able to use words and sentences appropriately. The letter must be coherent.

Once we have covered in detail the '**who, what, when and where' questions** and possibly included **why** and **how** and explored other **possibilities**, then we will have covered most requirements. If we get a phonecall from someone saying, "I'm at the shopping centre. Come and pick me up" then there is a lot of detail to be filled in, including "Er...**Which** shopping centre?" In writing or when speaking, **give details**.

General rules to follow include staying friendly and polite and telling the truth in a sincere way. In real life we may be sarcastic but in the IELTS we go on as if we want to retain the friendship or co-operation. Obviously, we write letters to best friends (informal); to people we are familiar with our boss for example (semi-formal); and to people we have never met (formal). For **semi-formal** openings or salutations we use Dear Ms Jones and close with '**Yours sincerely**'; to the electricity company, we open with Dear Sir (/Madam) and close with **Yours faithfully**.

In between, the **details** and **purpose** of the letter are clearly stated!

Teach yourself:

1. The first thing to do is to get org_nised. Start with dates.

2. Inform_tion must be communicated, transferred and understood.

3. For effective letter-writing we give (basic) det_ils, details, details.

4. __Why__ are you writing and __wh_t__ are you writing about?

5. __Identify__ yourself and the situ_tion: past tense, present and future.

6. __What__ h_ppened __when__? The situation now and recommendations.

7. __Ask for__ or give specific inform_tion. Make a specific suggestion.

8. __Communication__. Be the best communicator and st_y polite.

9. Give __good presentation__ especially regarding the letter's l_yout.

10. Refer to previous key words, letters or promises.

11. Make a f_vourable impression and impact. Be purposeful.

12. After a greeting and identific_tion: __come the point directly__.

13. From the outset build up an intention of a pe_ceful ending.

14. Be t_ctful and suggest conflict resolution incentives. __Both win__!

15. __How__ can we resolve the matter? H_ve you got the receipt?

16. **Who** are you? Address, telephone and cont_ct.

17. **How** did you meet? Wh_t is your subject or topic?

18. For formal letters demonstr_te the use of clear paragraphs.

19. The use of **numbers** is useful especi_lly in financial matters.

20. **Where** did you meet and **where** will you meet next time?

21. What do you w_nt done? **What is your suggestion**?

22. Is an altern_tive possible? Suggestion, resolution, suggestion.

23. What contribution can you offer? Do you need to be persu_ded?

24. Say either: 'I would appreciate it if' or 'I would be gr_teful if...'

25. 'I am writing reg_rding the...' or 'Could you be so kind as to...'

26. Aim at writing three or four or five par_graphs.

27. Open as a friend, close as a friend. We do not want our re_der to say: "I have filed your letter in the appropriate place." (The bin!) Appreciate our quality of "**assertiveness with polite humility**".

100.

Tautology: Taut = the same; - logy = the word or idea

We smile when we observe tautology: "**Those pregnant** women over **there** are **each** going to have **two** twins next month"? Tautology is a form of 'wordiness' and in this final chapter we use this example to repeat and to show why we KISS or Keep it Simple Sweetheart. **Tautology is when we say something twice when once is enough**. We have to allow 'pregnant women' while we frown at 'two twins.'

Some tautology is acceptable as we 'all' have many 'problems and difficulties' of the 'complex and complicated' kind which can hardly be understated. 'What do you mean by 'don't panic'? If you're not panicking then you don't realise the situation.' It helps to exaggerate or over-emphasise sometimes and so some repetition is allowed!

A common example of tautology or redundancy we have probably used is: 'I'm sorry, can you repeat that **again** please?' What about 'stand **up**' or 'rise up'; 'descend **down** the mountain'? We need not ask if someone will 'repay us

back the money' even though the loan was 'large in size'. We may be going to a sale where prices have been 'reduced down'. After all, it might be a '**very** unique opportunity' and other opportunities 'may possibly be few in number'. 'It is either a bargain or not' is 'adequate enough'; we do not have to add 'or it is not a bargain'. But we still want to 'hurry up!' to the 'ATM machine.'

We add emphasis by saying we 'absolutely disassociate' ourselves from such an action when the matter is serious. We probably feel awkward when referring to '**real life**', but when we have to tolerate so much teaching theory from university education departments we want to know if they have been in an actual classroom recently. There are theories, but those are washed away in the practicalities of **real** life.

Although not quite the same thing, when we make use of **ellipsis** we omit unnecessary or **redundant** words from our statements. It is amusing or annoying to see **tautology**; we are reminded to take care.

<u>Teach yourself</u>: **Find the following amusing and adjust if needed**:

1. There is only one thing in the world that is worse than being talked about and that is not being talked about. (Oscar Wilde)

2. The only thing that hurts more than paying an income tax is not having to pay an income tax. (Thomas R. Duwar)

3. What you have done is very unique. This is your one and only life.

4. You are the champion of the whole world, as well the universe!

5. If you want to notice tautology, then listen to your wife.

6. Reveille is at 6 a.m. first thing tomorrow morning before breakfast.

7. Your free gift is in close proximity.

8. IELTS test. PIN number. ATM machine. HIV virus.

9. When I'm good I'm very very good, but when I'm bad I'm even better. (Mae West) Too much of a good thing can be wonderful.

10. It was a game of two halves. I'm not sure of the finished result. The game isn't over until it's over.

11. (a) I'm not prejudiced but... I hate people who are intolerant. (b) I am free of prejudices; I hate everyone equally (W.C. Fields)

12. They talk most who have least to say. (Matthew Prior) The thoughtless are rarely wordless.(H.W. Newton)

13. When people criticise us are they commenting on us or revealing their own experience and how they think?

14. I assume that every one of us is unanimously agreed.

15. Are you a beginner or have you just started?

16. We'll cross over that bridge when we get to it.

17. I believe she's nearly or a little bit slightly pregnant.

18. The elderly are our first priority because they are often old.

19. Human beings and people naturally like to be appreciated.

21. Nostalgia isn't what it used to be.

22. Fresh produce for sale: untouched by human hand.

23. This is only a short summary of what actually happened.

24. Gently assertive people say: "I have stood up!" We must!

Language is like Love

Our attitude regarding **language** can be just like attitudes regarding love. We can treat it as being not much more than fun or regard it as having a **deeply fulfilling purpose**. Both language and loving are **forms of communication**. We may enjoy them all the time, whether alone or in company. The more **mature** we are about them then the sharing is all the **richer** and the more **fruit** they bestow.

Our **maturity** of approach determines the outcome. If we are tenderly respectful, careful and adopt a healthy attitude then we know that **communicating** through loving and speaking a language or two will bear a harvest of worthy fruitfulness and riches. In the debate about which came first: the chicken or the egg, the egg of **loving** has first claim.

Next is **conception**: the **generation** of **ideas** and of giving birth to **life**. A relationship is built. A society and a couple cement their union through common bonds: either language or union or both. Before IVF there was the conception of a baby beginning with the union of male and female. Similar is the mutual dependence of ideas and language on each other. In both, the development depends on our **responsible contribution**. We choose to see the beauty of our chosen road.

Becoming pregnant and subsequently giving birth is a peak moment of fulfilment for most couples, especially when we consider how difficult it can be to **conceive** in the first place. Our good command of language gives **fertility** to ideas and we might discuss how crucially the roles of masculinity and femininity affect cultures and conception.

A **respectful** and healthy **attitude** is essential both in a relationship and in the development of our language. To use a cliché: it's all in the mind. Poetical or **spiritual** experiences are accessible through loving and through language. Our duty is: to **select the right frame of mind and enjoy the journey, because we make beautiful things happen. We generate them through our connection and communication**.

Be Precise: Allow flexibility for overseas students and workers

Our good English is an asset in several ways. When we use grammar in a conventional way we want to be accurate and transmit our meaning with precision. We like order and structure in our life and, just as our religion or our job is for many of us, a belief in using English in a conventional manner is our supporting guideline.

It is unbelievable that the standards of English required of immigrants into Australia is being raised rather than allowances made. Grammarians should know that a sentence is divided into the subject and the predicate, but it is prejudicial to expect immigrants to be tested on Don Bradman and cricket. Ignorance of grammar and of this fact apparently makes a starving refugee an unworthy citizen!

It is not the end of the world if we use grammar unconventionally. The present immigration rules promote status seekers and those who feel they are superior. They were like this in the schoolyard and they find childish reasons to continue to be so. Therefore, regarding English, immigrant students should be aware of the mountain they have to climb if they are not to be looked down upon by legislators.

Australia denies itself the benefits of the talent of so many potentially academically and technically skilled immigrants. Overseas candidates are set ridiculously high bars or levels of English. Skilled trades-people such as bricklayers cannot be given entry if their English is not up to scratch. To rely solely on the 'fine judgements' of IELTS examiners is foolishly short-sighted. This policy is selfish or plainly prejudicial. We scorn excuses of 'there is not enough land.'

Using correct grammar is merely a convention. It is not a crime to misuse it, just as it is not a crime to speak a language other than English. To be fair, English speaking universities can reasonably expect its students to be proficient in this tongue, but it is both foolish and over-discriminating to raise the bars of qualification so high.

WORD LISTS
Add your own words to these lists:

State what used to happen. What is happening now?

I used to. I **didn't use** to…. There used to be… They used to…

EVERYTHING **CHANGES, we make and explain CHOICES; many things have CHANGED. For example…such as…**

Nowadays, we … there are…. has to be…. For instance

<u>SPECULATE</u> on the future with **modal verbs** about what should/ought/might/must happen. Can happen, could/would happen. May occur, (maybe), perhaps, possibly, probably, perhaps. Conclusion: Recommendations, planning and suggestions. One solution might be: Going to, shall, will. If it is a certainty then it is going to happen. Are we sure?

The Passive: The situation is serious; something must be done about it before it is too late.

<u>**COMMUNICATION and CONNECTIONS**</u>: Emphasise **key words**. Describe a technological device: three uses: 1st, 2nd, 3rd.

<u>Resources and communities</u>: transport facilities, food, markets, training, (further) education, police, hospitals, doctors, nurses, water supplies, electricity, gas, safety, security, road, rail, air, canals, sea, parks, sports, libraries, leisure facilities, fertile soil, livestock, industry, history, culture, music, dance, rivers, forests.

<u>Population</u>: 7 billion, crisis point, sustainable development, proportion of and care of the elderly, quality of life, environment, existence, consume, energy resources, trends, urgent action.

<u>Climate Change</u>: weather extremes, destructive, loss of, emissions of carbon dioxide, greenhouse gas, melting snow, cyclones, water, agricultural and fish supplies, farmers, economic crisis, cost.

Keeping fit: Hobbies: Sport: Cars: Housing: Family: Money.

CONNECTING AND BUT OR LINKING WORDS

<u>CONNECTING or Linking words</u>: Be comfortable using them:

Generally speaking, many of these linking words are VITAL. They help us make a smooth TRANSITION to a different theme and give us a direction: <u>BUT,....</u> <u>AND,.....OR,</u>....

<u>BUT</u>: Compared with, whereas, while, but, **by/in comparison**, in/by way of **contrast**, **on the contrary**, comparatively speaking, on the one hand, on the other hand, conversely, though, even though, relatively speaking, even if/though, instead (of), although, yet, still, (dis)advantage, nonetheless, (or) else, preferable, rather, only, while, after all, **HOWEVER**, nevertheless. **Add others if needed**...

<u>AND</u>: **In addition**, what is more (avoid 'what's more'), moreover, also, again, **furthermore**, first(ly), second, third, to begin with, then, next, above all, the next step, as well as, and to conclude, hence, **in conclusion**, in summary, to sum up, to summarise, lastly (not 'at last'), **finally**, equally, likewise, similarly, correspondingly, in brief, (respectively), overall, generally, **THEREFORE** (not 'so'), thus,

The cause, the effect of, the result is, (resultant) consequence, advantage, consequently, accordingly, due to, owing to, because of... Output doubled; saw twice as many; trebled. Period; annual; biennial; decade; fortnight; monthly. Half; halved; a quarter; an eighth; dozen.

With reference to, regarding, infer, assume, presume, implies,...

Incidentally, by the way, actually, in reality, really, to be practical

Either, neither...nor..., not only ... but also

OR: **Change or replace**: **Alternatively**, again, rather, realistically, another possibility is that/would be to, better, worse, on the one hand, on the other hand, advantage, in other words, in that/which case,

Create a list of favourites: **because, however, although, whereas**...

Use comparatives, superlatives and statistics

Use comparatives and superlatives and statistics to describe data, business and trade, population figures, graphs, charts, information and to distinguish trends. We present information to a blind professor.

We write coherently. We observe **growth**, dramatic growth of imports, they grew and have grown. Now they have reached a plateau and levelled off. The numbers reached a **peak** and peaked. We give examples. There had been a steady rise but then numbers climbed rapidly, dropped slightly, fell gradually and then **increased** sharply again by 34%. We cohesively move on to each new point we make.

By observing the **trend** we expect they will decline even more or remain constant. We can make forecasts, make projections regarding the future and predict or say what we expect will happen. However, it is not acceptable to appear to know the future. We 'hedge' or use **possibly** or probably; very rarely can we say 'certainly will…'

An important word is **'significant'**. When the Prime Minister visits another country we expect there will be significant talks and decisions made. The numbers or statistics or one particular number viewed will probably be most significant. Indicate exactly **when or where**.

In addition, we use linking words. **Firstly**, we have combinations of dramatic rises and falls, a recovery, sharp increases, prices that plummet or slump. **However**, production remains stable or constant.

Although we begin by giving an overall picture we then go into detail. We thankfully resist giving an opinion. There is 'the most noticeable aspect' and 'most significantly, there is a dramatic....'

We constantly refer to the graph and perhaps go in **chronological** order or select significant moments or movements. We refer to and mention virtually every word on the graph or diagram. Use four or five paragraphs with a short introduction and conclusion. First, give the **overall view**. **Observe details**. Finally, **highlight** the key factors.

It all Depends on which Team Turns up

Whether we succeed often depends on either how much we know or on how much we care or how we act. It is fine to respect and look up to universities such as Yale or Stanford or Oxford or Cambridge. But another dimension regarding the way we compare ourselves with these grand institutions is how much we believe we are just as good. We show our **worth** in our self-presentation, if only by believing that the population is also made up of very talented people: each of us!

A lot depends on the approach and belief of "I'm as good as you are." We are, but they have more experience in their realm and so they have a temporary advantage. We practise getting our presentation and ourselves organised. "You need me!" We learn not to compose a talk or essay of 27 interesting yet disjointed sentences. We group various ideas in common and **organise** them into about five parts.

When we face our interview or our audience we do not hunch up in a small ball but sit up straight with our hair tidy with the hint of a smile. We adopt the reasonably rightful attitude that we are potentially equal people. In fact, we turn it round to show that we are the carer and they need our talent and steady hand. We are the nurse and they are the patient rather than the other way round. We set the example!

This is why a series of ten interview failures is a bonus. We get to the point where we realise that we have overdone the giving of respect and of feeling we are a lesser person than these hitherto thought of 'gods.' Without getting above our station, without giving up our humility, we give up being over-respectful. We deserve respect too.

While they are in conference rooms debating issues we are the ones on the frontline. We are at least equals. And so we sit up straight, get our hair off our face, do not put our arms across us, but open up and give an example of facing the world. We are not the spectators who criticise. We are the ones doing it. They can't manage without us!

Vocabulary: Useful
Words for every essay

<u>Vocabulary</u>: Useful Words for every essay: <u>ADD</u> your favourites:

I want to marry someone cheerful and: Attractive, honest, truthful, beautiful/handsome, kind, considerate, interesting, fair, caring, stable, sincere, reliable, dedicated loyal, confident, desirable, **strong**, stands up and walks on, trustworthy, ambitious, wise, diligent, hardworking, mature, humble, sensible, encouraging, **bright**, persistent, patient, loving, optimistic, unique, intelligent, good, affectionate, successful, healthy, humorous, protective, modest, respectful, polite, responsible, thoughtful, joyful, understanding, capable, perfect, **resilient**, gentle, motivated, energetic, resourceful, compassionate, sensitive, dares to, committed, magnificent, radiant, fascinating, faithful, exemplary....

Words to use all the time: Change, communication, complex and complicated, **strong**, because, consistent, survival, environment, duty, information, direct, speculate, analyse, permission, privilege, advise, advice, suggest, challenge, creative, however, visible and clear manifestation, mitigate, cholesterol, **build**, bridges, fashion, rare, recommend, viewpoint, nurture, facility, facilitate, enhance, generate, awareness, private, fashion, advertise, physical, reality, serious, right attitude, enable, **conflict (creates discussion)**, effect, result, invaluable guidance, illustrate, possible, probable, although, furthermore, for example, ….

<u>We want to</u> grow, think, develop, mature, make progress, sit up, have determination, be practical, participate, be successful, be genuine, be worthy of praise, be versatile, be natural, show perseverance, feel safe and secure, live in harmony, share, have and fulfil our potential, feel worthy, impress, be **bright**, be disciplined, be economical, know joy, be punctual, have personality, have plans, be organised, perform well, show initiative, be purposeful, forgive, be cordial, be flexible, have experience, listen, have belief, be accurate, endure, be decisive, be exact, have vision, reap the benefits, be clear, be **strong**, have inner strength, have courage, have a sense of pride, like making lists, show gratitude, be innovative, make connection, set a good example,…add

Be a Pioneer

Two things become transparently clear when we try something new or adventurous. One is that we learn to **improve** and the other is that we find that people cannot wait to criticise. It is like opening a flood gate. There is a compulsion to criticise. Noticeably, the common factor is the critics have done hardly anything creative themselves. They can't stand us doing so! Therefore, pioneers: please, please: go ahead.

Our shortcomings are listed. It is strange that if 100 people give a list of what they know are our shortcomings then each list will be different. The conclusion or question is obvious: is this a list of our shortcomings or someone else's: theirs? They have unfulfilled wishes.

We are similarly criticised at work or in particular when volunteering. We show up for work and inevitably, when dealing with people, not everything goes as expected or as hoped by the debaters in the conference room. Other people have other agendas and there is no accounting for, say, childish stubbornness being a higher priority than the results of the project. What we thought we did sincerely and conscientiously to help turns out to be a vehicle for critics who wish they had the initiative to act. In the end, they do less than nothing.

It is as if we are as strong as a brick wall and our critics crash the disappointment of their own inactivity into us. Amazingly, despite how many critics crash into us we stand firm and solid as they display their deep disappointment of not using their own initiative. Their Ferrari or four wheel drive crashes into us with all its force; yet, it is as if their metal is but dust because we know our work is worthy.

The conclusion is: go ahead and improve. **Go ahead** and venture out and try to do the right thing; eventually find the right way of doing it. Do not wait for critics; they remain frustrated. Be like Elvis and sing in your style. Go ahead and set up a home to help others. You'll only be criticised by people with cars that have the impact on us of dust.

Exercise ANSWER PAGES

Answers:

1. a collection, an English, the characters, the charm, the books, an eager, the countryside, a child, a privileged, an early, a love, the natural, the Lake, a farm, a student, the tragedy, the Lake, The friendship, a romance, a village, a traditional, an extension, the farm manager, a beautiful, the scenery, a deep, a conservationist, the National, the impression, the countryside, a century.

2. a. i, b. u, c. a, d. e, e. o, f. a, g. o, h. a, i. a, j. h.

3. 1. o, 2. d, 3. o, 4. e, 5. o, 6. o, 7. u, 8. i, 9. a, 10. the, 11. the, 12. the, 13. the, 14. the, 15. the, the, a, the; 16. the, the, the, a; 17. the, the.

4. 1. O, 2—14 the.

5. 1. was, 2. couldn't, went, 3. happened, 4. sank, 5. flew, 6. was, 7. didn't, developed, 8. were, written, 9. was, respected, married, wrote, died, was buried, 10. been, 11. visited, been, 12. was given, was, felt, had, drank, knew, was, getting, had.13. went, studied, had been learning, toured, thought, was; 14. Could, understood, started; 15. Been, learnt; 16. Used, have.

6. Feel, have doing, can, rest, have, are, more, stay, help, keep, signal, give, look, release, oozes, dries, evaporates, draws, is, have, are, reduce, retain, produce, start, stand, are, trapping, acts. 1. i; 2. E; 3. O; 4. o; 5. E; 6. A; 7. O; 8. i; 9. A; 10. A; 11. U; 12. E; 13. U; 14. A; 15. i; 16. E; 17. E.

7. 1. Going, 2. Will, 3. Going, 4. I'll, 5. Will, 6. I'll, 7. Going, 8. I'll, 9.Going, 10. Going, 11. It'll 12. Going, 13. Will, 14. will, 15. will, 16. Going, 17.will, 18. Will, going, 19. Won't, I'll, 20. Will, 21. going 22.shall.

8. 2. E, 3. A, 4. A, 5. u, 6. i, 7. U, 8. O, 9. Y, 10. A, 11. U, 12. u 13. i, 14. a 15. O, 16. A, 17. O, 18. O, 19. O, 20. i, 21. A, 22. O, 23. A, 24. W, 25. E, 26. U, 27. U. 28. A, 29. E, 30. U, 31. U, 32. i, 33. A, 34. O, 35. O, 36. A, 37. U, 38. E, 39. A, 40. U, 41. i, 42. G, 43. Y.

9. 1. Did, doing, 2. Do, done, 3. Do, 4. Do, do, 5. Did, do, 6. Doing, 7. Done, do, 8. Does, doesn't, 9. Doing, 10. Do, 11. Did, do, 12. Doer, 13. Do, do, do, does, don't, 14. Doing, didn't, 15. Didn't, didn't, used, we, 16. Does, didn't, do, 17. Did, 18. Do, didn't, 19. Doesn't, 20. Do, 21. Do, 22. Did.

10. 1. For, 2. During, 3. From, from, 4. From, from, 5. From, 6. During, during, 7. Since, since, 8. For, for, 9. Until, since, during, since, for, since, for, from, since, 10. For, during, since, 11. For, before, during, since.

11. With, apart, for, throughout, of, from, with, by, in, to, after, if, up, of, By, on, with, by, at, up, with.   1. Up, 2. By, 3. Of, 4. Of, 5. About, 6. By, 7. About, 8. To, 9. For, 10. At, 11. About, 12. In, 13. Up, with, out, 14. On, on, 15. Out, with, for, in, 16. To, up, 17. Between, with, out, about, on, 18. To, off, 19. Of, of, 20. To, against, until, 21. In, 22. For, 23. With, on, 24. By. 25. For, out, of, 26. To, of, for, with, of, about, of, of, 27. By, with, of, out, of, 28. Of, of, of, to, on, in, 29. about, of, on, for, about, of, 30. On, for, by, from, of, for, on, 31. On, from, of, in of, into, about, 32. About, for, to, of, up, 33. To, of.

12. 1. Warmer, 2. Better, 3. But, 4. Easiest, but, 5. Strongest, 6. Or, 7. Greater, 8. More, 9. Loudly, inner, softly, 10. Honest, reliable, truthful, patient, serious, tolerant, responsible, persistent, persevering, diligent, respectful, respectable, upright, consistent, loyal, creative, 11. Twice, research, reliable, 12. More, less, 13. Higher, 14. Far, greatest, 15. Used, harder, harder, modern, significant, older, more, employment, otherwise, too, 16. Whereas, longest, 17. Generally, most, slightly, marginally, fractionally, different, 18. Considerably, dramatically, better, worst, 19. Which, more, substantially, less, least, 20. Better, ever, 21. Than, fate, death, 22. As, drop, dramatically, higher, higher, can, crashing, falls, market, 23. Improve, reverse, worse, regression, 24. Best, worst, wisdom, foolishness,

25. Contrasting, comparing, variations, opposites, conversely, contrary, contrast, comparison, however, nonetheless, though, of therefore. 26. Same, similarly, almost, same, exactly, 27. Peak, climaxed, decreased, enough, 30. Certain, predictable, changes. 31. Moral; 32. Like; 33. More; 34. Far.

13. 1. O 2. Due, 3. Consequently, 4. Reason for, 5. Otherwise, 6. Therefore, 7. Led, 8. Result, 9. Causes, provokes, leads, 10. Pretext, generate, set, brought, prompted, causes, stem, 11. E 12. Aim, 13. Result, 14. Purpose, vision, 15. Upshot, 16. Accordingly, costs.

14. 1. E, 2. I, 3. There's, 4. O, 5. Been, 6. Mice, 7. Strength, 8. A, 9. I, 10. O, 11. O, 12. A, 13. U, 14. A, 15. i, 16. U, 17. I, 18. U, 19. e, 20. A, 21. O, 22. V, 23. O, 24. O, 25. A, 26. O, 27. U, 28. E, 29. Otherwise, 30. A, 31. O, 32. A, 33. O, 34. O, 35. A, 36. E, 37. O.

15. 1. Effect, result; 2. Sparks, generate, 3. Effect, stimulation, save, giving, into, 4. Affected, bringing about, giving, 5. Used to, cause, leads, consequences, brighter, healthier, much happier, more resilient, motivated, decided, give; 6. Because, due, develop, Build, motivated, improve, cause, results, facilitates, therefore, 7. Causes, transported, sugar, 8. Produces, results.

16. 1. education, school, university, advice, 2. Flour, salt, water, beer, toothpaste, wine, 3. Chocolate, coffee, 4. E,

5. E, 6. Clothing, size, 7. Furniture, money, 8. Cheese, sugar, milk, rice, 9. Designing, machinery, 10. O, 11. Success, health, 12. Conduct, behaviour, 13. E, 14. Harm, work, nonsense, 15. Travel, sightseeing, 16. Co-operation, accommodation, 17. Experience, toleration, patience, 18. Unforeseen, permission, 19. Information, chaos, 20. Luggage, damage, baggage.

17. 1. alleged, 2. Was murdered, 3. Was, 4. Was disappointed, 5. Been, 6. Argued, 7. Broken, was, 8. Was murdered, kidnapped, 9. Born, 10. Closed, 11. Carried, 12. Were shown, 13. Found, fined, 14. Received, 15. Killed, was, was killed, 16. Enclosed, protected, collected, pumped, surrounded, known, referred, known.

18. 1. Have, 2. E, 3. O, 4. A, 5. A, 6. A, 7. O, 8. E, 9. A, 10. E, 11. A, 12. O, 13. E, 14. O, 15. O, 16. E, 17. A, 18. A, 19. A, 20. Six, 21. A, 22. I, 23. Y, 24. N, 25. E, 26. I, 27. A, 28. E. 29. A.

19. These answers may be open to different opinions: 3. Wanted to go to Italy. 4. Said that he/Mark wanted to go to G. 5. Would never forget being 22. 6. Would remember being/having been this age forever. 7. She said that she had really enjoyed being at university. 8. He noted that they had also graduated. 9. She said that she was having the best time of her life. 10. He said that he used to have been naïve. (??) 11. She said that she had learnt so much. 12. She said that some of what she knew she had learnt in the classroom. 13. …she had improved her singing. 14. … that she had always been good at it/singing. 15. She added that her singing teacher, Ann, had made her twice as good. 16. She said that she had improved because she had practised and concentrated on …. 17. She said that she had learnt some French songs. 18. She said that her confidence in speaking French had improved so much. 19. She said that she had also learnt a speech in French. 20. …. She had had to enunciate …. 21. ….that practice had certainly made … . 22. She said that when they had had that fortnight in Paris that she been really immersed in French. She had matured. And had grown up. 23. She would never forget the year she had been 22. 24. She really believed that experience meant that she was going to get far more out of life from then on. 25. She had developed so much confidence through doing all that.

20. 1. Whose, 2. Which, 3. Which, 4. Where, whose 5. Whose, 6. Which, which, that 7. Which 8. Which, 9. Whose, 10. Which, 11. Whereas, 12. Whatever, 13. Whose, whereupon, 14. That, 15. Which, 16. Which. 17. Who, 18. Which, 19. Whose, 20. Who, who, 21. That, 22. That, who, 23. Who, that, who, that, 24. That, 25. Who, 26. Who, 27. Which, which, 28. Who, which.

21. 1. Being satisfied, 2. Having closed, 3. Having, 4. Getting, 5. Acquired, that, 6. Looking, 7. Being, 8. Having, 9. Being, 10. Being, 11. Cried, 12. Which, 13. Though, who, 14. Since. 15. Regarded.

22. 1. A; 2. A; 3. U; 4. S; 5. E,a; 6.e; 7. due; 8. Owing; 9. Due; 10. Owing; 11. Due; 12. Owing, account; 13. Several reasons, because, due. 14. M

23. 1. O, 2. E, 3. E, 4. O, 5. E, 6. I, 7. A, 8. R, 9. r. 10. E, 11. a, 12. o. 13. A; 14. O.

24. 1&2. Burst, 3. Cooked, 4. Darkened, 5. Darken, 6. Develop, 7. Developed, 8. Grow, 9. E, 10. Dog, 11. A, 12. Begin, 13. O, 14. E, 15. i, 16. A, 17. I, 18. D, 19. O, 20. I, 21. O, 22. O, 23. O, 24. E, 25. A, 26. U, 27. A, 28. A, 29. A.

25. Insert 'c'

26. Insert 'o'

27. 1. A, 2. i, 3. E, 4. H, 5. O, 6. A, 7. O, 8. O, 9. i, 10. A, 11. Y, 12. O, 13.o. 14. U.

28. 1. o, 2. E, 3. O, both 4. E, 5. O, 6. O, 7. E, 8. O, 9. E, 10. P, 11. A, 12. W, 13. A, 14. i, 15. A, 16. V, 17. i.

29. S

30. 1. A, 2. U, 3. F, 4.v, 5. X, 6. U, 7. B, 8. A, 9. U.

31. Insert c

32. Insert 'c'

33. 1. i, 2. e, 3. A, 4. A, 5. A, 6. A, 7. O, 8. E, 9. i, 10. O, 11. A, 12. E, 13. O, 14. i, 15. N, 16. O, 17. Y, 18. O, 19. E, 20. A, 21. E, 22. O, 23. L, 24. i.

34. Insert 'from'

35. Up, up, with, out, up, together, off, up, on, out, on, to, off, to, up, in, apart, up, to, after, in, out, with, up, out, up, out, up, up, out, to, off, down, up, over, apart, out, on, up, off, from, down, in, out, between, up, over, in, for.

36. To, from, away from, up, away, with, out, up, out, forward, apart, forth, with, through, into, ahead, out, up, away, back, through, with, up, with, of, upon, up, out, from, ahead, for.

37. Insert 'o'

38. 2. E, 3. A, 4. O, 5. A, 6. C, 7. M. 8. U, 9. M, 10. U, 11. P.

39. 1, o, 2. C, 3. M, 4. D, 5. C, 6. H, 7. B, 8. U, 9. D, 10. C.

40. 1. o, 2. Q, 3. M, 4. B, 5. Q, 6. V, 7. W, 8. B, 9. i, 10. N, 11. P

41. Insert 'u'.

42. 1. Billion, 2. Good, 3. Karaoke, 4. Life, 5. Yacht, 6. Tallest, 7. Purpose, 8. Mature, 9. Roots, 10. Teenagers, 11. Future, 12. Survive.

43. 1——5: insert 'c' 6. (a) apparently; (b) suggest; (c) presume; (d) liable; (e) appears; (f) 7evidence; (g) recommendation.

44. 2. Remind you; admit to; bellow at; shout at; yell at; promise to; permit you; encourage you; order you; allow you; scream at; boast to; announce to; reveal to; command you; forbid you; roar at.

45. 1. To; 2.-ing, to; 3. To; 4. –ing; 5. To; 6. –ing; 7. –ing; 8. To; 9. To; 10. –ing; 11. –ing; 12. To, -ing; 13. –ing, to; 14. To, -ing; 15. To, -ing; 16. –ing, -ing; 17. –ing, to; 18. –ing, to; 19. To, -ing, to; 20. To, to, to; 21. –ing, to; 22. To, -ing.

46. 1. E; 2. T; 3. E; 4. E; 5. O; 6. i 7. o 8. i 9. A.

47. 4. Whom; 5. Who; 6. Which; 7. Who; 8. Whose; 9. When; 10. That; 11. Where, which, that/which; 12. Who; 13. When; 14. That; 15. That, which; 16. Whose, which.

48. 1. i; 2. E; 3. R; 4. O; 5. P; 6. U; 7. O; 8. W; 9. O.

49. While; so that; when; at the same time; while; so that; As; we did not which is better than last time; when; Because; when we heard; when I feel; tidy which is; twice since they; This dress is cheaper than that one; When I fall; You can have some more tea if you give me...

50. 1. Biggest, smallest, which; 2. Because; 3. Since, almost entirely; 4. But; 5. When; 6. As; 7. But, which, because; 8. Although; 9. and 10. Also, because.

51. R1. E; 2. O; 3. O; 4. S; 5. O; 6. H; 7. A; 8. A; 9. A; 10. U; 11. C; 12. M; 13. C; 14. F.

52. 1. Realistic; 2. Immersion; 3. Effectively; 4. Culture; 5. Turning; 6. Citizen; 7. Hatched; 8. Attitude; 9. Direction; 10. Obstacle; 11. Course; 12. Hobby; 13. Sense; 14. Hair; 15. Lethal; 16. foolish.

53. 1. O; 2. i; 3. O; 4. A; 5. E; 6. O; 7. i; 8. U; 9. U; 10. A; 11. O; 12. E; 13. i; 14. E; 15. A; 16. O; 17. T; 18. M; 19. Y; 20. O.

54. 1, diverted; 2. limited; 3. Closed; 4. Safe; 5. Behind; 6. new 7. Long; 8. Simple; 9. Cold, free; 10. O; 11. E.

55. 1. U; 2. A; 3. E; 4. O; 5. M; 6. Recently, lately, formerly, punctually, usually, Previously, finally, eventually, before, after, soon; 7. O; 8. I; 9. U.

56. 1. A; 2. I; 3. O; 4. O; 5.a; 6. A; 7. U; 8. E; 9. E; 10. A; 11. E; 12. E; 13. O; 14. E; 15. P; 16. A; 17. E; 18. A; 19. I; 20. i; 21. o; 22. i; 23. f; 24. O; 25. O; 26. A; 27. O; 28.e; 29. E. 30. E.

57. 1. O; 2. E; 3. A; 4. O; 5. O; 6. E; 7. E; 8. A; 9. E; 10. i; 11. i; 12. E; 13. A; 14. E; 15. I; 16. E; 17. E; 18. i; 19. O; 20. i; 21. A; 22. o; 23. O; 24. U; 25. E; 26. E; 27. W.

58. 1.a. situation/place; b. situation; c. situation/place; d. situation; 2. O; 3. O; 4. O; 5. O; 6. A; 7. I; 8; e; 9. U; 10. O; 11. E; 12. O; 13. E; 14. O.

59. 1. M; 2. O; 3. O; 4. A; 5. U; 6. A; 7. E; 8. e; 9. a; 10. O; 11. G; 12. V; 13. U; 14. M.

60. 1. O; 2. A; 3. A; 4. E; 5. A; 6. O; 7. I; 8. I; 9. E; 10. I; 11. E; 12. U; 13. O; 14. E; 15. E; 16. I; 17. E; 18. i; 19. i and o; 20. I; 21. A; 22. I; 23. A; 24. O. 25. i.

61. 1. O; 2. A; 3. I; 4. I; 5. I; 6. E; 7. U. 8. O; 9. U; 10. A; 11. O; 12. O; 12. A; 13. M; 14. R; 15. V; 16. M; 17. T.

62. 1. N; 2. S; 3. D; 4. E; 5. G; 6. T; 7. U; 8. E; 9. H; 10. O; 11. O, o; 12. U; 13. K; 14. G; 15. O; 16. E.

63. Insert a.

64. Insert o.

65. 2. a watch; b. intend; c. disappear; steal; d. sell; e. sleep. 3. a. u; b. e, I; c. e; d. o, o, u, u, a, a, u.

66. 1. Before, after; 2. Until; 3. Until; 4. Soon; 5. Before, then; 6. Just; 7. Before; 8. Before, after; 9. then; 10. Since; 11. Until; 12. After; 13. Just; 14. People, sporting, too.

67. 1. U; 2. E; 3. A; 4. O; 5. O; 6. M; 7. E; 8. A; 9. A; 10. N; 11. A; 12. A; 13. O.

68. Have, should, may, must, will, obliged, needs can, must, can, will, ought, must, will, should, can.

69. 1. Commander; 2. Judge; 3. Accept; 4. Hand; 5. Flu; 6. Therefore; 7. Comfortable; 8. Concentrating; 9. Technique; 10. Vivid; 11. Passionate.

70. 1. Blame; 2. Police; 3. Perfect; 4. Wisdom; 5. Give; 6. Bail; 7. Traffic; 8. Then; 9. Week; 10. Map; 11. Late; 12. Could; 13. Will; 14. Wrong; 15. Beach; 16. Ambulance.

71. 1. Police; 2. Save; 3. Airport; 4. Game; 5. Besides; 6. Visa; 7. Room; 8. Exam; 9. Crisis; 10. Apart; 11. Fish; 12. Excellent; 13. Teacher; 14. Desire; 15. Respect. 16. For example.

72. 1. O; 2. i; 3. A; 4. A; 5. B; 6. H; 7. L; 8. O; 9. U; 10. Y.

73. 1. Alternative; 2. sentence; 3. rather; 4. addition; 5. impact; 6. usually; 7. Extra; 8. Despite; 9. For instance; 10. Even; 11. Impression; 12. contrast; 13. Social; 14. English.

74. 1. S; 2. A; 3. T; 4. G; 5. E; 6. O. 7. U.

75. 1. A; 2. E; 3. i; 4. ea; 5. H oo; 6. A; 7. U; 8. p; 9. b; 10. O; 11. A; 12. F; 13. o.

76. 1. R; 2. U; 3. O; 4. A; 5. O; 6. Q; 7. R; 8. A; 9. W; 10. t; 11. M. 12. E; 13. G; 14. u.

77. Shot; married; had; wanted; rescue; found; killed; shocked; avoided; get; chased; cornered; helped; drew; told; bought; informed; escaped; discovered.

78. 1. Living, earnings; 2. A; 3. A; 4. i; 5. i; 6. R; 7. O; 8. K; 9. O; 10. U; 11. U; 12. E; 13. a; 14. a; 15. O. 16. O; 17. E; 18. E; 19. O; 20 a; 21. Oo; 22. E; 23. E; 24. A; 25. U.

79. 1. University; 2. Deaf; 3. Qualifications; 4. Seriously; 5. Whatever; 6. Art; 7. Advice; 8. Education; 9. Anything; 10. Seriously; 11. Time; 12. Quick; 13. Mature; 14. Mind; 15graduate; 16. The.

80. 1. By; 2. From; 3. For; 4. To; 5. From; 6. by; 7. Of, with, of, to, on; 8. Of; 9. Of; 10. In; 11. In; 12. F; 13. O; 14. With; 15. O; 16. From, of, on, from, to, of, by, for, for, from, at, of, of, in; 17. By; 18. About, about.

81. W; 2. S; 3. O; 4. A; 5. S; 6. U; 7. O.

82. 1. Invite; 2. Go; 3. Love; 4. Want; 5. Fun; 6. Think; 7. Back; 8. Much; 9. Like; 10. Won; 11. At; 12. Hate; 13. Just; 14. Rather; 15. Watch; 16. Volunteer.

83. 1. A; 2. A; 3. e; 4. O; 5. It, be, is, are, strengthened, disappointed; been; taken; made; are.

84. 1. Proposed; 2. Added; 3. Smiled; 4. Demanded; 5. Suggested; 6. Asked; 7. Laughed; 8. Muttered; 9. Exclaimed; 10. Agreed; 11. Enquired; 12. Continued; 13. Concluded.

85. 1. T; 2. C; 3. V; 4. i; 5. O; 6. R; 7. S; 8. O; 9. a; 10. i; 11. E; 12. A; 13. U; 14. U.

86. 1. Is; 2. Are; 3. Is; 4. Third; 5. Diabetes; 6. Ways; 7. Is; 8. Was; 9. Is; 10. Harem; 11. Is; 12. Are; 13. Me; 14. Is.

87. Insert 'o'. 1. Insert 'e'; 2. Insert 'i'. 3. E.

88. 1. Insert 'u' and 'o'; 2. Much, several, few, many; 3. Too much baggage; 4. Insert 'a'; 5. 'o'; 6. 'i'; 7. 'i'; 8. 'a'; 9. 'a'; 10. 'a'; 11. 'i'; 12. 'a'; 13. 'a'; 14. 'a'; 15. 'a'.

89. 1. A; 2. E; 3. i; 4. i; 5. a; 6. O; 7. A; 8. O; 9. U; 10. i.

90. 2. Threw; 3. Patients, patience; patients, patience; 4. Ate; 5. Son, sun; 6. Course, hear, coarse, course, missed, mist; 7. Fair, fare; 8. Write, paws, pause, pours, pores; 9. Rode, road, sails, rowed; 10. Sight, site; 11. Dear, aunt, dear, dear, deer; 12. Their, place, they're, there or not; 13. Steel, steal. 14. Know, principal, principle; 15. Stationary, stationery; 16. Peel, peal, mown, moan, wine, whine; 17. Scent, sent.

91. Has, punctuation, attractive, laughter, bonds, matter, serious, physically.

92. 1. Attitude; 2. Believe it when I see it; 3. Born yesterday; 4. The benefit of the doubt; 5. Foolishly; 6. Bigot; 7. Bravely and boldly; 8. Miraculously; 9. Gullible; 10. A pinch of salt; 11. Strangely enough and coincidentally; 12. Obviously; 13. Sadly.

93. —-

94. Insert 'a'.

95. 1. Alleged, fought; 2. Suggested; 3. Announced, declared; 4. Thought, taken, spoken; 5. Believed; 6. Forbidden, say, orbited; 7. Mentioned; 8. Collected, inspected, cleared, met, graced; 9. Confirmed; 10. Seen; 11. Launched; 12. Strengthened; 13.threatened; 14. Grown, promoted; 15. Shown; 16. Estimated; 17. Appreciated; 18. Broken; 19. Told; 20. Lost.

96. 1. Crashed; 2. Graph, axis; 3. Curve; 4. Always; 5. Results; 6. Possibly; 7. Why; 8. Research.

97. Blind, introduction, decreased, dramatic, chart, illustrated, significant, May.

98. Made, found, ruled, treated, pollination, primitive, employed, supplied.

99. Insert 'a'.

100. Be amused or remove words such as 'very' from 'very unique'.

BV - #0010 - 220426 - C0 - 229/152/28 - PB - 9781909544222 - Gloss Lamination